The Book of Klobucko; In Memory of a Martyred Community

(Klobuck, Poland)

Translation of
Sefer Klobutsk; mazkeret kavod le-kehila ha-kedosha she-ushmeda

Originally Published in Yiddish in Tel Aviv, 1960

A. Wolff Jasny   Redactor

This is a translation from:
Sefer Klobutsk; mazkeret kavod le-kehila ha-kedosha she-ushmeda

The Book of Klobucko; In Memory of a Martyred Community Which Was Destroyed,
Tel Aviv, by the Former Residents of Klobucko in Israel, 1960.

Published by JewishGen

**An Affiliate of the Museum of Jewish Heritage - A Living Memorial to the Holocaust
New York**

The Book of Klobucko; In Memory of a Martyred Community
Translation of *Sefer Klobutsk; Mazkeret Kavod le-Kkehila ha-Kkedosha she-Ushmeda*

Editor: Allan D. Mantel
Translation Project Coordinator: Allan D. Mantel and Ruth Wilnai (emerita)
Translators: Asher Szmulewicz and Gloria Berkenstat Freund
Layout: Sheldon Lipsky
Image scanning: Allan D. Mantel
Image Editor: Larry Gaum
Cover Design: Rachel Kolokoff Hopper
Map Design: Jan R. Fine
Publicity: Sandra Hirschhorn
Yiddish and Hebrew Consultant: Josef Rosin

Published by JewishGen, Inc.
An Affiliate of the Museum of Jewish Heritage
A Living Memorial to the Holocaust
36 Battery Place, New York, NY 10280

Printed in the United States of America by Lightning Source, Inc.

Library of Congress Control Number (LCCN): 2014959000
ISBN: 978-1-939561-27-5   (hard cover: 398 pages, alk. paper)

Front Cover: Memorial candle for the Martyrized Klobuck Community Sketched by
Adele Unglick
Back Cover: The Synagogue of Klobuck by Alele Unglick,
Both are in the original Yizkor Book
Cover background photo by Rachel Kolokoff Hopper is detail from the Warsaw
stone Monument at Stawki Street in Poland.

JewishGen and the Yizkor-Books-in-Print Project

This book has been published by the **Yizkor-Books-in-Print Project,** as part of the **Yizkor Book Project** of **JewishGen, Inc**.

JewishGen, Inc. is a non-profit organization founded in 1987 as a resource for Jewish genealogy. Its website [www.jewishgen.org] serves as an international clearinghouse and resource center to assist individuals who are researching the history of their Jewish families and the places where they lived. JewishGen provides databases, facilitates discussion groups, and coordinates projects relating to Jewish genealogy and the history of the Jewish people. In 2003, JewishGen became an affiliate of the **Museum of Jewish Heritage - A Living Memorial to the Holocaust** in New York.

The **JewishGen Yizkor Book Project** was organized to make more widely known the existence of Yizkor (Memorial) Books written by survivors and former residents of various Jewish communities throughout the world. Later, volunteers connected to the different destroyed communities began cooperating to have these books translated from the original language—usually Hebrew or Yiddish—into English, thus enabling a wider audience to have access to the valuable information contained within them. As each chapter of these books was translated, it was posted on the JewishGen website and made available to the general public.

The **Yizkor-Books-in-Print Project** began in 2011 as an initiative to print and publish Yizkor Books that had been fully translated, so that hard copies would be available for purchase by the descendants of these communities and also by scholars, universities, synagogues, libraries, and museums.

These Yizkor books have been produced almost entirely through the volunteer effort of researchers from around the world, assisted by donations from private individuals. The books are printed and sold at near cost, so as to make them as affordable as possible. Our goal is to make this important genre of Jewish literature and history available in English in book form, so that people can have the personal histories of their ancestral towns on their bookshelves for themselves and for their children and grandchildren.

A list of all published translated Yizkor Books can be found at:
http://www.jewishgen.org/Yizkor/ybip.html

Lance Ackerfeld, Yizkor Book Project Manager

Joel Alpert, Yizkor-Book-in-Print Project Coordinator

Title Page of Original Yizkor Book

ספר־קלובוצק

מזכרת כבוד לקהילה הקדושה שהושמדה

יזכור־בוך פון דער פארפייניקטער קלאבוצקער קהילה

רעדאקטאר – א. וואלף יאסני

ארויסגענעמם פון „ארגון יוצאי קלובוצק בישראל"

און קלאבוצקער לאנדסמאנשאפטן פון פראנקרייך

און פון אויסטראליע

תל־אביב תש״ך. 1960

Translation of the Title Page of Original Yiddish Book

SEFER–KLOBUCK

Respectful remembrance of the martyrized community that was annihilated Yizkor book of the destroyed Klobuck community

A. Wolff Jasny   **Redactor**

Published by "Organization of people originating from Klobuck in Israel"and by Klobucker countrymen from France and Australia Tel Aviv Tav Shin Chaf (1960)

Printed by "Arazi" Ltd. Tel Aviv Ayelet Hashachar 4 Street

אַרגון יוצאי קלובוצק בישראל:
יזכור־בוד־קאָמיטעט —

פאָרזיצער: יחיאל זיידמאַן

סעקרעטאָר: ברוך שימקאָוויטש

קאַסירער: חיים קורלאַנד

פאַרוואַלטונגס־מיטגלידער:

אברהם אושר	אברהם גאָלדבערג
יעקב שפּערלינג	אברהם ווייס
משה פּייגע	שמואל גאָלדבערג
שמשון זיידמאַן	בערעק יאַקאָבאָוויטש

קאָמיטעט פון דעם לאַנדסמאַנשאַפטן:

אין פּאַריז:

משה ווײנגמאַן, יעקב משה אונגליק, ישראל אייזנער נח ריפשטײן

אין אויסטראַליע:

אדעלע שאו (אונגליק) דוד קראָשקאַבסקיי, א״ד ביכוויץ אליהו רעזענטאַל
מענדיל שנײער

Translation of Previous Page

Organization of people originating from Klobuck in Israel:

Yizkor Book Committee

President: Yechiel Zeidman
Secretary: Baruch Szimkowicz
Treasurer: Chaim Kurland

Management members:

Avraham Goldberg   Avraham Osher

Avraham Weiss   Yaakov Szperling

Shmuel Goldberg   Moshe Fajga

Berek Yakubowicz   Shimshon Zeidman

Committee from countrymen:

In Paris:

Moshe Wajnman, Yaakov Moshe Unglick, Israel Azjner, Noach Rypsztein, Yaakov Szmulewicz*

In Australia:

Adele Shaw (Unglick), David Kroszkowski, A. D. Buchweicz Elihayu Rosenthal, Mendel Shniur

Foreword and Dedication for the Translation

During the six years from 1939 to 1945, life on earth in Europe was destroyed, burned and scarred beyond recognition. Out of the ashes, a few seeds survived, and were scattered around the world. Green shoots emerged from the destruction, and 70 years later, new forests stand.

We are the children and grandchildren of the martyred departed and of the survivors.

The translation of Safer Klobuck is dedicated to the memory of the martyred victims of the Shtetl Klobuck, who perished during the Holocaust because they were Jews, may they rest in peace, and to the courage and sacrifice of the few survivors, who enabled future generations to remember. "L'dor v'dor." Never Forget.

This translation has been made possible through the generous support of:
Hanan Weiss & Family, Haifa, Israel;
Gabriel Weiss & Family, Tel Aviv, Israel;
Miriam Mantel Paluba & Family, New York, NY; and
Allan D. Mantel & Family, New York, NY.

December, 2014

Acknowledgement

This translation would not have been possible without the dedication and commitment of Asher Szmulewicz, and his contributions are gratefully acknowledged.

Map Klobuck in Poland

Map credit: Jan R. Fine

Geopolitical Information:

Kłobuck Poland is located at 50° 54' North Latitude / 18° 56' East Longitude.

Alternate names: Kłobuck [Polish], Klobutzk [Yiddish, Russian], Klobutzko [German], Kłobucko, Klobutsk

Region: Piotrkow

	Town	District	Province	Country
Before WWI (c. 1900):	Kłobuck	Częstochowa	Piotrków	Russian Empire
Between the wars (c. 1930):	Kłobuck	Częstochowa	Kielce	Poland
After WWII (c. 1950):	Kłobuck			Poland
Today (c. 2000):	Kłobuck			Poland

Jewish Population in 1900:	1,027
Notes:	Russian: Клобуцк. Hebrew: קלובוצק 11 miles NW of Częstochowa.

Nearby Jewish Communities:

Kamyk 5 miles ENE
Truskolasy 5 miles WSW
Miedzno 6 miles NNE
Krzepice 10 miles WNW
Częstochowa 11 miles SE
Działoszyn 15 miles N
Mstów 17 miles ESE
Nowa Brzeźnica 17 miles NE
Pajęczno 18 miles N
Olsztyn 18 miles SE
Aurelów 18 miles E
Lubliniec 19 miles SW
Olesno 22 miles W
Sulmierzyce 23 miles NNE

Praszka 23 miles WNW
Gorzów Śląski 24 miles WNW
Pławno 24 miles ENE
Dobrodzień 24 miles WSW
Gidle 24 miles E
Radomsko 25 miles ENE
Janów, (near Częstochowa) 25 miles ESE
Przyrów 26 miles ESE
Żarki 27 miles SE
Osjaków 27 miles NNW
Wieluń 27 miles NW
Myszków 28 miles SE

A Short History of Klobuck

Klobuck is a small town, located in the south-west Silesian region of Poland, approximately 20 kilometers from the city of Czestochowa. The famous Cathedral of the Black Madonna is located in Czestochowa. Pope John Paul II was a native of the region.

For more than 200 years before World War II, Klobuck had a thriving Jewish community of approximately 500 families, consisting of approximately 2000 individuals. As a market town, Klobuck had developed a sucessful mercantile class of trades people, who in turn, had created and nutured thriving religious, educational, charitable, social and cultural institutions.

On September 1, 1939, the first day of World War II, the Nazis invaded western Poland, and the town of Klobuck was immediately over-run, torched and occupied. The cohesive Jewish society that had exisited for generations was completely eradicated and ceased to exist; no Jews have lived in the town since the War.

The overwhelming majority of the Jewish inhabitants of Klobuck were murdered, starved or worked to death by the Nazis during the Holocaust. Several hundred Jewish Klobuckers survived the War. They made new lives for themeselves, and started new families. The Survivors resettled mostly in Israel, the United States and Europe.

This is their beloved memories of their lives before the War. The Rabbis, teachers, and charitable towns people, who helped the sick and poor, are brought back to life.

This book also containts their eye-witness, harrowing, accounts of the six years of horrors and tortures inflicted on them and their families during the Holocaust.

As it was originally intended by the publication of this Remembrance Book in 1960, the stories recounted herein are meant to stand the test of time for all generations.

May it be their will.

Allan D. Mantel
New York, NY
2014

Notes to the Reader:

Within the text the reader will note "{34}" standing ahead of a paragraph. This indicates that the material translated below was on page 34 of the original book. However, when a paragraph was split between two pages in the original book, the marker is placed in this book after the end of the paragraph for ease of reading.

Also please note that all references within the text of the book to page numbers, refer to the page numbers of the original Yizkor Book.

The original book can be seen online at the NY Public Library site:
http://yizkor.nypl.org/index.php?id=2318

Table of Contents
Table of Contents of the Translation

Translated by Gloria Berkenstat Freund

The Economic Life

The First World War and its Effects on Klobucker Jews

The Jewish Communal Life

Cultural Activities Between the Two World Wars

Types and Images

Klobucker Jews in Extermination Camps

Attempts at Resistance in the Camps

Episodes from the Time of Extermination

Experiences of Klobuckers in France During the German Exterminations

German Exterminations

Necrology

Table of Contents of the Original Yizkor Book

Translated by Gloria Berkenstat Freund

Klobucker Righteous Gentiles

Anti-Semitism in Klobuck

The German Extermination of Jewish Klobuck

[Page 1]

SEFER–KLOBUCK

Respectful remembrance of the martyrized community that was annihilated Yiskor book of the destroyed Klobuck community

A. Wolff Jasny   Redactor

**Published by "Organization of people originating from Klobuck in Israel"
and by Klobucker countrymen from France and Australia
Tel Aviv Tav Shin Chaf (1960)**

[Page 2]

**Printed by "Arazi" Ltd.
Tel Aviv
Ayelet Hashachar 4 Street**

[Page 3]

**Memorial candle for the martyrized Klobuck community
Sketched by Adele Unglick**

[Page 4]

Blank page

[Page 5]

Organization of people originating from Klobuck in Israel:

<u>Yizkor book committee:</u>
President: Yechiel Zeidman
Secretary: Baruch Szimkowicz
Treasurer: Chaim Kurland

<u>Management members:</u>
Avraham Goldberg
Avraham Osher
Avraham Weiss
Yaakov Szperling
Shmuel Goldberg
Moshe Fajga
Yaakov Szmulewicz
Berek Yakubowicz
Shimshon Zeidman

Committee from Countrymen:

In Paris:

Moshe Wajnman, Yaakov Moshe Unglick, Israel Azjner, Noach Rypsztein, Yaakov Szmulewicz*

In Australia:

Adele Shaw (Unglick), David Kroszkowski, A. D. Buchweicz, Elihayu Rosenthal, Mendel Shniur

[Page 7]

To our Brethren from Klobuck
wherever they may be

by the Committee of people from Klobuck

Translated from Hebrew to English by Asher Szmulewicz

We are a group of people originating from Klobuck. We took it upon ourselves to establish, willingly and with devotion, a "Yad Vashem" (Remembrance) to the victims of our town, who were persecuted and tortured, and to those that died from unnatural death, together with the six million Jews, by the Germans, the Nazis and their collaborators, impure and damned. Everything disappeared and is no more. Indeed, a tombstone of paper must be erected. Day and night the saints and the pure come with a silent claim. Brethren and Sisters! The ones who survived! Do not forget. Tie us with the knot of life. We establish for them a modest and simple remembrance, and by doing this we honor their memory by writing their memories in Yiddish, the same language they lived with for generations, (the language) they were created with and also (the language they) went to the furnace and burned with.

Dear Brethren from Klobuck.

When you browse through the pages, do not look for beautiful literature, for a novel or for genius or for science. This is a book about blood and tears, described by simple and ordinary people, who worked for a living. Each one did his and her best. These memories are from days of youth, full of nostalgia, days of the past that are gone; (memories) from the coachman with the whip in one hand and a psalm book in the other hand; from the student, and Torah scholars navigating through the sea of Talmud and Chassidut; from the breakthrough of the Enlightenment into Jewish towns; from the limited Intelligentsia of the villages, the libraries, the zionist political parties and social political parties who cared for the future. All of them good and dear Jews, with a heart and a soul, and now there is only a vacuum! We, the survivors, have to erect a sanctuary of paper to consecrate their souls. We do not have any historical documents left, so we had to use our memories and with the passage of time, errors occur or we become forgetful.

That is why Brethren and Sisters,

We apologize for the living and for the dead. If some facts are not completely accurate, some of the inaccuracies and errors introduced here and there, will be corrected afterwards by the historians.

[Page 8]

This modest book should be a remembrance for our small town Klobuck, and a pillar in the "Yad Vashem" building that the People of Israel are erecting in the Land of Israel. We will remember for our entire lives our small town, and mourn together with the People of Israel the great destruction that occurred in our generation. With the building of our nation, bringing back the survivors being attached to the People and the Land, we will find our consolation.

Please, receive this book of remembrance, should it be an eternal true kindness[1] for our community.

Committee of people from Klobuck
Translator's Footnote

1. Chesed shel Emet (This expression is used in Hebrew for the last respects given to a dead person, it is a true kindness because the deceased will not be able to "pay back")

[Page 9]

Preface

By the Committee of people from Klobuck

Translated from Yiddish to English by Asher Szmulewicz

It is said that when the Germans were about to kill the martyr historian Simon Doubnov, he shouted to the people around him: "write and describe!"

We, the Klobucker survivors, who built our homes in Israel, took it upon ourselves to fulfill the last words of this martyr and scholar. We undertook the difficult task of gathering all of the materials, testimonies, and memories of the suffering and persecutions that the Klobucker Jews went through by the Germans, into a Sefer Yiskor (Memorial Book), which will remain for the generations to come as a memorial document to describe the bestial behavior of the Germans against the Jews.

It was not easy to fulfill this sacred mission. We could not get the archive materials that described the history of the Klobuck Jewish Community (Kehilah). The Germans also destroyed the Jewish Archives. That is why we made the strenuous effort to induce the people originating from our town to write their memories: those who survived the German extermination of the Jews should describe their pain, the hard labor, and the extermination camps where the Klobucker Jews were.

Our endeavor bore the expected results: the Jewish survivors of Klobuck did not forget their annihilated community (kehilah), and in the "Sefer Klobuck" they described the lives of those Jews and their communities: the religious ones, the national-cultural and social institutions, the charity organizations and the varied political parties that constituted the society's political life of the Jews in this little shtetl.

[Page 10]

The Klobucker survivors fulfilled their duty to the murdered ones: the living Klobucker Jews made public their descriptions of the memories of the German extermination. Unfortunately there is no exact statistical data and no full list of names to assert the number of the exterminated Jews. But from the memories alone we get a clear picture of the great destruction of our community of Klobuck.

It is our duty to express our gratitude to all of the people originating from Klobuck who helped us assemble the Sefer Klobuck – the secretary of the association of people originating from Klobuck: Baruch Szimkowicz, who did not spare anything and gave all of his free time to gather memories and organize the fund raising to finance the expenses; Mrs Adele Unglick in Australia, who drew the memorial candle, the Klobuck synagogue, the map of the shtetl and did other things in favor of the Yiskor book; the people originating from Klobuck living in France: Moshe Wejnman, Yaakov Moshe

Unglick, Noach Rypsztein and Israel Azjner; and the association of people originating from Klobuck in Australia.

We thanks our friend A. Wolf Jasny for his devotion and initiative while editing our book about Klobuck.

With profound respect we present the "Sefer Klobuck" to our people originating from Klobuck, who carry in their hearts the memories of our martyrs. In the Jahrzeit for our martyred community, standing close to the memory candle lit to elevate their souls we will read chapters from the Yiskor book, in order to reunite with our dear relatives who succumbed to sanctify the Holy Name and the People.

The Commitee

Jewish Klobuck

Historical Notes and Memories
by Baruch Szimkowicz
Translated by Asher Szmulewicz

The settlement of the Jewish town of Klobuck or Klobucko, according to the "Evreiskaya Encyclopedia",[1] is in the distant, foggy past. The first Jews that constituted the shtetl and built the community did not leave any records. The archives of the shtetl were destroyed by the Germans during World War II. Therefore we did not have any evidence of the exact date of the creation of the Jewish settlement of Klobuck.

The tradition, handed down from the Jews in the shtetl, said that the first Jews of Klobuck came from Dzia□oszyn (Zaloshin), a shtetl with an older Jewish settlement, located approximately 30 kilometers north of Klobuck.

There was an old, unused, cemetery in Klobuck. No one knew how old the cemetery was. On Tisha B' Av[2] when people traditionally went to their ancestors' tombs, they also visited the old cemetery. There was a tombstone, covered with moss, that the old people of Klobuck said was the tombstone of the first Rabbi of Klobuck, Reb Yitzhikel z"l (of blessed memory). After him, Klobuck had three other Rabbis until the destruction. Calculating the tenure of each of the religious leaders that served in the Rabbi's position, it was determined that the Klobuck Jewish community existed for more than 200 years before the German extermination of the Jews.

Additionally, it was not well established how old the Shul (Synagogue) was, or the Batei Midrashim (Houses of study), which also were all destroyed by the Germans. From various opinions, the Shul stood approximately 80 years before it was destroyed. It was not the first Shul. The Batei Midrashim were even older.

[Page 12]

About the history of the shtetl of Klobuck, our Landsmann (fellow countryman) Moshe Weinman who lives in Paris, wrote:

"In 1935 Klobuck celebrated the 800th anniversary of the creation of Klobuck. The historian Jan Dlugowicz, who lived in Klobuck for a long period, declared that the name Klobuck came from when the foundation of the first house in Klobuck was laid. At that time, a hat was found, and a hat is called Klobucko in old Polish, and that is how it became the name of the shtetl.

There is no precise date when the shtetl was created. Some historians said the creation date of the shtetl was 1135, others said it was 1185. In any case it can be said that Klobuck was one of the oldest shtetls in Poland. The antiquity of the village can be proven by the fact that the church, which was built over a large area, was built on the remains of an older church that was destroyed in the big fire in 1796."

*

The first verifiable news about Jewish life in Klobuck is from the year 1808. At that time, Luszczewski, the Finance Minister from the Grand Duchy of Warsaw, decreed that Jews had to have all their printed books stamped, and pay a special tax on each book.

The burden of organizing the stamp tax payment fell on the Jewish communities. The town of Czestochowa sent to each of the communities within the Czestochowa district an announcement dealing with the stamp decree. Among the list of the communities, Klobuck was mentioned. Dear Sir Dr. Szaczki (of blessed memory) wrote about this in his historical work "Jews of Czestochowa Until the First World War", which was published in the Yiskor Book of Czestochowa, "Czestochower Jews" (published in New York under the editing of Raphael Maler).

[Page 13]

From Szaczki's publication we know that there were Jews in Klobuck in the year 1808 under the administration of the Czestochowa community.

*

In the "Evreiskaya Encyclopedia" at letter kof (k) there is the following information about Klobuck:

"A village close to Czestochowa, within the Piotrków province, but because the village was in a border strip (between the Russian-German border) difficulties existed for Jews to establish themselves there. In 1856 there were only 444 Jews in Klobuck. From the 1897 census there were 3576 inhabitants including 1027 Jews in Klobuck, or 28.6% of the overall population.

*

I left Klobuck in 1923, when there were more than 450 Jewish families, comprising approximately 1600 people. From 1923 to the outbreak of World War II, the Jewish population virtually did not change. In general, a majority of the young Jewish people left Klobuck between the two World Wars, and moved to bigger cities, the land of Israel or emigrated to various foreign countries.

Klobuck, at the crossroad between Czestochowa and Krzepice, was a beautiful village surrounded by orchards, gardens, a stream called "Jike" and ponds. The entire area was covered with forest land, and meadows, which in the spring were blanketed with green grass. During my childhood the other young boys and I cut green plants for Shavuot. Close to swampy ponds in the harvest season, we cut green Hoshanot (willow twig) for Sukkot.

In summer time, in the evening, the young people would swim in the ponds from one bank to another; it was joyful and lively. On the Zavader pond there was a watermill, with its big wheel, that was turned by the power of the water.

[Page 14]

The watermill belonged to a Pole with a long beard. He looked like a Jew.

At the end of the summer the Czestochowa fishmongers rented the swampy ponds, removed the water and took out the fish. The swampy ponds were full of tenches and pike fish. In the winter, when it was very cold, a thick layer of ice covered the ponds, and the landlord of the soda factory, Itshe Unglick, hired peasants to cut the ice in cubic blocks,which were saved for the summer.

There was another neighborhood named Zagorz, which was in a forest close to the village, that was related to the Klobuck Jews, but more precisely with the young boys of Klobuck. On Lag BaOmer[3] the teachers with theirs pupils went to Zagorz and played "war" with wooden swords, one Cheder against the other.

In Zagorz the imperial castle was located. The Russian Royal Prince used to spend a few days in the castle - according to the tales of a few Jews.

So the shtetl remained embedded in my memory.

The Rabbis of Klobuck

As stated earlier, the Klobuck community had four Rabbis until the extermination of the Jews by the Germans. Even the oldest town's people did not remember the first Rabbi, Reb Yitzikel, of blessed memory. We only knew about his good deeds for the community, and that he was a genius Torah scholar. He published a book that did not survive.

After Rabbi Yitzikel, the Rabbinate seat was occupied by Rabbi Yoshua Israel, of blessed memory. Several (Klobuck) Jews knew (and remembered) him well. He was a parent (in-laws) of Rabbi Yitzik Djalowski. When he passed away, the well known Tzadik (righteous) Rabbi Yankele, of blessed memory, became the Rabbi of Klobuck, and because of him the Klobuck (Jewish) community became renowned. About Rabbi Yankele there were various wonderful stories.

[Page 15]

Rabbi Yaacov Rabinowicz, righteous of blessed memory, was simply called Reb Yankele by Jews who loved him. He was the son of the Radomsker Rabbi "Baal Chesed le Avraham" and a grandson of the "Baal Tiferet Shlomo". When Rabbi Yankele became the Rabbi of Klobuck, Klobucker Jews lived in a "Splendid Period". Making a living was easy, and Jews from others villages came to Klobuck to listen to Rabbi Yankele's interpretation of Torah, or to receive a blessing, or to ask for advice from him about various subjects. On Shabbat and in particular during the Days of Awe (High Holidays), Jews from the surrounding villages came to Klobuck to davenen (pray) together with Rabbi Yankele.

My grandfather, Avraham from Krzepice, said that he only went to Klobuck for Rosh HaShana to davenen (pray) with Rabbi Yankele, and to hear his sighs and the "Oy Veh" of his "Peh HaKadosh" (sacred mouth), which enabled my grandfather to achieve a state of repentance.

When Reb Yankele became the Rabbi of Klobuck, he was very young. Nevertheless he could exceed all of the great Torah scholars, and was proficient in Shass (Michnah and Talmud) and in the Tanach verses. Savant Rabbis wrote to him to ask him about various difficult questions. They decided their conflicts in accordance with his answers. The questions and answers are part of his book, "Emet LeYaacov" (Truth of Yaacov).

Rabbi Yankele established new rules for davenen (to pray). He stated that in the Shabbat morning prayer the "Kedushah" should start with the word "Nekadesh", according to the Ashkenaz tradition. The "Kedushah" of the Shabbat Mussaf prayer should start with the word "Keter". This was contrary to the prior local traditions, when Jews used to say "Nekadesh" for the "Kedushah" of the morning prayer and "Naritzach" for the Shabbat Mussaf Kedushah. His decision remained in place thereafter, because the Rabbi who succeeded him did not want to change the decree of the Righteous Rabbi.

The young Rabbi from Klobuck, Yankele, contracted tuberculosis. He was brought to Otwock (a famous Polish spa). From there he went to the closest shtetl, Kortshew (Karczew), where he passed away, at only 29 years old, in year 5662, 21st of Iyar (1902).

For the Jews of Klobuck and for his followers from other shtetls, after his death Rabbi Yankele was revered as a model. During every hard time, disease, epidemic, or Heaven forbid, pogrom, when the community was saved from trouble, we believed that the merit of Rabbi Yankele, Righteous of blessed memory, protected the shtetl.

[Page 16]

Book "Emet leYaacov" (Truth of Yaacov)
From former Rabbi of Klobuck:
Rabbi Yankele with Haskamot
(Endorsements) from Rabbis

[Page 17]

Book "Emet leYaacov" (Truth of Yaacov)
From former Rabbi of Klobuck:
Rabbi Yankele with Haskamot
(Endorsements) from Rabbis

[Page 18]

His Yuhrzeit (death anniversary), the 21st of Iyar, was a special day for the Jews in Klobuck. Every year, for his Yuhrzeit, in the great Beit HaMidrash (House of Study), a special remembrance lamp was turned on, which consisted of the symbolic carving of the Kohanim hands raised up, blessing the people. That was in recognition of the fact that Rabbi Yankele was a Kohen. Also, there were two lions resting on a Magen David (Star of David) beside a carving of the year and the day of his passing away.

Every Jew in Klobuck felt a duty to come to the Beit HaMidrash on the Yuhrzeit of Rabbi Yankele. On this day the Beit HaMidrash was full of Jews. In addition to the big lamp, as described, hundreds of candles were lit, and people recited Mishnayot for the peaceful resting of his soul. Less educated people read Tehilim (Psalms). This occurred every year until the German extermination of the Jews.

A few years after his passing away, when the Klobuck community had to hire a Shochet (ritual slaughterer), the will of Rabbi Yankele was taken into account. The Radomsker Chassidim devoted themselves to serving as the Shochet, because the Rabbi of Radomsk said it was the "will" of Rabbi Yankele, and so it was. Reb Moshe Zander was thus hired to be the Shochet, and he was a scholarly Jew, with an easy and accommodating manner, and good humor.

Rabbi Yankele's wonders and good deeds

Jews from Klobuck said about Rabbi Yankele the following:

When his first baby boy was born, later the well known Reb Avramele, people came to the Beit HaMidrash to announce the good news and wish him mazal tov. Rabbi Yankele, the young father was sitting and studying with his students, and said that he would first finish the lesson and then he will go see the baby.

[Page 19]

So it was - half an hour later, together with his students he came to the new mother, and while looking at the baby he immediately said that the baby would be a great genius. One of his students, an insolent teenager asked: "Rabbi, how do you know that he will be able to study"? Rabbi Yankele answered: "watch closer and you will see". The insolent teenager didn't stop and said that he was watching but did not see anything.

The teenager indeed did not see, but Rabbi Yankele had the greater insight. This baby became the famous scholar, Reb Avremele.

*

Once Rabbi Yankele was invited to Działoszyn to participate in a Din Torah (Judgement according to the Torah) with two other Rabbis. Reb Yankele stood close to Reb Shimon Szilit.

When Reb Shimon Szilit came in the room, Rabbi Yankele asked him if he needed anything. Reb Shimon answered immediately that he made a good living, thank God, he was healthy and that he did not need anything. Twice Rabbi Yankele asked the same question and received the same answer.

When Rabbi Yankele prepared himself to leave and travel back to Klobuck, Reb Shimon, while saying goodbye, asked him for a blessing. Rabbi Yankele answered: you missed the opportunity, when I asked you before if you needed anything. The time to ask was before the davenen; the davenen was a favorable moment to ask a wish of the Master of the World; now it is too late".

This story was told by Reb Moshe's son, whose name is Yankele and lives in Jerusalem.

*

[Page 20]

A poor man came to Rabbi Yankele and complained that it was winter and he did not have warm clothes to wear. The Rabbi called his wife and told her that since he had two coats, she should give one away to this poor man. The Rabbi's wife acted accordingly and gave the poor man a coat.

On Shabbat, the Rebbezin (Rabbi's wife) realized, to her distress, that she gave away the better coat. She told her husband, the Rabbi, about her grief, but he calmed her down and said: "it does not matter, since this poor man will be warm, I also will be warm."

*

Rabbi Yankele, who sat day and night studying, never had time to meet with the village community leaders. Shmuel Szperling and Feivel Mass decided that they needed to meet with the Rabbi to discuss community issues. They arranged a meeting with the Rabbi by telling him that he was going to get a raise.

As soon as it was announced, the meeting was scheduled. Both Jewish community leaders came to the Rabbi and told him that they wanted to give him a raise in his salary of two rubles. The Rabbi cut them short and said: "I don't need a raise, anyway the Rebbezin will spend it. If you have an important charity matter, you can spend this money on that instead."

*

Finally I will relate a tragic event in my own family which is related to Rabbi Yankele:

My uncle Levi had a great misfortune. My aunt Rachel, his wife, gave birth to a son, but she passed away just before the Brit Milah. My uncle lived on the Shule street, where Rabbi Yankele also lived. People went to the Rabbi to ask what they should do about the Brit and the funeral.

Rabbi Yankele while listening to the tragic event, moaned and said Baruch Dayan HaEmet (Blessed the Truthful Judge)[4] and asked them to come back the next morning. He needed time to think about this overnight.

[Page 21]

The next morning, when the people came to him, he ordered that the Brit occur first, after the corpse's purification, in the same room where the deceased mother laid. So it was done. Rabbi Yankele was the Sandak (Godfather) and the baby was circumcised in presence of his dead mother, who was laying on the purification bed, covered with a black cover. Rabbi Yankele sat in front of the deceased mother, and asked everybody to drink LaChaim (to the life) and to congratulate the mother, who was present at her son's Brit Milah.

The Rabbi gave the baby two names - Reuven Binyamin, an allusion to the story of our Matriarch Rachel when she gave birth to Binyamin. Almost everybody came to this strange Brit.

*

The Last Klobuck Rabbi

The last Klobuck Rabbi, who was exterminated by the Germans together with his community, Reb Yitzhak Henech Goldberg, of blessed memory, came from a great family. He was a grandson of the famous genius and first Gerer Rebbe -Baal Chidush Harim. Rav Yitzhak Henech was very concerned with Torah studies. He studied with teenage students. His students were: Yaacov Granek, Emanuel Charjewski, Leizer Kleinberg, Avraham Mendel Liefer from Truskolasky and the writer of these lines.

Translator's Footnotes

1. Chesed shel Emet (This expression is used in Hebrew for the last respects given to a dead person, it is a true kindness because the deceased will not be able to "pay back")

2. Tisha BeAv 9th of Av is the anniversary of the destruction of the two temples in Jerusalem and is a fast day

3. Lag BaOmer or the 33rd day of the Omer is a festive day marking the end of the epidemic that killed 24,000 students of Rabbi Akiva

4. Baruch Dayan HaEmet (Blessed the Truthful Judge). This sentence is said when learning about somebody passing away.

Synagogues and Houses of Prayer

The Klobuck Synagogue

by Adele
Translated by Gloria Berkenstat Freund

The Synagogue of Klobuck
Drawn by Adele

In far away Australia, the Klobuck Synagogue, destroyed by the defiled Germans, begins to shine before my eyes in the brightest light. No, it is not burned - somewhere this holiness exists, somewhere the divine piety of my childhood years flutters.

The sunlight piously, modestly radiates through the high windows with the colored windowpanes like the silent prayer of *Shmoneh Esreh* [central prayer of Jewish worship]. These colored rays of sun that light up every corner of the synagogue still shine today in my heart.

Past experiences and childish excitement on Friday nights and holiday evenings in the synagogue emerge in my memory, chandeliers and extra bright oil lamps pour their light over the *Shabbos* [Sabbath] and holiday Jews who all are joined in holy prayer to the Creator of the World.

And there is the God-fearing *Kol-Nidre* [*All Vows* - the opening prayer recited on the eve of Yom Kippur - the Day of Atonement], the hot tears of Jewish Klobuck, the prayers of the men and women pour into the clear, warmed lightness. The *Kol-Nidre* singing rolls and reaches higher and higher; it appears that the synagogue becomes higher. The sacred painted ceiling disappears and the gates of heaven have opened.

On *Tisha B'Av* [the ninth of Av], the night of the destruction of Jerusalem, dark shadows spread in the synagogue; the mourning Klobuck Jews sit removing their shoes from their feet and near a small candle they cry out their *Book of Lamentations* song at the destruction of the Temple.

[Page 24]

And after all of the sadness of the people - it again becomes animated with the beaming joy of the people: Klobuck Jews rejoice with the Torah - *Simkhas Torah* [holiday commemorating the completion of the yearly reading of the Torah and the start of the reading for the new year]. Light, joy, religious ardor merged the individual Klobuck Jews into one congregation that filled the synagogue with singing, dancing in honor of the Torah.

* * *

The Klobuck Synagogue, the small Temple, was destroyed with the *kehile* [organized religious community]. However, it lives in my heart and soul with those closest and dearest, who were cruelly tortured.

I have tried with a weak effort to bring this synagogue again to paper so that its appearance and its memory will never be removed from our eyes and hearts.

[Page 25]

The Rise of the Synagogue

by Gitl Goldberg

Translated by Gloria Berkenstat Freund

My mother, Rayzl Leah, of blessed memory, often talked about the Klobuck synagogue and how difficult it was to build and, later, to finish the synagogue.

Before there was a synagogue, everyone prayed in the small house on Zawada where all of the Jews were once concentrated. The plot with the small house belonged to Reb Ahron Wajs, the grandfather of Reb Wolf. Reb Ahron gave this small house as a house of prayer. They prayed there for many years.

They approached the building of the synagogue with very little money. However, they immediately found a generous donor who took upon himself the holy duty of helping to build a house of prayer. The generous donor was – Reb Shimeon Weksler, a wealthy man, who with his wife leased the alcohol factory in Zagorsz. With Reb Shimeon's money, they first properly approached the building of the synagogue. When the walls and the ceiling finally were erected, they again lacked money. Therefore, they made collections in the *shtetlekh* [towns] around Klobuck. Meanwhile, they prayed in the uncovered four walls.[1]

It took a long time until the completion of the synagogue and the women's synagogue to which led many steps.

The name of Reb Shimeon Weksler, the generous donor, of blessed memory, was carved over the ark for all time.

Translator's Footnote

1. The author uses the word "ceiling," but she is probably referring to the roof. She also contradicts herself; she indicates that the "ceiling" had been completed, but then writes that walls were uncovered.

[Page 26]

The Synagogue – the Prayer House of the Klobuck Jews

by Borukh Szimkowicz

Translated by Gloria Berkenstat Freund

The Klobuck synagogue had a reputation in the area as the tallest synagogue. And in truth the synagogue was very high, sturdily built with long windows. Several wide steps led to the entrance to the synagogue; beautiful wide doors opened into the anteroom. The anteroom was spacious and had three doors: one led out onto the synagogue courtyard, the second – to a small house of prayer and two wide, thick half doors opened into the synagogue. The large anteroom also was used on *Shabbos* [Sabbath] for the public reading of the Torah.

One entered the synagogue by descending several steps in order to fulfill the saying, "From the depth I call to You, God." The *neyr-tomed*, a perpetual flame, six-sided with a brass *Mogen Dovid* [shield of David – the Star of David] hung from the ceiling a little further, dark red, blue glasses from which always shone a dim light. From my childhood years I remember how we *kheder* [religious primary school] boys interpreted the words *neyr-tomed* – the light burns by itself through a miracle, because we could not understand how the *shamas* [synagogue caretaker] could reach and light the *neyr-tomed* when it hung so high and there was no ladder in the synagogue.

The eastern wall had three small windows with half round, blue, red and green panes high up. Two dark brown lions carved out of wood stood over the *Aron Kodesh* [ark holding the Torah scrolls], leaning on the blue tablets on which the Ten Commandments were engraved in golden letters. A little lower, on both sides of the ark, stood two large flowerpots with fruits.

The ark was deep into the wall. Many Torah scrolls were located inside, as were *posle* [sacred books and pages no long considered fit for use] wrapped with *avneytim* (cloth bands). They were used only on *Simkhas Torah* [holiday celebrating the conclusion of the annual Torah reading and the beginning of the new cycle of readings] for *hakafos* [procession of Torahs encircling the synagogue]. There were several steps to go up to the ark that were on both sides. One went up on the right side and down on the other side. There were two important "seats" on both sides under the ark.

[Page 27]

The rabbi always prayed on the right; on the left, the respected property owner Mendl Guterman prayed. It seems that he inherited his "seat" here.

Near the ark stood the large synagogue's lectern over which hung the *Shivisi* [first word of the chapter in Psalms that begins, "I stand before God..."]. The *sheliekh tsibei* [representatives of the community before God] – Reb Dovid Hirsh and Reb Moshe Zander, both *shoykhets* [ritual slaughterers] – always prayed at the lectern.

Reb Dovid Hirsh, with his stately appearance and long, patriarchal beard stood before the lectern during the Days of Awe for over 40 years and was the reader of the prayers of the Klobuck Jews. Many tears poured out here in the synagogue when Reb Dovid Hirsh wrapped in his *talis* [prayer shawl] and in his *kitl* [white coat worn on special religious occasions, which also serves as a burial shroud] sincerely prayed and sang his cantorial pieces with flourishes. An apprehensive stillness engulfed the synagogue when the cantor, with his powerful voice, shouted: "Fearsome and awesome almighty One". His sons stood on the steps on both sides of him and helped him sing the melodies of the Days of Awe.

Reb Moshe Zander, my former teacher, prayed *shakharis* [morning prayer] at the lectern. He had new melodies every year that he brought with him from the Radomsker Rebbe. It was known in the *shtetl*: if Moshe the *shoykhet* had been in Radomsk before the Days of Awe, they would hear new melodies. His singing drew the musical ones in the *shtetl* who, because of this, especially came to the synagogue to pray to hear Reb Moshe's new melodies. His praying on *Shabbos* and his welcoming of *Shabbos* was sweet.

When one thinks about the Klobuck synagogue, the Synagogue Street swims into one's memory. This was not just any street that led to a synagogue, but a sort of "antechamber" to the house of prayer. Since a Jewish *kehile* [organized Jewish community] was established in Klobuck, generation after generation, every Klobuck Jew walked through this street many, many times. In addition, to the synagogue and house of prayer, where they went to prayer three times a day – in the morning and *Minkhah-Maariv* [afternoon and evening prayers] they walked through this street to get to the *mikvah* [ritual bathhouse]. The *khederim* [religious primary schools], where mothers led their small children during the summer to learn the *alef-beis* [the Hebrew alphabet, the basics of education] and where older boys went alone to study Torah, also were located in the Synagogue Street.

[Page 28]

Let us here remember the *melamdim* [teachers in religious schools] of the Synagogue Street: the teachers of the youngest children were – Reb Itshe Ber with the nickname Kurczak [chicken] and the lame Leibele; Itshe Lewkowicz, Yosef Buchwajc, Moshe Szajowic (Deitsch) and Moshe Yakov Rozental taught *Khumish* [books of the Torah] and Rashi and to older children.

The *hakhnoses orkhim* [hospitality for poor *Shabbos* guests] and the Gerer and Aleksanderer *shtiblekh* [one room prayer houses] were also located in the Synagogue Street. At that time, the famous rabbi and righteous man, Reb

Yankele, may the memory of a righteous man be blessed, lived on the street and his *yeshiva* [religious secondary school] was located there.

Right after the synagogue stood the small stooped little house of Ayzyk Chlapak. There was prayer and the reading of the Torah there every *Shabbos*. The Torah reader was Yitzhak Zajbel. The worshippers created a *gmiles-khesed* [interest-free loan] fund. Three blind women, Zlata, Nakhela and Ritshl, lived in a small room in the house. Reb Ayzyk Chlapak served them as a *mitzvah* [commandment, often translated as good deed]. Thus appeared the Synagogue Street in Klobuck.

The Young Men of the House of Prayer

In addition to the synagogue, Klobuck also had two houses of prayer – a large one and a small one. The large house of prayer, which really was big, did not rest – not winter and not summer. Day and night. Here they prayed and studied, recited Psalms and simply conversed. The writer of these lines also spent many years in the house of prayer pressed to a bench, studying.

My Klobuck house of prayer remains deeply engraved in my memory... The long, thick, planked benches and tables. The large cabinet of religious books, old books with yellowed pages, the various Talmuds and several set of the *Shulkhan Aruch* [*Code of Jewish Law*]. The young men who studied with me remain in my memory: Emanuel Chorzewski, Yakov Granek, Leyzer Klajnberg, Ahron Wajs, Yakov Dawidowicz, Yehiel Rozyn, Yakov Ahron Bloj, Mendl Lipier and Leibl, Moshe the *shoykhet*'s brother-in-law.

We were then the house of prayer's "middle" young men. In addition to us, there were the "bigger" students, that is, the older young men to whom we looked with particular respect.

[Page 29]

The sons of the members of the clergy belonged to this group: Moshe the rabbi's son, Shlomo Menakhem – son of the *shoykhet* Yakov Borukh, Moshe Rudek, Avraham Mendl Dudek, Levi Wajnman, Levi Kurland.

There was another group of house of prayer young men, "beginners," very young, who had just begun to engage independently with the Torah. Avraham Goldberg, Mendel Chorzewski, Hilel and Yosef Leib Zoltabrocki, Chaim Dzialowski, Yosef and Yehiel Guterman and Moshe Zelkowicz belonged to this group.

We came to study at the house of prayer at four o'clock in the morning. The first worshippers came an hour later: Yitzhak Lipszic, Yitzhak Szuster, Yehiel Kraszkowski, Shmuel Szperling, Ahron Zajdman, Yakov Fishl Rozental, Yitzhak Zajbel, Ahron Saks and Kh. M. Goldberg. They were the first *minyon* [group of 10 men required for organized prayer]. The young men-students moved to the small house of prayer as soon as they began to pray.

Every year, *Rosh Khodesh Adar* [the start of the month of Adar – February-March], the words *Mishenikhnas Adar Marbim B'Simkhah* [When Adar arrives we increase our joy] were written in large calligraphic letters on the eastern wall of the large house of prayer. Moshe the *shoykhet* interpreted the acronyn of the word *b'simkhah* [joyfully]: "*Bronfn shtarkn muzn Hasidim hobn*" [Hasidim must have strong whiskey]. A long table reached from the eastern wall to the door. The *yeshiva* young men sat around the table swaying over their *gemaras* [Talmudic commentaries] and called to one another with: "Rava said and Abba said" [references to Talmudic sages]. The table also was used for the large *kehile* [organized Jewish community] meetings. Every year, during the time of the Days of Awe, Reb Kasriel the book-seller would spread out his *Mokhzorim* [holiday prayer books], prayer books, all sorts of books, story books of miracle workers, thick and thin *havdalah* [candles – used at the conclusion of *Shabbos*].

Reb Kasriel was not from Klobuck. He especially came with his holy books for the Days of Awe. When several days passed and he had not taken in any money, he created a "lottery." He raffled off a dozen *Khumishim*, a *Sheyver Muser* [18th century treatise – *Rod of Chastisement*], a *Kav Hayosher* [18th century moral treatise – *The Just Measure*] that I could win for only three *kopikes*. After Reb Kasriel had gathered a sum that the books cost, a drawing took place.

[Page 30]

A number was drawn from a long small bag and whoever had the luck, received the book.

The small house of prayer also was not empty. Here one studied only during the summer and prayed on *Shabbosim* and the holidays throughout the year. The worshippers were mostly sellers of livestock and horses. They always stuck together as a society, drank and played cards together.

An old well was located in the synagogue courtyard. A large bucket was attached to a long iron chain that served for washing the hands before entering the house of prayer. The clear water of the well was always filled with small stones that "customers" threw in to see how the water bubbled.

I remember how every year, *erev* [eve of] *Yom Kippur* before *Kol Nidre* [opening prayer], Reb Dovid Hersh washed his dressy slippers with the bucket. It was said then that this is a Strikower custom because Reb Dovid Hersh was a Strikower Hasid.

The Community Bathhouse and the *Mikvah*

A small enclosure was also located in the synagogue courtyard that was feared by the children. Inside the enclosure stood the casket for the dead and the black wagon with which Jews were taken to their eternal rest at the cemetery. When it was seen from the distance that the door of the enclosure was open, it was known that there was a funeral today. The *kehile* did not own a horse with which to take the bodies; they always had to borrow a horse from a wagon driver.

On the left of the synagogue courtyard, not far from the casket for the dead, was the *mikvah*. Pious, observant Hasidim immersed themselves almost every day in the morning before praying, both summer and winter. Almost all of the Klobuck Jews went to the bathhouse Friday afternoon. The entire week the *mikvah* also served the observance of the laws regulating marital life... On the days of *Slikhes* [penitential prayers recited before the Days of Awe], many pious Klobuck Jews went to immerse themselves in the morning before saying *Slikhes*.

[Page 31]

The *mikvah*, which was very near the young men of the house of prayer, had the first effect of awakening heretical thoughts... The young students began to say among themselves that the *mikvah* was terribly dirty and they had complaints for the rabbi – how could he justify such an unclean *mikvah*?

The Klobuck bathhouse consisted of a large room with an entry, where the bath attendant, Shlomo Rozental (Uliarsz) always was found chopping wood for heat and to warm the water. One paid to use the bathhouse. There was no established price, one paid as much as one wanted to give – from two *kopikes* to 10 *groshn*. Whoever paid more received another bucket of warm water.

It was always dark in the bathhouse because of the steam. As one became accustomed to the darkness, he first noticed the benches nailed to the wall. One had two choices in undressing: either waiting until someone would get dressed or to lay the package of things on that person's package. Later, when getting dressed, a search began. The clean shirt that they had brought with them to change into often lay dirty on the wet floor. With no other choice, one had to put it on in order to change the shirt one had worn for the entire week.

The bathhouse also possessed three bathtubs in which two or three men at a time would sit. They sat, told stories, mocked and enjoyed themselves. Whoever had time meanwhile waited until they could also slip into the bathtub. After getting out of the bathtub, the bath attendant treated them by pouring a half bucket of water over them... Shrewd men secretly went up to the faucet and took another bucket of water behind the bath attendant's back. The water in the bathtub as well as in the *mikvah* was rarely changed.

[Page 32]

Ghosts in the *Mikvah*

by Batya Zajbel-Izraelewicz

Translated by Gloria Berkenstat Freund

The *mikvah* [ritual bathhouse] bordered our meadow. The *mikvah* water flowed through a specially created canal onto the surrounding meadows. Streams were created at various places in which our ducks splashed.

Once, on a Thursday night, the ducks disappeared. We looked for them all over and, not finding them, we were sure that they had been stolen. My father, as always, when something unusual happened, responded with a saying, "Never mind, a *kapore*[1] on the ducks, as long as we have other fowl."

However, it happened: There was a pious Jew in Klobuck, a God-fearing person, an Aleksanderer Hasid, Reb Yudl Ahron, who went to the *mikvah* every day to immerse himself. On that Friday morning, when he entered the dark *mikvah*, he suddenly heard splashing in the water. In his imagination, he saw images moving on the surface of the water.

Frightened, he quickly ran out, went home and, later in the *beis hamedrash* [house of prayer], said that he had seen ghosts in the *mikvah*... Several bold Jews, among them my father, took a chance and went into the *mikvah*. Here they saw our ducks swimming in the *mikvah*. They were given the nickname, Kosher ones, immersed ducks.

Mrs. Gitl Goldberg talks about the *mikvah* in her memoirs: My father-in-law always spoke about the problems the Klobucker Jewish residents had in building the *mikvah*. It seems that gentiles were afraid of the Jewish *mikvah* that was being built and twice they burned the building that was being built.

A delegation of esteemed Jewish Klobuck businessmen went to Piotrkow to the governor and obtained permission for the regime to protect the religious facilities of the Jews. The Klobuck police turned to the Polish managing committee at the city hall and made it responsible for every case of setting fire to the *mikvah*. This had the effect that the building of the *mikvah* was completed.

Translator's Footnote

A *kapore* is a fowl used as a scapegoat in a ritual before Yom Kippur in which one's sins are transferred to the fowl.

[Page 33]

The Klobuck *Kehile*

Translated by Gloria Berkenstat Freund

As in all of the cities and *shtetlekh* [towns] of Poland and Lithuania of the past, Klobuck had its own *kehile* [organized Jewish community] that was led by three or four people, the so-called *dozores* [synagogue council]. They decided and carried out all of the communal business matters and managed the revenues and expenditures, consisting of the *etat* [communal tax] and the like. They consulted with the rabbi in religious matters, for example: in ordering the Passover flour for matzos, in creating *eyrovim* [wire boundaries indicating a "private area"] to enable the carrying of things on *Shabbos* [Sabbath]. Such matters were decided only with the rabbi's ascent.

There also were exceptional cases when meetings were called, as for example: when the synagogue or the house of prayer had to be repaired or a new fence had to made around the cemetery and for this purpose money was needed – the entire *kehile* was called to a meeting. Friday night after the prayers, the *shamas* [synagogue sexton] banged on the Torah reading table and announced that the *dozores* had called a meeting that would take place on Sunday afternoon in the house of prayer. Only the leading citizens, the finest business owners in Klobuck were called when hiring a rabbi or *shoykhet* [ritual slaughterer]. The *shamas* would receive a list of names from the *dozores* of who had to be invited to the meeting.

The expenditures of the Klobuck *kehile* at that time consisted of: the salaries for the rabbi, *shamas* and *shoykhet*; heating during the winter and lighting (candles, kerosene) in the houses of prayer; support for the *hakhones-orkhim* [hospitality on the Sabbath and on holidays for poor travelers], the *mikvah* [ritual bath] and the cemetery. The main source of revenue was the *etat*, that is, the yearly tax that every Klobuck Jew had to pay to the *kehile*. Only those about whom it was known that they were "reduced to a loaf of bread" were freed of paying the *etat*. There was an evaluation of the income of each and every one and the level of the *etat* that he could pay was done by the *dozores* themselves. The list of the tax payers was sent to a high Russian official in Czenstochow by the leaders of the *kehile* and the general czarist tax administration collected it all.

[Page 34]

In addition to the *etat*, the *kehile* had income from the ritual slaughtering. There was a special fee from butchers for slaughtering; this payment also was taken from each family. A "receipt" had to be obtained from Ahron Zajdman for the slaughter of poultry. When the *shoykhet* received such a "receipt," he was permitted to slaughter. The receipts cost: four *groshn* – for a goose or a duck, for a chicken – three *groshn*. The income for the *Resh Khet-Shin* (for making use of the clergy – *Rov*, *Khazan* and *Shoykhet*)[1] was an exceptional part of the *kehile* budget. A special fee was required for weddings, *brisn* [ritual circumcisions], registering the newborn and *eybodl lekhaim* [words said between the mention of birth and death to separate them] and registering of death. This income went only to the clergy: rabbi, *shoykhet* and *shamas*.

The clergy also had a traditional holiday income. It was the custom in Klobuck that on the day of *erev* [eve of] Yom Kippur both *shoykhetim* went from house to house to slaughter the *kapores* [chicken used in the pre-Yom Kippur atonement ritual]. Every Jew would properly [pay] for the efforts and performed the *mitzvah* [commandment] of covering the blood after the slaughter. On Purim, each head of household knew that he must send *shalakhmones* [gifts of cakes and drinks] and Purim money to the rabbi and *shoykhet*. The same for Chanukah – Chanukah money.

I remember the *dozores* from my young years: Meir and Shmuel Szperling, Moshe Shmulewicz, Feywl Mas, Dovid Ziglman, Shimsha Lichter, Ahron Mas, Moshe Szperling, Ahron Zaks and Avraham Jakubowicz.

The Jewish communities in the villages around the *shtetl*, such as Miedzno, Kocin, Ostrowy, Najdorf, Walenczów, Libidza, ☐obodno, Z☐ochowice, Wr☐czyca and Kamyk, also belonged to the Klobuck *kehile*.

The *Kehile* During the First World War

The Klobuck *kehile* leadership began "to reform" itself during the German occupation during the First World War. The three *dozores* at that time were: Avraham Jakubowicz, Ahron Zaks (the tall Ahron) and Moshe Szperling. The head of the *kehile*, Avraham Jakubowicz, began to introduce reforms: notices from the *kehile* were not delivered by the *shamas* in the synagogue, but through announcements in Yiddish that were hung up in the house of prayer.

[Page 35]

Jakubowicz also reformed the special help given by the *kehile* so that the needy person did not feel humiliated and that the business owners not use the *shamas* and the rabbi for assignments that did not belong to their offices. The head of the *dozores* organized the first inexpensive kitchen for the poor and required that the *kehile* ask advice on all important questions through frequent meetings.

The rabbi was not happy with these reforms and a conflict arose between him and the democratic *dozor* [member of the synagogue council]. However, Jakubowicz was sufficiently bold and declared that there need not be agreement with everything that the rabbi said.

Translator's Footnote

Resh Khet-Shin is an acronym composed of the first letters of the words *Rov* [rabbi], *Khazan* [cantor] and *Shoykhet* [ritual slaughterer

[Page 36]

The Melamdim [Teachers] in the Shtetl [Town]

Thus We Studied Torah

by Avraham Goldberg

Translated by Gloria Berkenstat Freund

My first rebbe [teacher] was called Reb Moshe Yakov Rozental, a former Radomsker Hasid. He lived in the Synagogue Street, across from the Great Synagogue. The *kheder* [religious primary school] in which we studied was in the courtyard and the only window, which gave light, looked out onto Leib Zajbel's stall. The horses in the stall looked in sadly equine, through the window and listened to "the voice of Jacob from the nursery school children."

The kheder room also was used for other purposes. A machine stood there to press oil from flax seeds brought by the peasants. The waste from the pressing of the oil was sold in the form of four-cornered "cakes" as food for the cows.

The pious song of the Rosh Hashanah and Yom Kippur prayers spread from the *kheder* during the Days of Awe. My rebbe was very talented in music and song; he had a sweet voice. He traveled as a leader of prayer to the *kehilus* [organized Jewish communities] in the surrounding areas. He had a "choir" of choirboys. When he sang out *Yareiti Biftzoti* [I am in awe] and "*Unetanneh Tokef*" [liturgical poem - part of the liturgy of the Days of Awe] with flourishes together with the choirboys, people came running in wonder.

There was a room near the *kheder* in which the daughter of the *melamed* [teacher] had her workshop. The sons also worked somewhere in a large city but, despite all of this, my rebbe was a very poor man.

We *kheder* boys felt very good with the rebbe, Reb Moshe Yakov. To the extent that I remember, we had pleasure from the vivid environment; a few dozen meters from the *kheder* there was the river along with wide meadows

[Page 37]

on which cattle grazed. Moshe Borukh's orchard was not far away, full of apples and pears during the summer, which tempted us and drew us to them. However, an "angel of death" in the figure of Kopl Mantil, Moshe Borukh's son-in-law, stood at the orchard. He persecuted us without mercy. Woe to the child who fell into his hands.

Besides the orchard, we children had another recreation, which I remember today with an unpleasant feeling: not far from Reb Moshe Yakov's *kheder* lived the crazy Fradl, a lonely woman, whose hysterical shouting resounding in the street. We *kheder* boys teased her, which gave us wild pleasure.

[Page 38]

Reb Moshe Yakov had a reputation as a good teacher in Klobuck. When my parents brought me to *kheder* the first time, the rebbe welcomed me with fatherly tenderness. Immediately, upon learning the first letter [of the Hebrew alphabet], the "angel" began to sprinkle candies and nuts, of which there were enough for me and for my new friends who, because of this, immediately took me in as one of there own. I learned the holy letters with joy and then entire words. Reb Moshe Yakov quickly made me into a "Hebrew-reading boy" and after a half year of studying I had to leave my dear, good *kheder*.

*

Khol Hamoed Sukkous [the intervening days of the Feast of Tabernacles] Reb Itshke, a Jew, a boorish man, came to our house. He was what we called a "handy man." We studied with him - *Khumish* [Torah] with Rashi, *Gemara Bava Metziah* [Biblical commentaries - *The Middle Gate*], writing a Yiddish letter, as well as Russian. The *kheder* was located in Podkamenicer Road, hidden deep in a courtyard in a half room, half house with a small window. On a bleak day it almost was dark there. Here we also had our childish joy, which was always disrupted.

Reb Itshke's kheder room was located in a peasant's courtyard, packed with agricultural tools. Cows stood ruminating hay. Small calves learned to run, springing over stones and tree stumps. Learning did not go into our heads here. We quarreled outside. But when we tried to do mischief with the calves, we were brutally driven back into the *kheder* room.

Reb Itshke and his *kheder* left the room under pressure from the students' parents. He rented a large room with two windows. A large table with long benches was installed. We students of Reb Itshke also had a "devil" here who disturbed our learning. The "devil" was the pear tree that appeared through the window in the *kheder* courtyard that was covered in juicy pears during the summer. We went to it and tore off the tasty fruit at every opportunity.

.[Page 39]

Woe to the student who was caught in a transgression. Reb Itshke did not know any mercy. He lay the fellow over the bench, pulled down his small pants and Reb Itshke counted the blows of the whip according to his discretion. After such an execution, the rebbe was pale. He gasped and his stomach rose and fell. The heavy penalty did not help. We again tore pears and there were always new "victims."

Reb Moshe Yakov Rozental with his wife

In general Reb Itshke was included among the best *melamdim* [*kheder* teachers] and had more students than the other *melamdim* in Kolbuck. In addition to the teaching profession, Reb Itshke also was occupied with sock manufacturing and commerce. In the *shtetl*, he was considered a respectable person who made a good living, particularly after he bought his own house and continued to carry out his teaching and his commerce there.

*

Reb Yisroel Lapides, a smart Jew, a man of stately appearance with a beautiful patriarchal beard was my third teacher, who taught me Torah. Both the students and their parents were satisfied with this teacher. He was the only *melamed* in Klobuck who gave to his students a clear Hebrew with an understanding of the meaning of the words. Reb Yisroel did not let the praying be gobbled up. We had to stop at each verse.

Reb Yisroel had his system for the study of *Khumish* and Rashi: we began to learn a Torah portion on Sunday, and on Tuesday afternoon the best student repeated the entire portion of the week. Everyone listened. Everyone had to repeat the portion according to the example of the best student. Everyone knew the portion of the *Khumish* and Rashi at the end of the week. On Friday we read the weekly portion with musical stresses and learned *Targum Onkelos* [Aramaic translation of the Torah] translated into Yiddish. During the summer, we also studied The Ethics of the Fathers.

The learning of Hebrew as a language to speak was new in Lapides' *kheder*. He endeavored to teach the students Hebrew words, which could be used in speaking. Simultaneously, he also taught how to write a Yiddish letter. He had a beautiful, elegant handwriting and required

[Page 40]

of the students that they copy him. The punishments in Reb Yisroel's *kheder* also were different. He did not have a whip but two rulers: one a thick one and the other a thin one. The students received a slap on the hand with the thin ruler for a light "sin." A greater punishment was a slap on the back with the thick ruler. Despite the light punishments, the discipline in *kheder* and the respect of the students in the street was extraordinarily strong.

Reb Yisroel was not a scholar. He had not studied *Gemara*, but what he gave his students was complete. He tried to give each *kheder*B, boy the simple day-to-day *yidishkeit* [a Jewish way of life]. In addition to *Khumish*, Rashi, Hebrew, writing a Yiddish letter and fulfilling the commandments such as: "Honor your father and your mother," "Love thy neighbor," he also implanted the love of prayer in his students. He taught us the songs of praise and liturgical poems from the holiday prayer book for each holiday. We had to know them just as we knew *Ashrei* [prayer recited three times a day] and to understand every word.

In addition to his stately appearance, Reb Yisroel also made an impression on us with his long pipe. We knew what kind of mood the rebbe was in by the way in which he let out the smoke. As soon as he smoked quickly, we knew that a storm was coming and every boy tried not to anger the rebbe.

After "exhausting" the education of Reb Yisroel, I entered the *kheder* of Reb Meir, the son-in-law of Shloma Dovid Hirsh, the *shoykhet* [ritual slaughterer]. He was a pious Jew with wide orthodox knowledge, a grammarian. He did not move without *Tanakh* [The Five Books of Moses - the Torah]. His students were grown young men. I was the youngest among them. There also was a female student in the *kheder* - Hena, the rebbe's daughter, who later became a well-known teacher.

It was then during the First World War that the Germans stood at the gates of Warsaw. In addition to the lesson from the Torah, our rebbe gave us a *shiur* [lesson on a subject of Torah] in the field of strategy and instructed us in the war tactics of Prince Leopold of Bavaria. The Rebbe, Reb Meir also awoke in us the idea of the "return to Zion" that he explained to us in his way.

[Page 41]

From *Kheder* to the *Yeshiva*

Reb Meir, the son-in-law of Shloma Dovid Hirsh, the *shoykhet*, was my last *melamed*. From him I went to the house of study, to the *yeshiva* [secondary religious educational institution] that had just been founded in Klobuck. Those studying in the *yeshiva* were mostly from the Klobuck artisans and shopkeepers. The *yeshiva* was too restricted for me. The learning was dry and I was no longer interested in the "Laws of an Egg Laid on a Holiday" [from the *Shulchan Aruch* - codification of Jewish law]. Yet, I studied, in order to [please] my parents who wanted nothing else than for me to be a scholar.

We sat in the house of study and studied the *Amora* [scholar] Rabbah and the *Amora* Abbaya with the old melody. We arose very early and we studied in the house of study until late at night. We often were questioned by the rabbi or by other learned men. We never stopped studying. My greatest aspiration was to be able to study without the help of the older young men. In addition to studying we also were employed in serving the *yeshiva*: gathering money to memorialize the dead, making the lanterns for the *yarhzeit* [anniversary of a death] of Rebbe, Reb Yankele, adorning the house of study in "days of celebration," etc.

The founding of the *kheder*, *Yesodei haTorah* [Foundation of Torah] that was led by Reb Zisha Bornsztajn, a great scholar and affable to people, revived the small *yeshiva*. A number of the young men went to study in the highest class of the *Yesodei haTorah*. Our rebbe was Reb Avraham Kanapnicki, a manufacturer merchant, a former student of Rebbe, Reb Yankele. He had an ascetic face and never smiled. However, his teaching of *Gemara* captured me. In addition, the students were chosen - the sons of the best scholars in the *shtetl*, among whom also were the rabbi's two sons, Shmuel and Binem, sons of those competent to decide matters of rabbinical law, the scholars from the Dudek family.

Despite his strictness, Reb Avraham never lifted a hand to a student. His look and word were enough that we would study with diligence. Such were my teachers. I learned Torah and respect with them, which remained with me for my entire life.

[Page 42]

My *Melamdim*

by Borukh Szimkowicz

Translated by Gloria Berkenstat Freund

When I was four years old, my father led me to the *melamed* [teacher] of the youngest children, Reb Itshe Ber, who was called the *kurczak* [chicken]. He lived in the synagogue street. I began to learn the *alef-beis* [alphabet] there. Reb Itshe Ber was an angry teacher and imposed a fear on the children with his screaming. Therefore, the students did not like him and only learned under the pressure of fear.

My hostility to my first teacher was so great that once when I received monthly money (tuition) from my father for the teacher, I hid it somewhere under a stone and did not give it to the *melamed*. Of course, when the matter came out, I paid with spanks and tears.

After two years of torment with Reb Itshe Ber, I arrived in the *kheder* [religious primary school] of Reb Moshe Deitsch (Moshe Szajowic). We learned *Khumish* [the Torah], Rashi and *Gemara* [commentaries] with him. He also crammed the Torah into our heads with a whip. He mostly let out his anger to a student when he suddenly asked him where we were [on a page] and the [student] could not find the right place in the *Gemara* that we were studying.

The Reb carried on a "second war" with us during the wintertime. Of the 30 students who studied in the *kheder*, many often "disappeared." The teacher knew where to look for them. He left for the frozen *rzeka* [Polish – river], as we called the river, with his whip under his long coattails and when he found his students there, he let them have it and chased them until they came back to the *kheder*.

In addition to the river, we *kheder* boys had another spot where we "carried on winter sports." This was the hill that led from the market to Shlomo Aliarczik's house. We started down the frozen and snow-covered hill with ice skates or small sleds that had been provided for us by the son of Avrahmtshe the tinsmith, a student in our *kheder*. We also met the rebbe's [teacher's] whip on the frozen hill. However, here we succeeded in running away and arriving in the *kheder* before the rebbe. When he found us sitting at the table, he began an investigation: which boy had skated. He did not rest until he found the "criminal" and the whip did its [work]...

[Page 43]

The ice skates and the small sleds were the main *yetzer hara* [evil inclination] that tore us away from the holy Torah and brought on us the rebbe's whip. We quietly carried on a trade with the skates and sleds in the middle of learning. We hid the goods in Moshe Borukh's stall that was located not far from the *kheder*. Asher, his son, who studied along with us, protected our dear sports things. In return, he received half a bagel and an egg that we brought with us to the *kheder*. A boy often ran to check if our dear treasure had been stolen.

Thus – in playing and in pranks under the rebbe's whip – I grew and became serious. I also was given a serious teacher, Reb Berl Borukh, who taught Torah to only a select [group] of students. We were eight boys in his *kheder*. Several names remain in my memory: Yakov Ahron, Yehiel Rozen, Emanuel Charzowski, Leyzer Klajnberg, Yakov Granek, Henekh Fajga. We studied *Gemara* with commentaries with Reb Berl Borukh.

Several of us went away to study after studying for a few terms with the teacher. Layzer Klajnberg and I left for Praszka, where we studied with the Praszka rabbi, the author of *She'erit Yakov [Remnant of Yakov]*. In time I came home again, and with Emanuel Charzewski, studied with Moshe *Shoykhet* [ritual slaughterer] and in the Klobuck house of study. We repeated the tractates with commentaries with diligence. We learned "as a pair" and alone in the morning hours and in the evenings. We debated the fine points of Talmudic law and absorbed God's Torah.

My Friend in Learning

Of all my *kheder* and house of study friends, Emanuel Charzewski is engraved in my memory. We went to *kheder* together, studied together with Moshe Dajcz, with the rabbi, and in the grey mornings

[Page 44]

we went to the house of study to learn God's Torah. Our sisters also became friends through our friendship, my sister, Toba and his sister, Fraydl Leah. They always were close together.

We grew up, and left our childhood. My friend Emanuel was industrious in his studies, a dear person, a sensible person; one could consult with him about various questions. We both became Zionists. Reb Meir Shlomo Hirsh, the Klobuck Hebraist and grammarian, had an influence on both of us. We both studied Hebrew. My friend remained devoted to his religious belief and belonged to the *Mizrakhi* [religious Zionist] organization in Czenstochow.

During my departure for *Eretz-Yiroel*, I arrived in Czenstochow at six o'clock at night to say goodbye to my friend of many years, Emanuel Charzewski. He already was a father then and had a small, dear little girl – Chana'le, who today lives in Israel. I was supposed to leave at eight in the evening, but my friend would not let go of me, I should remain over night and leave early in the morning. Emanuel also wanted so much to go to *Eretz-Yisroel*, but something did not go well for him in this respect.

I stayed with him at night. We spent the entire evening together. We went to say goodbye to our teacher, Reb Meir Shlomo Hirsh, who then lived in

Czenstochow. We slept very little that night. We paged through our entire past. Emanuel promised me that we would meet in *Eretz-Yisroel*.

When I already was in the country, I received *l'shanah-tovah* [for a good year] cards from him every year and once he wrote to me that he was ready to come to *Eretz-Yisroel*. However, fate wanted something else.

[Page 45]

Memories of My Childhood Years

by Fishl Fajga

Translated from Yiddish to English by Asher Szmulewicz

As a small child, I moved with my parents from the village of Lipie to Klobuck. My parents established themselves, and when I was four years old, my father brought me to the "Cheder" (Jewish traditional elementary school) of the "lame Leibele" (the teacher). When I think back about this first "school" of mine, I can remember and see before my eyes Reb Leibele's "Cheder". (There was) a copper "quart" (water jug), with the two big handles to scoop out the water, (which were so big) that we almost were unable to hold with our little hands. The quart always stood on a kind of "scoop holder," made of two pieces of wood. There also was the portrait of the Russian Czar, Nicolas II on the wall, which was next to an authorization to run a "Cheder"

From the "lame Leibele", during the first year I learned the letters of the Alef–Bet (Hebrew alphabet), and the "Mode Ani" (the first prayer in the morning upon waking up).

In the second year, my father brought me to the Cheder of Rabbi Henech "Rantshkele". He taught us very little because he always was busy chopping wood for cooking, and preparing himself for the winter, which was difficult for him because of his disability; thus the Rebbetzin (the Rabbi's wife) always kept us busy.

The Rebbetzin, Gutshe, was a tall, thin woman, who was always busy peeling potatoes, or plucking (chicken) feathers. The pupils often helped her, and sometimes we played tricks (on her). She used to chase us, shouting: "shiksim, lobuses" (rascals, little devils). In spite everything, we managed to learn to read a little Hebrew.

After a few trimesters of studying in several "Chadarim", I came to Rabbi Reb Itshke. There both younger and older boys studied. We learned Chumash, Rashi and Gemara. I stayed in this Cheder for a few trimesters.

*

[Page 46]

I still have in my memory the "Lag Baomer war", which ended for us, the Cheder boys, very sadly. It was during the second or the third year of studying in Reb Itshe's Cheder and just after Pesach, that we, the pupils who knew each other well, decided to organize a "Lag Baomer war". As our adversary we choose the pupils of the Cheder of Reb Moshe Daitsh. As was usual, in this case, our Cheder sent an invitation for the "war" to the other Cheder boys, and they accepted it.

The students of Reb Itshke's Cheder prepared themselves thoroughly for the "war", and not with the usual bows and arrows, but with "modern armament". We had a specialist in our Cheder, Aizik Mass, who made out of wood "real looking rifles" and "artillery" on small wheels. Until "Lag Baomer" the "military" from both Chadarim had skirmishes in all of the places where the boys of both Chadarim were to be found, and we planned to fight each other, but we soon became victims.

Finally, the long awaited day of Lag Baomer came. I could not sleep the night before, and like a "soldier" I thought about the next morning's "battle" and about the victory of the boys of Reb Itshke's Cheder. The next morning we gathered at Aizik Mass' place, where our armament repository was found. From there, each of us marched with a "rifle" with prominent "bayonets". The four "soldiers" carried the "artillery", two in front and two behind.

We went out on the Zagorz road. The "military" of Moshe Daitsh Cheder marched through the Grodjisker road. We planned to meet at the sawmill of Yitzhak Chade. The "battle" was supposed to be held there. Suddenly when we arrived at the end of march, a bunch of shiksim (non–Jewish hooligans) came out of the chimney sweep (station) . They jumped on us, punched several of us, and took all of our armament. We ran back to the shtetl crying. We found on our way to Moshe Szmulewicz. He asked us what happened. We told him the whole story, and he went with us to see the chimney sweep. The chimney sweep took from his sons, (the shiksim), our armament and gave it back to us. The "war" was already postponed. It never happened.

*

[Page 47]

In 1913–1914 I studied in the Cheder of Rabbi Reb Moshe Shayowicz, or how we used to call him, Reb Moshe Daitsh. Only chosen children attended this Cheder, like Leibel, the Rabbi's (son), Yitzhak Fajga, Moshe Zelkowicz, Yeshaya Enzel, Arie Dudek, Yossef Leib Zaltebrawski, two twin brothers Yossef and Yechiel Arie Guterman, Mendel Charzewski, Leib Szmulewicz and others.

We learned Chumash, Rashi and Gemara, and each week the Rabbi sent the teacher a list of important well to do landlords, Chasidim, to whom the pupils were sent for an examination. The landlords had to report to the Rabbi as to which pupils were learning well or were not.

Reb Moshe Daitsh did not hit his pupils. We were 10–11 years old, and the Rabbi had respect for us. In this Cheder I studied until the outbreak of the First World War, when we stopped our studies. Reb Moshe died at the beginning of the war.

My last teacher was the "yellow" Moshe (blond). In addition to Gemara and Tossafot I was also learning how to put on the tefilin (phylacteries). There were 10 students in the Cheder. The Rabbi also had 10 sons, so it was a "big Cheder".

The classes started very early in the morning. During the short winter days we went to the Cheder when it was still completely dark outside. Once, I awakened in the middle of the night. My watch had stopped, and I thought that it was already early morning. There happened to be a full moon that night. I dressed silently, said "Mode Ani" (prayer when coming up), took my tefilin and went to Cheder.

On my way I knocked on the window of my friend Leib Szmulewicz. He also thought that it was time to go to the Cheder. He got dressed and we went (to school) together. Suddenly a pack of white dogs attacked us. We could not escape from them. Due to our shouting Yonathan Kortzbard came out. He chased away the dogs and asked us where we were going in the middle of the night. We told him that we were going to the Cheder.

[Page 48]

It was in fact one o'clock in the morning. We were afraid to go back home, and we sat all night and until the morning at Yonathan's table. My friend Leib was shivering, and shared with me with a secret. He forgot to wear his talit katan (small talit with four tzitzit that is worn under the shirt), and he said that the dogs were certainly "ghosts". We actually "proved" (the theory) because on the side were we held our tefilin, the dogs didn't attack us.

When we came to the Cheder in the morning, we told the story of the "ghosts". Over time, the shtetl came to accept and believe the story that "devils" attacked two boys who went to the Cheder at one o'clock in the morning because they didn't know what time it was. For a long time I was very afraid and frightened to go out at night. I was sure that the white dogs were "ghosts".

Longing for Education and Knowledge

by Sura Bratt, Paris

Translated by Gloria Berkenstat Freund

I was born to simple, pious parents. My father was an honest Jew, a *Kohen* [priest]; my mother – a quiet virtuous woman. My father, Zalman Brat [Polish spelling], never had any great ambitions. He lived in another world and had one answer for his difficult life: "This is only a vestibule to there"... to the other world of holiness and eternal life in *gan-edn* [paradise]. Because of this belief he always was stoic about his poor life and was proud of his fulfilling the *mitzvah* [commandment] to give the priestly blessing [in the synagogue].

He never used a watch during his entire life. He would wake up in the morning, look into the sky to see if one was permitted to put on *tefillin* [phylacteries] and pray.

He would go to sleep just as the sun went down. My father did not have the least burden for providing for someone in this world. He had as many children as God gave and did not take care of them; not even when it was necessary to report the newly born "person" and get a birth certificate for him.

[Page 49]

[Page 49]

When I reached the school years, I wanted with pleasure to take this first responsibility and obligation that every child had, namely, to study in school. However, my first dramatic experiences began here.

To be able to send a child to school at that time in Klobuck, one had to be the head of a household with three acres of land. This was supposed to be a guarantee of tuition. Because the school had no more than two rooms, the rich children were accepted first. I also had to take upon myself the entire struggle to enter the school because my parents did not recognize the need for it.

After a great deal of effort and tears, I finally entered the school. A week later, I was asked for my birth certificate. I spared no effort and went to the city hall alone for the document. The official searched in his books for a long time and finally said to me in an angry tone that I did not <u>exist</u>. That is, officially I had not yet been born. As a child I already had the experience of the value of such a small paper...

That I was a girl and my father did not care about my getting a birth certificate was the reason for the problem with the arrangements for getting it. However, I pleaded with my mother that at least she should be able to remember the year of my birth.

– Wait my child – she said – I think it was three weeks before the new year...

– This is not important, Mama, only the year. – I said with a tremble in my heart.

Alas, my mother wracked her brains and finally with a victorious tone said:

– It was then 40 degrees of frost... A bit later, the Czar had issued an order that all Jews who lived in the villages had to leave and go to the *shtetlekh* [towns].

With a great deal of difficulty I was just able to learn that my birth fell on a historic date. Namely: the Russian Revolution of 1905. And the birth certificate was filled out with my year of birth.

I grew in my longing for education and knowledge for which, sadly, my parents did not have any understanding.

[Page 50]

Jewish Celebrations in Klobuck

Shabbosim, Holidays and Weddings

Borukh Szimkowicz

Translated by Gloria Berkenstat Freund

Very early Friday, the arrival of the holy Shabbos [Sabbath] already was felt in Klobuck.

Women and girls hurried with cakes and challahs to the bakers. Apple cakes or cakes filled with black berries, which were beloved in Klobuck, were prepared in the houses. They also baked egg cookies that served as a snack at the Shabbos morning kiddush [blessing of wine after prayers]. In addition to the egg cookies being tasty, they also had the virtue that we did not have to wash [and say a prayer, as one does when eating bread] and could eat them right away, as soon as we returned from praying.

The fisherman, Yakl Ripsztajn, stood near the sidewalk near Dovid Zigelman's house with a choice of various sorts of fish: carp, giant perch–pike, bream and other small fish. The fisherman was surrounded by almost all of the women in the shtetl, each wanting to be the first to buy. They shouted, made noise, bargained, but no one went home without a fish. In Klobuck, it could not happen that there was a house that did not have fish for Shabbos.

Friday at around one o'clock, the first Jews were seen going with small packages of underwear to the mikvah [ritual bath]. The first mikvah–goers were: Moshe Dombier, (Zigelbaum), Yehiel Kraszkowski, Dovid Zigelman, Harcka Guterman and Emanuel Wilinger. All of the men of the shtetl went to the bathhouse after them.

[Page 51]

When they returned from the mikvah, Shlomo Shamas [assistant to rabbi] already was calling them to the synagogue. He had his well–worn path: from Moshe Szmulewicz to Avrahamtshe Blachacz. At Shlomo Shamas' call, Jews made their last purchases in the shops. Zelig, the kerosene maker sold out his last quart of wine, which he carried to the houses. Girls hurried to the bakers with the pots of cholent [stew cooked overnight for eating on Shabbos]. It began to get dark and the holy Shabbos arrived in the shtetl.

Candles lit up the windows in all of the Klobuck Jewish houses. Fathers and children went to pray – in shiblekh [one–room prayer houses] and in the synagogue. We boys were drawn to the synagogue where Moshe Shoykhet already was welcoming the Shabbos. After welcoming Shabbos in the synagogue, kiddish, was made over a glass of wine and we children drank from the glass. The Shamas made sure that every boy received his portion of wine. When a boy drank too much, he never again received a taste of the kiddish.

When we left the synagogue, there already were orkhim [guests invited for Shabbos and holiday meals] waiting, poor Jews, from outside the shtetl, who remained in Klobuck over Shabbos. Almost every head of a household took home a guest.

The Jewish streets emptied very early on Shabbos and the strictly observant Hasidim appeared in silk or velvet robes. They went to the mikvah with slow steps. They went right to the synagogue after the mikvah, said the blessings and took a look at a commentary in a religious text. Of these strictly observant Hasidim I remember the names Reb Josef Buchwajc, Reb Yakov Fishl Rizental, Reb Makhel Dudek, Reb Yeshaya Bachinek, Reb Yitzhak Chada and Reb Itshe Meir Sztiler.

They came to the synagogue to pray very early. However, it lasted until 11 o'clock because they waited for the rabbi to arrive in the synagogue for [the prayer,] Shokhen Ad [He Who abides forever]. And they again waited for the rabbi to end the prayers with the Krias Shema [Shema Yisroel – Here O Israel – declaration of faith] and Shimoneh Esrei [the 18 benedictions].

Shabbos, after prayers, the Klobuck Jews did not rush to eat. Mainly, they did not go around with empty stomachs: they said the blessing on the wine and snacked on eyerkikhl [egg cookies] and they could wait a while. They waited for the cholent [Sabbath stew], which were not given out so quickly by the bakers. All of the wives had to gather in each bakery so that each could identify hers. So that, God forbid, there would not be a mistake.

[Page 52]

The children usually went to the bakers. However, although it was Shabbos, the mothers were not idle. Chopping was heard from all of the houses; with a cleaver they chopped the onions that every Klobuck Jew had to have as a second food after the fish.

They went to sleep for two hours after the midday meal – Shabbos repose. During the summer, after sleeping, they ate Shabbos fruits that had been provided by Yakl the fruit seller. Young people went into his orchard, which Yakl [leased] every summer from the Polish doctor, and ate apples, pears and plums that had been obtained for credit there. Yakl was a pious Jew and understandably did not take any money on Shabbos.

At the same time as the young spent time in Yakl's orchard, several Jews left for the shtiblekh [one room synagogues], for the large synagogue, where they devoted themselves to study. In the summer they studied The Ethics of the Fathers with commentary and Midrash Shmuel [commentary on the Book of Samuel]. In the smaller houses of prayer, the respected members of the middle class – Reb Shmuel Szperling, Reb Ahron Meirs, Reb Meir Szperling and others – took a look at books of ethics: Tiferes Shlomo, Khesed l'Avraham, Kedushat Levi and Avodas Yisroel.

When the evening shadows began to spread over the shtetl, they said the evening prayers in the shtiblekh and in the houses of prayer. The young then would stroll along the roads that led to the surrounding villages. Pious Jews had their roads for strolling – the length of the Shul Gas [Synagogue Street] to the river and large "sidewalk" that connected both corners of the pond.

*

The preparations for Passover in Klobuck began during Shabbos Shirah.[1] After the prayers on Shabbos Shirah, it was announced in the synagogue that, God willing, everyone should come to the rabbi where the holiday flour would be sold. An auction took place in the rabbi's house. Whoever gave more received the supply contract for flour. A month before Passover, the flour was brought to Klobuck. It was hidden in a special room and the rabbi took the key.

[Page 53]

Two Weeks Before Passover

In the shtetl they began to feel that the great holiday of the Exodus of the Jews from Egypt was approaching – they began to bake matzo. The bakers – my father and Chaim Yehoshaya the bagel maker, Yakl Ribsztajn and Yehezkiel Mejtes, Moshe Mendl and Kopl the baker – were busy making matzo. They heated the ovens at night on Shabbos. After eating on Sunday morning, the rabbi went to look over the ovens to see if they had been properly koshered for Passover.

The rabbi had a system with which to test if the ovens were kosher. He rubbed on the bricks with a long piece of iron and, if sparks spurted, the oven was kosher. However, the rabbi was a sickly man and the iron would fall out of his hands and no sparks were seen. Then the oven would have to be heated again – until the weak hands of the rabbi scraped sparks from the bricks. The rabbi received three or four rubles for his efforts.

The supervisor of the bakeries was Reb Yudl Ahron Gad, a pious, strictly observant Jews and an Aleksander Hasid. He came to examine the utensils that had a connection to the baking of matzo several times a day such as the kneading basins, the water pails, the tables covered in tin, rolling pins and the perforators for the rolled matzos. Pious and healthy "gentile girls" were mostly employed for the rolling. As soon as Reb Yudl entered, the gentile girls immediately moved from the tables. They knew that as long as they stood there, Reb Yudl would not approach the tables. After scraping the rolling pins with glass, Reb Yudl Ahron indicated to the "gentile girls" that they could approach the table.

Water for the matzo bakeries was taken from the river. It was called mayim shelonu waser [water that has remained in a vessel overnight]. Every night in the pre–Passover weeks, they went with water cans and pails to draw water that was carried to the bakeries. There the water was filtered into barrels, covered so that it would cool off until morning so that it was worthy for baking matzos. Every Klobuck Jew felt it was a mitzvah [commandment or religious obligation] to take part in the gathering and carrying water to the matzo bakeries.

[Page 54]

Shmura matzo [matzo made under close religious supervision] was sold by several Jewish Hasidim; Berl Baruch, the supervisor Reb Yudl Ahron and others. There were two kinds of matzo shmura: that which was baked right before Passover and only used on the Seder nights and matzo shmura that the Hasidim ate all through Passover. The Hasidim baked the truly watched matzo shmura on the eve of Passover. The baking itself was a bit of a holiday. Those taking part in the holy service came in holiday clothes. They sang Hallel [songs of praise taken from Psalms] and Hasidic melodies when the matzo was placed in the oven.

Once a case occurred with Reb Berl Baruch that incited the entire shtetl. Reb Berl Baruch hid the shmura flour in the attic so that no one would touch it. Before Passover, when he took down the flour, it was completely wet. It was said cats had searched for a resting place on the flour... The flour was banned and the price of shmura matzo rose terribly in Klobuck.

In the houses of the Klobuck Jews, they began to prepare for Passover at Purim. In addition to scouring, washing, rubbing and scrapping every corner of the house, every woman of the house was busy preparing beet borsht. They purchased herring casks, small and large, several weeks before Passover. They were scrubbed well at the river and then they were left to soak in the water for two weeks. Close to Passover the holiday knife was taken out. The beets were cut and they were stuffed into the casks. The full casks were covered with clean linen and were placed in a corner of the house. The children were told to be sure not to touch the casks and threatened with great punishment from heaven.

Three days before Passover the cask was opened and the borsht was tested; if it poured thickly it was a sign that the borsht was successful.

The "first born sons" ran to the synagogue and houses of prayer on the morning of the eve of Passover to celebrate the completion of the collective reading of the Talmud [commentaries]. The young men of the houses of prayer already were there with copies of the Gemara [Talmudic commentaries] and showed the "first born sons" where to complete the last lines of the Tractate [section of the Talmud]. They drank a toast and the young man was redeemed.

After the burning of the hometz [foods not kosher for Passover], they waited impatiently for the sun to set somewhere in the unknown distance and the joyful holiday night would envelope the shtetl.

[Page 55]

Days of Awe, Succos, Hashanah Rabah and Simkhas Torah

The arrival of the Days of Awe already was felt during Rosh Khodesh Elul [the first day of the month of Elul – August or September]. The blowing of the shofar [ram's horn] at the close of prayer reminded the Jews that the Day of Judgment was arriving. Almost every Jew in the houses of prayer studied a page of Gemara because if an illness occurred, a woman had a difficult labor, the shofar could be used to drive away the illness...

Kasriel the bookseller appeared in Klobuck as soon as the first sound of the shofar was heard in the shtetl. He emptied his sack of books near the door of the house of prayer and then arranged them on a long table. He had an assortment: makhzorim [holiday prayer books], sidurim [prayer books], musar–seforim [books of ethics] and storybooks. There were new almanacs with calendars, in which were "prophesies" of when there would be snow, frost, rain and sunshine. The sale of esrogim [citrons used during the Sukkos services B,– Feast of Tabernacles], which were brought to show the rabbi for his appraisal, also began during Rosh Khodesh Elul.

During the days of slikhos [penitential prayers said during the days preceding Rosh Hashanah] the preparations for the "Day of Judgment" increased. A fear descended over the shtetl. Everyone, including women with their small children, came to the first slikhos in the synagogues and houses of prayer at four in the morning. Pious Jews went to the ritual bath before slikhos.

The fruit sellers, who took the fruits to Czenstochow, came to slikhos. Jews from all of the surrounding villages in the Dzialoszyn area came. They filled the prayer houses at the grey dawn and heartrendingly prayed in words not understood by every worshipper.

Everyone entered the synagogue very early on Rosh Hashanah to hear Reb Nota, the shoykhet, recite the verses of the songs of praise; the Jew who prayed at the reader's desk during the morning prayer always was Reb Yeshaya Buchinik, until the arrival of Reb Moshe, the shoykhet in Klobuck, who became the usual khazan [cantor].

[Page 56]

They went to the river for tashlikh ["casting off" – one's past sins are symbolically "cast off" into a flowing body of water] after the afternoon prayers. Every strata of Jews had its spot at the river: middleclass Jews stood to recite tashlikh across from the synagogue courtyard; Hasidim went farther, where the water was deeper and the currents would carry away the sins more quickly... Radomsker Hasidim had a claim at the river close to the lake. Thus, each Klobuck Jew had his spot at the river in Klobuck and was sure that the river actually removed all of the sins and carried them away to the sea.

Right after Rosh Hashanah, the trade in kapores [chicken used in a ceremony in atonement of one's sins] began. The peasants from the surrounding villages knew what kind of kaporens [fowls] they needed to bring to each house: for a pregnant woman – a chicken and a rooster, for a Hasidic family – white chickens.

At two o'clock in the afternoon Erev [on the eve of] Yom Kippur, the entire shtetl felt itself in a Yom Kippur mood. They went to the afternoon prayers and brought candles with them to the synagogue that were placed in sand boxes. After eating the last meal before the holiday, a cry was heard from each house when the mothers blessed the candles. The children were blessed; best wishes were given to neighbors and the best wishes were accompanied by loud laments.

Everyone went to Kol Nidre [prayer recited on the eve of Yom Kippur]; the large neshome–likht [candle lit in memory of the dead] was left burning and was watched over by an older child. They went to the synagogue, the houses of prayer and the Hasidic shtiblekh wearing kitlen [long white linen robes worn by men on holidays and also used as a shroud] and talisim [prayer shawls], in socks or in slippers, with dread and fear of the Day of Judgment. Here they really cried at the tfile–zake [prayer said on the eve of Yom Kippur]. Then there was a restrained silence.

The rabbi and Reb Nota the shoykhet took out the Sefer Torah [Torah scrolls], hugged them to their hearts and, during a procession around the Torah reader's desk, sang in weak, heartfelt God–fearing voices: "Light is sown for the righteous; and for the upright of heart, gladness [Psalm 97:11]." Then came the singing of Kol Nidre by Reb Dovid Hersh[2] the Shoykhet, which infused each worshipper with great respect and a God–fearing shiver.

The day of Yom Kippur passed in Klobuck as in all Jewish shtetlekh at that time. The Jewish streets and alleys were as if everyone had died. No non–Jews appeared there. The yellow flame of the neshome–likht disturbingly poured out of the windows of every house into the daylight. The heartrending voices of the worshippers, who pleaded with God Almighty for a good year, health and income, drifted from the prayer houses.

After sunset, when the prayers ended, after an entire day of fasting, the pious Jews did not hurry to go home. They remained to recite the blessing for the new moon and again wished each other a good year.

[Page 57]

Reb Dovid Hirsh the shoykhet and khazan

The Jews in Klobuck were already busy preparing for the Sukkos holiday the morning after Yom Kippur. All became master construction craftsmen. They sawed boards, nailed together walls and at almost every Jewish house a sukkah [temporary structure in which one has meals and may sleep during the holiday of Sukkos] grew. At the same the trade in esrogim and lulavim [unopened frond of date palm tree – used during prayers on Sukkos], which were brought from Czenstochow, took place.

The eight days of Sukkos passed joyfully with songs of praise that ended with the great joy of the Torah – Simkhas Torah [holiday celebrating the conclusion of the annual cycle of Torah reading and the start of a new one] – the true people's holiday for small and big, for women and men, a people's demonstration with adorned flags, burning candles [in] children's hands in honor of the Torah. These holidays, the Days of Awe and the joyful decorative sukkahs, glowed and lightened the heavy, grey fall and winter that long and painfully spread over Klobuck.

[Page 58]

Klobuck Wedding Customs

Every shtetl in Poland had its wedding customs. And the weddings often were transformed into a folk entertainment in which almost half of the shtetl took part. Not everyone was an invited guest, but the majority of Jews in the shtetl celebrated with the families whose children married.

If the groom was from Klobuck, the celebration began with him being called up to the Torah. Relatives and friends of the family were invited to the synagogue early on Shabbos for prayers. The groom was called up to daven maftir [read the last part of the Torah portion and the haftarah – related portion from the books of Prophets]. Reb Dovid Hersh sang a joyful march after the blessings and sugar candies, nuts and raisins were thrown on the groom from the women's section.

[Page 59]

When the groom was from another city, they went up to halfway on the road to meet him. For example: the Klobuck in–laws had to meet a groom from Czenstochow halfway on the road in Grabowka. Both families met there; they drank a toast of l'khaim [to life] and everyone joyfully entered Klobuck together. If the groom and his family did not come on time, the in–laws on the bride's side were very insulted and the shame of the insult hovered over the entire wedding. The mothers–in–law particularly felt the hurt.

Klobuck did not have its own klezmorim [traditional east European Jewish musicians]. There were two bands – the Dzialoszyner and Wloyner. The Wloyner were thought to be better. Their band consisted of five people. Therefore, they were paid two rubles more. The Dzialoszyner only had four musicians. They were called "di grimplers" [tuneless strummers] in the shtetl. Klobuck also did not have its own badkhen [wedding entertainer or master of ceremonies, who often recited improvised rhymes]. Therefore, they would bring Arye Marszalek or the lame Kopl from Czenstochow.

[They were led] to the khupah [wedding canopy under which the marriage took place], which was placed in the synagogue courtyard, during the dark hours. Candles were placed in the windows on the streets through which the wedding procession passed with music. The entire shtetl almost always stood at the khupah. There was joy and gladness, delight and rejoicing, as is said in the wedding blessing.

Translator's Footnotes:

1. This Sabbath falls either in late January or early February. The Torah portion, Beshalah from Exodus, is read on this Sabbath and is about the Exodus of the Jews from Egypt.

2. The name is spelled both Hersh and Hirsh in this article.

[Page 60]

Stories from Ancient Times

A "Confusion" That (Threatened) Against Jews

By Nechemia Starszynski
Translated from Yiddish to English by Asher Szmulewicz

Two Jews told me the following story:

It happened in year 1896. At that time there was a teacher in Klobuck, a Jew and a Torah scholar, named Reb Moshe Zalman. This teacher loved to drink strong alcoholic beverages, and he often was drunk; he was recognized by his red nose.

During Purim, when Jews are permitted to drink alcohol to the point that they cannot tell the difference between Mordechai and Haman, (the characters of the Purim story), of course, Reb Moshe Zalman went on a binge. Together with his son, Mordechai, and his grandson, Mendel, they wandered through the streets drunk and rejoiced. They hung a puppet made of old clothes, representing (the villain), Haman, on a hook used to draw water from the well, and sang: "Arur Haman, Baruch Mordechai" (Cursed be Haman; Blessed be Mordechai). So as to be understood by the Polish inhabitants of the shtetl, they sang also "Haman wiszy na szubenica" (Haman is hanging on the gallows).

This angered the non–Jews very much, seeing that Jews were happy about their victory over their enemy, and they told the priest that in Klobuck Jews were making fun of Jesus, and that they were carrying him through the streets and calling him "Haman". The priest gave sermons in church, inciting threats and retaliation against Jews.

Immediately Reb Moshe Zalman and his son were denounced. They were arrested. There was an oppressed atmosphere among Jews. Jews started to fear that a pogrom was going to happen.

The fear about a pogrom was increased when Jews saw that in the wood pile in Jagelski's yard, long knives and other weapons were being hidden, and were being made ready to make a blood bath on the Jews. People realized that the situation was bad and it was decided to send a delegation to the Governor in Piotrkow. The delegation constituted Hartzke Fajga, Meir Mayerczak, and another Jew.

The Jews went to the Governor in Piotrkow, and persuaded him that he should not allow a pogrom to occur. Shortly thereafter, several Russian officers went to Klobuck. They investigated. Understandably, it was proven that the non–Jews made a mistake and created a confusion. The officers warned the priest that he would be responsible for each person arrested who acted against the Jews. If a pogrom occurred in Klobuck, a troop of Dragoon–Cossacks would be dispatched. The guilty ones would be sent to Siberia.

The warning helped. The arrested people were freed, and the Jews were relieved.

[Page 61]

Cutting Off (A Woman's) Hair at the Birth of Her Child
By Borukh Szimkowicz
Translated from Yiddish to English by Asher Szmulewicz

Dvorah, Nechemia Mayerczik's wife, was the first wife in Klobuck to uncover her hair. People told the following story about her:

The shtetl was "boiling" over this offense, (religious, married, Jewish women did not appear in public without covering their hair). How was it possible for a married woman to go around without a wig, which was the way it should be for Jews? But nothing could be done against the offender. An "opportunity" soon arose to remove this sin from Jewish daughters.

Dvorah had a difficult labor (before childbirth). Her moaning and yelling could be heard all over the shtetl. Jews, full of compassion, forgot about her sin, and started to recite Tehilim (Psalms) and prayed to God that He should save her from her difficult childbirth. However, the women did not forget Dvorah's sin, and they came to the conclusion that until somebody cut Dvorah's the hair, God would not forgive her sin and she could, God forbid, go from this world to the other (die), together with her child.

The courageous wife of the Gabai, Hinde Myriam Green, took it upon herself to save the woman with the difficult childbirth. Hinde came to Dvorah and without listening to her crying and screaming, she cut Dvorah's hair.

[Page 62]

A Women Rebellion Against the Rabbi.

I don't remember when it happened, but the following happened:

People came to the Rabbi during Pesach, and told him that several teenager girls from Klobuck ate Chametz, (un–kosher for Passover food), drank beer and the like.

The Rabbi held a meeting with several well to do Jews, and it was decided that the Rabbi would speak in Shul against the frivolous young women, and that at Rosh HaShana and Yom Kippur, the women would not be allowed to enter in the women's aisle (in Shul to pray) because they did not keep their daughters from committing sins.

And so it was: On Rosh HaShana in the morning, when the women came to pray, they found the door to the women's aisle locked. The observant women did not keep quiet, but made a commotion, and entered the men's aisle and interfered with the men's prayers.

Several eminent, well to do, Jews intervened, and asked the Rabbi to authorize the opening of the women's aisle. The Shamash (Synagogue care-taker) opened the door of the women's aisle and the rebellion calmed down.

Fires and the Jewish Firefighters.

Klobuck, like the majority of the Jewish shtetls with wooden houses, often had a visit from the "Red Rooster" (fire). Jews in Klobuck, didn't seem to pay much attention to their fires, and people always spoke of fires in the neighboring village of Kamyk. As soon as there were red fire flames, people used to say: "it is burning in Kamyk".

[Page 63]

Klobuck had its Jewish Firefighters. As soon as a fire broke out, everyone could see the fireman, Hershl Krzepicki, in the streets with a big trumpet. He walked through the small streets to the market, blowing his trumpet and making a lot of noise. Leibke Sznajder was with him, with a smaller trumpet, cursing and calling the inhabitants to be aware of the enemy fire. Soon the other firemen gathered: Yankel Rypsztajn, Mordechai Rosen, Baruch Lewkowicz, Chilke Maites, Itzik Elyahu Besser, Baruch Szperling and Herztke Fajga, the commander of the firemen.

At the same time the Polish firemen also came running. When everybody was in place, they had to harness a horse to bring water.

When a fire broke out during a market day, they took a horse from the peasants that came to the Klobuck Fair. The peasants knew what was coming, and as soon as they heard the trumpet, they left the shtetl. Most of the time they had to take a horse from a local coachman, and they took the horse out of its stable, without asking its owner. With the horse they went to the Firemen's shed in the marketplace to get the barrel, and then they ran to the "Jike", which was the name of the shtetl's stream, in order to bring water.

By the time everything was in place, and until the rubber hose was ready, the fire already had spread from one house to the next. Most of the time everything was burned. I remember a fire on Shabbat, during the day, in the house of Reb Machel Dudek.

Reb Machel came out from the fire with two chalot (Shabbat bread) in his hands. When people asked him later: Why did you only save the two chalot?

He answered: according to the Shulchran Aruch, if a fire breaks out on Shabbat, nothing is allowed to be saved, except the chalot for the meal.

But the common people thought otherwise, and they removed everything from Reb Machel's house. The house burned completely.

Page 64]

The Economic Life

Sources of Income
by Moshe Wajnman, Paris
Translated from Yiddish to English by Asher Szmulewicz

The livelihoods and sources of income of the Jews of Klobuck were of varied. Like in all of the shtetls, the specific Jewish trades were prominent: ready to wear tailors, sold their products in the market; custom tailors, had their customers in the shtetl among the well to do Jewish and Christian populations; milliners, produced all types of hats: "litsipetkes"[1], winter hats, Jewish kerchiefs, and velvet hats; shoemakers, who cobbled new shoes or boots, and shoemakers that only repaired footwear; and gaiter-stitchers, which was a respectable trade, and was a craft and trade primarily for the Chasidic Jews.

Almost all of the businesses in the shtetl were in Jewish hands. The Jewish dry-goods store carried woolen fabric, white linen, peasant checkered fabric for blanket covers and pillow cases, flowery head scarves, and heavy winter shawls. Also the colonial food shops were mainly held in Jewish hands. The mills that ground wheat and rye, and provided electric light for the shtetl and electricity for the three sawmills that cut beams and boards also belonged to Jews.

The Jewish means of making a living also included the peddlers. They sold among the poorer villages, and dragged themselves on the roads during the heat and the cold, and hardly made a poor living. A special source of income for a significant number of Jewish families was the result of the trade with the nearby town of Czestochowa. Coachmen transported

[Page 65]

the traders to Czestochowa, and they returned in the late evening with the goods from the town. Also in the shtetl were Jewish tea-houses; orchard men "sadownikes", who rented orchards from rich peasants and landowners; hairdressers; butchers; an ice shop; and the Jewish religious trades: shochatim (ritual slaughterer); melamdim (Jewish teachers); Jewish judges; and the Rabbi.

During these years Klobuck had also a special category of Jews who made a good living by smuggling goods from the nearby Germany (distant of 17 kilometers from Klobuck) to Poland (that is to say Russia). Tobacco, saccharin and silk were smuggled.

Translator's Footnote:

1. I think it is a Borsalinoy.

[Page 65]

Jewish Artisans and Merchants

Borukh Szimkowicz
Translated by Gloria Berkenstat Freund

The Klobuck Jewish artisans were mostly pious men of the people who in the very full fervor of work would leave everything, wash their hands, put on their cloth smock and run to the synagogue to prayer in a *minyon* [prayer group of at least 10 men]. If someone was a bit of a *bel-tefillah* [the cantor or man who prays for the congregation at the lectern], a *baal-koreh* [man who chants from the Torah], he did not miss the opportunity to go to the lectern or reading desk to read the *Sefer [Torah].*They went home satisfied – having given to God in heaven what was His.

These simple Jews gave away their last *groshns* for their children to study Torah with the best teachers. *Machn di kinder for mentshn* [turning their children into responsible people] was a sacred obligation for each of the toiling Klobucker Jews. And the Klobuck Jewish community did not have to be ashamed of its people. Here there were learned men, heads of *yeshivus* [religious secondary schools], good tradesmen, great merchants, party leaders and community workers. It is worthwhile to immortalize in our memorial book the types and personalities of the toiling, sensitive Jewish community.

Avraham Leib Chorszewski belonged to the branch of tailors by appointment. He was a tall Jew with a small beard. He was called the Wreczycer tailor because before he settled in Klobuck, he had lived in Wreczyca. Arvaham Leib mainly worked for Christian high government officials who lived around Klobuck: in Zagorze, in the "imperial court" and for nobles in the area.

The tailor by appointment was a Radomsker Hasid. His son, Emanuel, was a good student. Avraham Leib's son and three daughters, Ita, Pesa and Yehudis live in Israel.

Lipman Holcman and Zindl Zigleman, tailors by appointment, only were busy with new Jewish garments: beautiful cloth jackets, furcoats, overcoats, *meshilange* [full length silk kaftans worn by pious men] and satin kaftans.

[Page 66]

**Avraham Leib Chorzewski [spelled Chorszewski below] and his family;
two daughters and a son remain – [they] live in Israel)**

[Page 67]

The so-called inferior-quality tailors, who worked for the market, were in great number in Klobuck. They bought balls of goods in Czenstochow, mainly on credit, and made suits, overcoats that they sold at the fairs in the surrounding villages and *shtetlekh* [towns]. If there was a large market day, they had the money to pay the merchant for the goods and a fine profit remained. And if they stood the entire day without revenue and still had to pay travel expenses – it was bitter. There was nothing with which to pay the merchant and there was hunger in the house.

Reb Lipman Birenbaum was an interesting type among the inferior-quality tailors. He was very beloved by the peasants who bought from him because of his good relationship with them. When Reb Lipman stood at the market selling his goods, he always had small boxes of snuff with him. When a peasant went by, Reb Lipman honored him with a bit of snuff and with it "recited" in Polish: "Do not be so hard on yourself; take a whiff of snuff." With such a joyous welcome, the peasant customer let himself be measured for a suit and agreed to the price. In addition, Reb Lipman said to his wife: "Bayla, pack up the suit quickly, bind it well with a lot of string"...

Rep Lipman had sons who were scholars, leaders of prayers. One son, Shlomo, is one of the oldest Klobuckers in Israel.

Hershl Ripsztajn worked sewing women's clothing. Yitzhak Zajbel was one of the most esteemed sewers of linens. He was the *gabbai* [assistant to the rabbi] of the *Khevra Kadisha* [burial society] for many years. Yitzhak was knowledgeable in the traditional Jewish texts and their study. His ambition was to pray at the synagogue lectern and to read from the *Sefer* [*Torah*]. His daughter Batya lives in Israel.

The life of the shoemakers was difficult. Almost all of them were very poor. If there was no one to earn money with poultry and fruits, he did not have any income. Despite their poverty, the Klobuck Jewish shoemakers always provided for their children to be able to study. They took money needed for food to pay the *melamdim* [religious school teachers]. The shoemaker, Jakov Goldberg, had a son who was called the Wloyner prodigy, because he lived in Wloyn. He was the author of several religious books.

[Page 68]

The Jews in Klobuck were represented in almost all of the craft trades. There were trades which employed only two or three people: there were three gaiter- quilters – Jakov Fajga from the old city, Niedziele, who lived in Zawada and Chaim Zajdman, whose son lives in Israel; two tinsmiths – Beser and Mendl Fajga. Beser worked on gutters for houses, covered roofs. From time to time he made repairs on the roof of the synagogue, which was a religious service for him. Mendl Fajga was occupied with domestic work such as fixing bathtubs, washtubs and pots. On Chanukah, he made various Chanukah lamps. Of the two hatmakers, one, Itsikl Lapides, worked for Christians, mainly fur winter hats, and he had a good income. The second one – Ayzyk Zagelman – had Jewish work. He traveled to the market and it was difficult for him to earn a living. Despite this, he always was in good humor, loved a witticism, a joke and never complained about his fate.

Two Jews were dyers: Reb Meir Hersh, a tall, quiet, modest Jew, and Shlomo Rozen, whose son lives in Israel. Both dyers had village work. The dyed wool was always seen hanging from poles in front of the houses of the artisans.

There were two Jewish oil pressers. They had great difficulty with income and had to have additional employment. One of them – Moshe Yakov Rozental taught, working with children learning *Khumish* and Rashi. In addition, he was a barber every Friday. He cut [hair] mainly for Hasidim. The second one was called Shlomo Rozental or Shlomo *Olejarz* [Polish word – oil man]. Both oil pressers had work from the village population. Peasants brought linseeds from which the oil pressers extracted the oil by primitive means. The greatest season was "Lent" time when the Catholics did not eat meat and used a lot of oil. The oil pressers then worked day and night. With great difficulty, they extracted their income from this season for an entire year.

[Page 69]

A good trade, which provided income, was the baking trade. Klobuck had several Jewish bakeries. The majority of them were named for the wives of the bakers, such as: Gitl Kopl's [Gitl, Kopl's wife], Brayndl Zalman's, Perl Lipman's. In addition there were bakeries with men's personal names, such as Moshe Dovid Ripsztajn, Josl Beker and Avraham Itshe Holcman.

The Jewish bakeries baked: bread, challah, rolls, bagels, *rogalkes* [horn-shaped loaves], *kajzerkes* [Kaiser rolls] – braided rolls and the like. The Christian taverns and restaurants bought from the Jewish bakers in addition to the usual purchasers of baked goods. This lasted until the Poles opened a bakery and took away all of the Christian customers from the Jewish bakers. It is interesting that the Polish baker employed a professional Jewish [baker] because he was not able to compete with the production of the Jewish bakers. He also wanted to win Jewish customers through the Jewish baker.

The Jewish bakers were afraid of the Polish competition and sought help from the rabbis. Bakers traveled to the rabbis from Radomsk, Rozprza and Czenstochow and asked for prayers that the gentile's baked goods would not succeed. One of the righteous men assured them that the Christian baker would close his bakery. So it was: the Jewish journeyman left his Christian boss. The Polish baker's baked good did not succeed during the year-end holidays. A second time the baked goods were burned. Finally, he closed the bakery. Naturally, Hasidim saw this as a miracle from the righteous man. Later, another Christian bakery opened.

The four Klobuck Jewish butchers – Mordekhai Unglik, Wolf Gelbard, Kopl Golard and Mentshe Unglik – were very charitable men and observant Jews. They took part in all of the institutions and helped the poor. Mentshe's wife, Rodl, stood in the butcher shop with her husband on Thurdays and during her free time did a great deal for the poor. Their daughter, Adela, who lives in Australia, visited Israel some time ago. Wolf Gelbard's son, Avraham, lives in Israel.

[Page 70]

In addition to the listed professions, Klobock also had: a Jewish carpenter – Reb Josef Gliksman; a glazer – Reb Berish; his daughter lives in Israel; and a watchmaker – Reb Meir Blau, a Radomsker Hasid.

The carpenter and the glazer had great difficulty earning a living. It was better for the watchmaker, who raised his children in the spirit of Torah. His oldest son, Yakov Ahron, was a learned man. Reb Meir Blau's daughter, Bluma, lives in Israel.

Klobuck also had two Jewish master-craftsmen who made clay pots (earthern). They were called: Mendl *Teper* [pot maker] and Borukh *Teper*. They brought clay from the Podkamienicer road and they produced various pots, flower pots using all of the primitive machines, such as a cutting machine worked with the feet. There were also several wagon drivers, porters, fruit traders, orchardists and Jews who were involved with agricultural; they [did the] seeding, plowing and cutting themselves.

Food Stores and Cloth Shops

The food stores belonged to the Hasidic Jew. They mainly were former *kest-eydems* [sons-in-law who were supported by their fathers-in-law for the first years after their marriage] who, when they became "on their own," had small food stores arranged for them by their in-laws. The *kest-eydems*, former habitués of the houses of prayer, or young *yeshiva* men did not have any trade. Therefore, they had to become teachers or storekeepers.

Jews in Klobuck, as in the majority of the *shtetlekh* [towns] in Poland, had almost all of the commerce in their hands, such as: cloth shops, grain stores, shoe businesses, confectioners and the like.

The Klobuck "steam" mill belonged to the partners, Josef Meir Kurland and Moshe Zylberbaum. The owner of the water mill was a Pole. The two sawmills (*zegwerk*) belonged to two Jewish partners – Hasidic Jews. Each sawmill had two partners who traveled to different rebbes.

The Klobuck Jewish horse and cattle merchants represented a particular stratum. The horses were sold in various places in Poland and brought to neighboring Germany. There they were sold to the German horse traders. The Klobuck Jewish horse merchants were divided into two groups. Each group had its partners. Those involved in this commerce had a respectable income.

[Page 71]

The cattle merchants were divided into groups. Each group had its partners. The cattle were bought at the markets in Poland and brought to Klobuck by "specialists" – drivers.

The Klobuck Jewish horse and cattle merchants were respected men. *Dozores* [members of the synagogue council] and *gabbaim* [assistants to the rabbi] were recruited from among them. They were Jews, scholars. We saw them for almost the entire week dusty, in crude clothing, cowhide boots with long sticks in their hands to drive the horse and cattle. The holy *Shabbos* arrived and they were other people. It was *lehavdl bein kodesh leChol* [distinguished between the sacred and profane]. When we passed in front of Hershl Zaks' window on *Shabbos*, we could notice how he sat over a *Midrash Rabbah* [the collected writings on the Five Books of Moses and the Books of the Song of Songs and Ruth, Esther, Lamentations and Ecclesiastes]. On *Shabbos* night, Reb Meir Szperling could be found in the house of study near the book closet looking for a good book of moral edification.

Meir Szperling

It then was difficult to believe that the middleclass, pious Jews were horse traders. The same with the cattle merchants, Yakov Fishl Rozental, Shmuel Szperling with the beautiful beard – on *Shabbos*, they did not want to hear about any business. They raised scholars and had sons-in-law who were devoted to Torah and *mitzvus* [commandments].

This is how the economic life of the Klobuck Jews appeared. The largest majority of them obtained their income with great effort.

(Information received from Gitl Goldberg, of blessed memory and Moshe Fajga)

[Page 72]

In the years up to the First World War, August 1914, Klobuck under Czarist rule, was not a *shtetl* (*miasteczko* [town]), but a settlement (*osada*). At the head of the settlement stood the village mayor and two village magistrates. In the years of my youth, that is, before 1914, I remember the village mayor, Suchajnski, a tall gentile with long sideburns and the village magistrates, Riepac and Djemba.

The leading citizens of Klobuck from the past with two Jewish representatives right: Emanuel Wilinger;
left: Dovid Zigelman and between them the village mayor, the priest and village magistrates

[Page 73]

The administrative office was the local "government house," where all of the meetings took place at which all of the business of the settlement was discussed and decided. Often, three or four Jews were invited to such meetings, particularly when decisions had to be made about new taxes.

Klobuck also had a notable arrest-house that was called the *koza*, as in all of the *shtetlekh*. Petty "criminals" sat there, such as, for example: those who received a month's arrest for fighting, for having given false weight, and Jews – for keeping their shops open on Sunday during the hour when [people] were going to the Catholic Church and, also, for not whitewashing the gutters and the like.

The *koza* was located near the administrative office. The guard for the "arrestees" was named Wilk, the tooth-puller, because in addition to being a guard, he also was employed with pulling teeth. He had a residence in the house of the administrative office. When Wilk needed to go to take care of his concerns, he let out the arrestees for an hour or two and asked them not to be too late because the chief could come and it would not be nice if he found an empty *koza.*

Wilk had particular rights with the bakers and butchers, who received punishment for charging too high a price or for not keeping the bakeries and butcher shops clean. Such "criminals" were let home for the entire night, the bakers to bake bread and the butchers to prepare the meat for sale. This had to be done with the knowledge of the "sergeant," as the local police-commandant was titled.

The Klobuck police at that time consisted of a "sergeant" and five to six policemen (*straznikes*), three gendarmes and three *smotsznikes* [police spies], a sort of border guard, who fought smuggling that came from the German border, 17 kilometers from the *shtetl.*

Printed notices were not yet known then in the administrative office. The local "news" was provided for the population through a drummer. When he began to play the drum, everyone came running and followed him. The drummer led the crowd to the pump opposite Hertske Guterman's [house]. There he again drummed and in a hoarse, drunk voice shouted out the "news." That is to say, the Piotrkow governor would be coming to the *shtetl* for a visit; the celebration (*galuvke*) in honor of the Czar or the wife of the czar was being postponed because of an illness; about the delivery of the horses for branding and about lost pigs that they were obliged to give to the owner.

The policemen were Russian. No Poles were taken for service. This is how things went on in Klobuck until the outbreak of the First World War, that is – until August 1914.

[Page 74]

The Market Place in Jewish Hands

by Batya Zajbel-Izraelewicz

Translated by Gloria Berkenstat Freund

In my time, four Jews - Zaynwl Rybsztajn, Leibke Inglik, Leib Zajdel and my father, Ayzyk Zajbel - rented the market place (Targowisko). I remember that we had a good income from our partnership in the market. My father saved money and bought the meadow near the synagogue courtyard.

A market day took place every second Wednesday. Guards stood at the gates and took payment for entering the market.

Later, during the time of the Polish state, the anti-Semites from the city managing committee did not permit Jews to rent the market place. It went over into Polish hands. One by one the Poles took over other means of income in the *shtetl.*

[Page 75]

The First World War and its Effects on Klobucker Jews

Fear of a Pogrom During the Bellis Trial

by Moshe Wajnman

Translated from Yiddish to English by Asher Szmulewicz

The effects of the Russian-Japanese war in 1904, and the revolutionary movement in 1905 were not felt in shtetl. A few Jews from Klobuck, who served in the Russian army and took part in the war, talked about their experiences, when they fought against the "Japanishkes" (derogatory name for Japanese), many years afterwards in "Port-Arthur". The Jewish "Achdut" (Jewish socialist movement) had no special influence in the year 1905. Very few people from Klobuck, who became active in the socialist party in Czestochowa, were arrested and deported to Siberia.

In 1912-1913 Jews in Klobuck felt a special shock during the blood-libel trial of Mendel Bellis in Kiev. Bellis was charged with murdering a young Christian boy in order to use his blood to prepare (Passover) Matzot. During preparations for the trial in the summer 1913, as always, during the harvest, religious Poles went to the "Holy Mother" in "Jasna Góra"[1] in Czestochowa. At that time the Jews in Klobuck lived with deathly fear. On all of the roads to Czestochowa there were processions (of Poles displaying) holy images. In Klobuck people waited for their arrival and anticipated and prepared for a pogrom.

Despite the (highly charged atmosphere), no pogrom actually occurred. People said that a pogrom was averted because the religious, anti-semitic, Poles had something else to divert their attention. During the preparations of the Bellis trial, another trial was being prepared against a high level priest from Czestochowa, Macoch[2] (pronunciation Matzoch), who was accused of stealing a jewel from the eye of the "Holy Mother" in "Jasna Góra".

[Page 76

During these times, when non-Jews shouted at us (young boys): "Bellishe", we answered back with: "Macoch". Later, after the exoneration of Bellis, we added a rhyme in Polish: "Bellis ¿ywy, a Macoch zgni" (Bellis is alive and Macoch is rotting). This was an allusion to the fact that Bellis was freed of the blood-libel accusation, while Macoch was rotting in jail.

T

ranslator Footnotes

The Jasna Góra Monastery (Polish: Jasna Góra, Luminous Mount) in Czêstochowa, Poland, is the most famous Polish shrine to the Virgin Mary and the country's greatest place of pilgrimage – for many its spiritual capital. The image of the Black Madonna of Czêstochowa, also known as Our Lady of Czêstochowa, to which miraculous powers are attributed, is Jasna Góra's most precious treasure. (source Wikipedia)

Damazy Macoch was a monk in Czenstochow's Pauline Convent. He killed his cousin and confessed to the murder, which took place after the monk, his cousin and his cousin's wife had committed a robbery at Jasna Góra, desecrating the robe and diamond encrusted crown of the "Black Madonna" and stealing and selling the jewels (source Jews in Czêstochowa Up to the First World War, Yiskor Book of Czêstochowa). He died in prison in 1916.

The Difficult Experiences of the First World War

by Moshe Wajnman

Translated from Yiddish to English by Asher Szmulewicz

The Jews of Klobuck lived through a difficult time at the beginning of the First World War, in August 1914; the shtetl made almost no preparations for the coming war. Very few people read the newspapers then. We spoke about a war in the future. Although nobody believed it would happen, the Jewish population's hearts were filled with fear. Jews saw in the red flares of the sunset, a sign of a coming war.

Suddenly, on a Sunday morning in Av we heard unusual thunderings. It was the morning of the outbreak of the war. The German army got closer to Klobuck, and took strategic positions around the shtetl, while shooting at the Russian garrison, which was fortified in the Zagorz "Prince Castle". Klobuck, from the first days of August 1914, experienced all of the horrors of the war.

The battle lasted for more than two hours. There were dead and wounded people. Houses of Podkamenicz were burning, the flames rose, the sky was full with black clouds of smoke. The Germans invaded Klobuck. Their first order was to give all of the inhabitants two hours to leave the shtetl. This resulted in a panic. Rumors were wide spread that the village would be torched by the Germans, so as to drive away the Russian military and the spies that were supposedly hiding in the houses. Anyone that was found hiding would be shot.

[Page 77]

Everyone ran away, filled with fear. Everyone took what he could carry from his apartment, and ran away, without looking back. The roads leading to the neighboring villages were full of the refugee waves. Fully packed carts were dragged, and filled with the small part of the lives of poverty that could be saved. Sick and tired people were scattered throughout the country; the hungry and thirsty, knocked on peasants' huts and asked for a piece of bread or some water.

The few Jews that did not want to leave their home, afraid that their possessions would be looted, were found by the Germans. All of the hidden Jews were gathered and brought to the Christian cemetery to be shot. This was before Hitler's time, and during the First World War, so then, things were different. The Germans were not caught up in an anti-Semitic madness. The Landowner of Libidcz, who had German origins, intervened on behalf of the Jews with the German Authorities. The executions were postponed. In the end all of the Jews were let go and expelled from the shtetl.

The front moved eastward. Two weeks later, we slowly came back to our homes, to find that that they were looted. Slowly by slowly, life progressed on a war standard of living. Some of the traditional tradesmen and newcomers adapted to the new situation, and became involved with smuggling foodstuffs and trading with the military. A number of Jews worked for the Germans. But the vast majority of Jews from Klobuck were left without a livelihood. They were starving. A typhus epidemic broke out, and many people died.

Although the German occupation then did not specifically focus on the Jewish population, the Jews endured many harsh decrees. Jews had to keep their shops open on Shabbat so that German soldiers would be able to buy goods. Another decree ordered that observant Jews were required to be photographed, bare headed, for their identification papers. Jews were also ordered to cut their beards when they underwent delousing at the Zagorz distillery building, which, during the Russian period, produced liquor called "Monopolke".

The groceries and bakeries had a lot of trouble from the German sanitary inspector. The officer, a little man with a short beard, that Jews called "Dos Beardel" (the small beard), harassed all of the groceries and bakeries for the slightest speck of dust. For the smallest infringement he closed the food enterprise for eight days. Slowly, the Jews became used to the German occupation authorities of that time, and it was better than the Czarist pogrom reign.

After the defeat of the German army and the armistice, Poland became an independent country and for the Jews in Klobuck a new political and economic era started, based on the equality of rights that the Jews received from the Polish Authorities.

[Page 78]

Memories of the First World War

by Baruch Szimkowicz

Translated from Yiddish to English by Asher Szmulewicz

Tisha BeAv 1914, Thursday morning, the German army marched toward Czestochowa without encountering any resistance from the Russians, who had left the city earlier. The Russian forces also left Klobuck, and the firemen (stra□ak), together with the Poles, Klepacz, Socinski and Dzemba, assumed leadership and took over the administration of the shtetl.

The Jewish population lived with great fear. People anticipated attacks on Jews, and the fear increased because of the wide spread rumor that organized gangs, who called themselves "Kosarjes", because they were armed with scythes (koses)

[Page 79]

and sticks, were in the region. People did not know who these gangs opposed; but we were sure that the first scapegoats would be the Jews.

For approximately one month, Klobuck was administered by the firemen. Then without warning, a German scout section, which was comprised of several horsemen, arrived in the shtetl. They summoned the leaders of the village, and asked about the whereabouts of Russian soldiers. The Germans requested that the leaders assure and encourage the population to stay calm, and immediately report to the Germans if Russian soldiers were present. After this announcement the scout section left, and Klobuck remained under the watch of the firemen, who guarded the village during the night.

Two weeks before Rosh HaShanah (New Year), on a Sunday morning at 8 o'clock, Russian Don Cossacks[1] entered Klobuck, and marched through the village in the direction of Dzialoszyn. The inhabitants were full of fear. We knew that nothing good could come from this. There was nowhere to go because the roads were filled with the military personnel of both sides. Two hours later we saw that the German cavalry was coming from the direction of the Czestochowa road. A few of them entered the village, and ordered the people to remain inside their houses.

I looked outside from a crack in the window, and saw how the Germans took positions in the streets along the walls. Soon a troop of Cossacks came from the Zagorz road, and shooting from both sides started, which lasted for two hours. A daughter of Yaacov Fishel, Yaske Berlin's wife, was killed from a stray bullet.

When the shooting stopped we saw dead Russians and horses lying in the streets. A rumor spread that the Germans were going to shell Klobuck, and so it was. Around three o'clock the cannons thundered. The sky became red from the flames and black from the smoke. Fire surrounded Szmulewicz's house. When the cannon fire subsided, people panicked, and started to flee from the shtetl. People ran by foot or by horses on all of the roads that led to the surrounding villages. All of the Jews left. Only Reb David Hersh Shochat stayed with his family. He said: "Here neither drowse nor sleep the Guardian of Israel" (Verse of the Psalms). They had a very bad night. The Rabbi of Klobuck (finally) left with his wife and children (and went) to his family in Warsaw.

[Page 80]

The next day, when things calmed down, little by little people started to come back to the shtetl. In the evening people returned to where they came from. At the end (of the day) a few people took the risk of staying overnight in their dark houses, under the (blasts from) the artillery guns. My father, with the entire family, also stayed overnight.

We had a bakery and seeing that people were coming back, we took the risk to bake bread, using flour taken from our strongly locked storage room. We were right: The Klobuck inhabitants came back to the shtetl, and carefully life in the shtetl returned, but we still did not have a stable leadership in Klobuck.

Rosh HaShanah and Yom Kippur went by calmly. Jews prayed in the Synagogue and in the House of studies. Before Sukkot, a section of Germans soldiers came with gendarmes (country police), and took over the buildings of the former Russian authority, and we found ourselves under German occupation.

After Sukkot the German Military went through Klobuck. The shtetl was an important stopover. The first decree from the German Authorities was that every household must accommodate German soldiers. The requisitioning depended on the number of rooms of each apartment. The population did not oppose this measure. An officer led groups of soldiers, and split them among apartments.

[Page 81]

The Germans of the First World War had not reached the awful level of genocide. They did not have any biased attitude towards the civilian population or the Jews. In Klobuck war means of living were set up. People did business with the Germans. At that time, the butchers and the bakers earned very well by providing meat and bread to the German army. The German Authorities provided flour for the bakers and cattle to the butchers.

However, the Germans wanted to force Jews to desecrate the Shabbat.

Close to Chanukah the Jewish population representatives were notified to appear before the Commander of Klobuck. The representatives, Avraham Jakubowicz and Aaron Zaks, went to the Commander. They received an order that the Jewish bakers and butchers had to work on Shabbat. The Commander stated: "This is war time, the military must have bread and meat, so therefore the bakers must bake during Shabbat, and the butchers must slaughter and prepare the meat on Shabbat."

The observant representatives did all that they could to revoke the decree. People went (to the Commander) to plead (that he reconsider), and ultimately it was agreed that the Germans would supply their people on Shabbat to work in the Jewish bakeries and butcher shops instead of Jews. I remember how comical it appeared in our apartment during Shabbat: we came back from Shul; my father said Kiddush at the Shabbat table; we sang zemirot (Shabbat songs); and in the bakery, bread was baked and the oven was operating. It was like this for several weeks.

A machloket (controversy) in shtel.

When the Germans took over Warsaw, The Klobucker Jewish refugees in Warsaw came back home, having left during the panic days. Among the returning people was the Rabbi of Klobuck, Rabbi Henech Goldberg. Upon his return a bitter controversy started in the shtetl. The controversy arose because the Rabbi requested that the shochatim (ritual slaughterers) pay him his part of the slaughtering fees during the full time he was not in the shtetl.

The shochatim objected and argued: "How come? Why is the Rabbi such a Rachash (Hebrew initials for Rabbi, Chazan, Shochet)". First, the money was already spent, and not on luxuries, but merely to survive; second, he was not in Klobuck, so how could the Rabbi make such a claim and request?

[Page 82]

The main controversy was between the Rabbi and Reb David Hersz Shochat. Moshe Shochat[2] did not want to get in trouble with the town Rabbi, who taught him how to be a shechita (ritual slaughter) in Klobuck. Soon there were two camps: The Chasidim and their supporters, who sided with the Rabbi, and maintained that he was entitled to get his part of the slaughtering fees, even for the time he was not in Klobuck. The common home owners from shtetl sided with Reb David Hersz Shochat, and defended him in his stance against the Rabbi, and not to give back any money.

The German demand to take photographs and the Jewish opposition on religious grounds.

In the beginning of the summer,1915, the German military had left Klobuck. A few gendarmes (country police), with a sergeant, remained and guarded the shtetl. Suddenly a new decree was issued to the Klobucker Jews: a notice asked that on a determined day all of the inhabitants of Klobuck had to bring a personal photograph of a specific size. For those who did not have a photograph, they had to come at 10 o'clock in the morning to the empty square next to the doctor, where designated photographers from Czestochowa would photograph the public.

This decree fiercely angered the observant Jews, who believed that photographing people violated Jewish law, because Jews should not make copies of people (or worship images). In addition, the non-observant were not thrilled to "be a human image". In Klobuck, people were not photographed often. There was a Jewish photographer, Motel, the son of Gertner, but he worked only for non-Jews.

Although Jews were reluctant to be photographed, on the scheduled day, Monday at 10 o'clock in the morning, Jews gathered in the square next to the doctor, and they were photographed by groups of ten. For this we had to pay 50 pfenning (100 pfenning equaled one mark) per person. On that occasion it was the first photograph taken of the majority of the Jews in Klobuck. Later, Jews received a German passport and became citizens of the German occupation Authorities.

Translator Footnotes

Don Cossacks were Cossacks who settled along the middle and lower Don. They had a rich military tradition, playing an important part in the historical development of the Russian Empire, and successfully participated in all its major wars. (source Wikipedia)

There was two shochatim (ritual slaughterers) in Klobuck David Hersz and Moshe. Shochat may not be their family name, they are called by their trade.

[Page 83]

Quarrels Because of a Chazan [cantor] and Shoychet [ritual slaughterer]

by Moshe Wajnman

Translated from Yiddish to English by Asher Szmulewicz

A great scandal erupted due to social differences when the old chazan and shochet, Reb David Hirsz Dawidowicz[1], passed away.

Reb David Hirsz was of small stature; had a long white beard; was vivacious like quicksilver; and was profoundly loved by the common people. Virtually the entire shtetl attended his levayah (burial). Eulogies were made in the great synagogue where Reb David Hirsz was the Chazan for many years. The Rabbi also made a funeral oration.

Reb David Hirsz was survived by his sons and daughters. One son was a shochet in a small village, and did not make much money. (Many) Jews from Klobuck wanted that Shlomo, (the son), should replace his father. Two other sons, Yankel and Shmuel went to the Rabbi and asked that their brother become the chazan and shochet of the shtetl. The Rabbi refused to give his approval.

A quarrel flared up in shtetl. There were two camps. On one side were the Rabbi and the chasidim, and on the other side were the craftsmen and the poor tradesmen. Shlomo came to Klobuck and started to perform the duties of a shochet. The Rabbi forbade the eating of the meat from his shechita (ritual slaughter). A few observant butchers, nevertheless, sold the forbidden meat. Each day the controversy spread.

One Friday evening, Shlomo took the pulpit and prayed as chazan in the great synagogue. Although he was not a great cantor, he was popular with the common people, due to his Kabalat Shabbat (prayer songs on Shabbat eve). The congregation sang together with the chazan, and they were happy with his victory. The Rabbi, it seemed, did not want to exacerbate the quarrel during Shabbat, and so he did not come to the great synagogue. He prayed with the Gerer Chasidim.

The controversy lasted for another few weeks and in the end, the orthodox group stopped the quarrel, and Shlomo remained both shochet and chazan. His appearance reminded us of his father, and with this he gained the sympathy of his fellow citizens.

Translator Footnote

It seems that it is the same person as Reb David Hersz Shochat from the previous chapter.

[Page 84]

The Jewish Communal Life

The First Charity Institutions and Torah Scholar Groups

by Borukh Szimkowicz

Translated from Yiddish to English by Asher Szmulewicz

The social life in Klobuck, like in other shtetls, started with charity institutions and Torah learning groups.

Remembering the old Jewish philanthropic institutions that were active in Klobuck, I recall the religious devotion, and the good deeds done for the community by the old time Jews, who were engaged in social activities. It was indeed a selfless activity, done for itself, and not for any money. This moral integrity, by those involved in public affairs, was the foundation that was transferred to the modern Jewish cultural institutions and the political parties, that were active in Klobuck.

The oldest Jewish institutions in Klobuck were "Chevra Chaye Adam" (Society for Human Life), and its predecessor, "Chevra Lomdei Torah" (Society of Torah Learners). According to tradition, this institution was created by Rabbi Yankele, righteous of blessed memory, cited in previous chapters. The goal of the institution was to provide Torah learning, Torah's laws and religious devotion among non-educated Jews. Thus, they learned the most important principles that every Jew should know: Knowledge of Moshe's Torah, Jewish Laws and Jewish Traditions.

The institution, "Human Life," had a shtibel (room to learn Torah), where Shabbat and Holiday prayers were conducted. Before davenen (prayer) in the morning, people were taught the Torah's laws for two hours, according to "Chaye Adam"[1]. After the Shabbat "tshulent", and before the afternoon nap, people studied again: in summer time, Pirkei Avot with the "Midrash Shmuel" explanations, and in winter time, various Torah reading portions with "Midrash Tanchuma".

[Page 85]

The so called "Rabbis" of the institution were: Yeshayahu Bachinek, Yosef Buchweitz, Yitzhik Chadi, and Shlomo Birenbaum, the son of Daniel Katsav. There also were Gabaim (everyday managers of a Jewish institution), who were elected in an interesting way.

Every year at Hoshanah Rabah, during the tikkun (late night Torah learning), five arbitrators were nominated, and they in turn, chose three new

Gabaim. On the afternoon of Simchas Torah, when everybody was tipsy, all of the members of the institution gathered, and the arbitrators selected the new Gabaim. Their names were not announced, but instead, the newly elected Gabaim were lifted up in the air. The first one lifted up was the First Gabai, and the other ones according to their order.

As I remember, the following people were part of the "Chaye Adam" institution: Moshe Szperling, Yitzik Tshuchne, Eliyahu Weichman, Eliyahu Mass, Hershel Szperling, Yossel Szimkowicz, Itshe Unglick, Itshe Wilkowietsker, Avraham Lubitsky, Hershel Rypsztein, Wolff Gelbard, Yunes Kirtsbard, Zalman Yossel Szwiertszewki, Chilke Kirtsbard, Moshe Mendil Friedman, Mordechai Unglick, Leib Szperling, Kopel Rosenszweig, Leib Zeibel and Kopel Weichman.

"Bikur Cholim" (Visiting and comforting the sick people)

"Bikur Cholim" was one of Klobuck's oldest institutions. According to the regulations of the institution, the goal was to provide poor and sick people with free medical help, such as, a doctor, or a barber (old time barbers were also surgeons), and also to provide medical equipment, such as a thermometer, cupping glass, rubber waist belt, and the like. The medical equipment also was lent to well to do people, who paid according to their use.

The "Bikur Cholim" members sustained the institution, as follows: a membership fee was paid by everyone, according to their means, which was collected every month by the shamash of the Beit Midrash, and from nedarim (promises to give money), when being called for an Aliyah to the Torah Reading. The majority of the members prayed on Shabbat morning at the large Beit HaMidrash. They were always together. Those who prayed in the Chasidic shtiblech were expected to pray at least once a month

[Page 86]

in the Beit HaMidrash, and promise to give money for the "Bikur Cholim" institution. The Chazan (cantor), Reb Moshe Zander, took it upon himself to pray in the Beit HaMidrash several times per year: on Shabbat Rosh Chodesh, and Shabbat Chanukah. His prayer services were always well attended, and consequently many nedarim (promises to give money) for the "Bikur Cholim" institution were made. Also, Reb Moshe Zanger personally promised to give money to the institution, because he could not perform the mitzvah of "Bikur Cholim", by going at night to visit the sick people, which was one of the highest obligations of the institution.

One of the founders and the eminent leader of "Bikur Cholim" was Chaim Zeidman.

Chaim Zeidman and family, one son lives in Israel

Every year on the Sunday of Parashat Vayera, (the Torah reading "Vayera"), during which it is told that the angels came to visit our Forefather Avraham, who was sick (just after Brith Milah), the society "Bikur Cholim" organized a "Seudat Mitzvah" (Festive meal), which was always attended by Wolf Gelbard, one of the first Gabaim. He always brought a veal, ritually prepared, for the festive meal. The celebration started with the Maariv (Evening) prayer in the Great Beit HaMidrash. During the prayer all the lights were on. During the "festive meal" Moshe Shochat sang Shir Hamaalot with a festive tune.

Several women also participated in the activities of the "Bikur Cholim". They raised money and looked after the sick people. The main activity of the institution was to look after sick people and serve them.

"Bikur Cholim" was a modest institution, whose members fulfilled their duty for the poor and sick people with a great "Ahavat Israel" (love for the Jewish people).

[Page 87]

"Gemilut Chasadim" (Charity)

The "Gemilut Chasadim" (Charity) was located in Aizik Klopak's shtibel, where every Shabbat people prayed and read the Torah. From the nedarim (promises), made by people called to the Torah reading, a considerable sum of money accumulated. The congregation, of mostly young married couples and young men, didn't know what was to be done with the money, and they decided to establish a fund to help the needy. The fund was later called "Chevrat Gemilut Chasadim" (Society to Help the Needy).

In the beginning the "Chevrat Gemilut Chasadim" helped needy people with a one time "loan" of money, that was not meant to be repaid. Later, the institution left the shtibel of Aizik Klopak and rented another shtibel for the prayers. The "Gemilut Chasadim" society then started to give interest free loans.

**Asher and Gitel Goldberg,
both died in Israel**

[Page 88]

The first members of "Gemilut Chasadim" were: Beril Klopak, Itzik Zeibel, Asher Goldberg, Aaron Zaks, Leib Zaks, Leib Weichman, Itzik Szperling, Aaron Weichman, Itzik Rypstein, Zeinvel Rypstein, Chaim Berl Weichman, Chaim Mendil Mass and Chilke Weissfelner.

*

In Klobuck there was also a society "Hachnasat Ochim" (Hospitality), which was in Yeshayahu Bachinek's house. The "Hachnasat Ochim" consisted of two large rooms, with several camp beds for poor travelers. Travelers passing through received a place to sleep overnight, and an evening meal. The lame, Leibele Melamed, was the ever present gabai.

The "Society of Young Men" who fought against the "Progress"[2] in the shtetl

The "Progress" in Klobuck started with establishing a library, organizing conferences and conducting a theater play in the Firefighter hall. As far I can remember, the first theatrical presentation was from a theater company that came to Klobuck from Lodz. I was one of the young men from the Beit Hamidrash who decided to fight against the "Kefirah" (Heresy), that was creeping into Klobuck.

At that time there were the Chasidim and the Rabbi. We started by trying to influence the parents to forbid their children from going to the library to read the "tereife psoles" (impure and unfit), which were the banned books in the library. The Rabbi called an assembly in the Beit HaMidrash, and warned the Klobucker Jews against the present danger created by the heretics, and announced a "formal ban" not to go to a theatrical production.

[Page 89]

I acknowledge today my guilt – I was one of the fanatically-observant Beit HaMidrash young men, who strongly supported and acted on this – to remove the "heresy". At first we tried to peacefully convince the founders of the clubs and the library to close their sinful activities, and return to the "right" path. When our appeals to morality did not work, we then started to use more constraining means. The arguments boiled over and came to a fight. Such an outburst of violence occurred on Simchas Torah, just after the Hakafot, (dancing with the Torah around the ark). In the small Beit HaMidrash an argument started between observant young men and the progressive young men. Soon fists became part of the argument, and it became "merry and joyful" (dramatic irony meaning the contrary). The whole Beit HaMidrash became a "battlefield". The observant young, including myself, received support from the Chasidim shtibel, and it became a big scuffle.

The community leaders could not calm down the crowd, and the police was called. About twenty people were arrested, including my father and myself. We were not under arrest for long. Later there was a trial. I don't remember who conducted the trial. In court, both sides decided to make peace.

Thereafter, the young observant men started to fight the "enemy" with their own tools. A society named, "Tiferet Bachurim" (Splendor of Young Men), was established, with the goal of attracting the youth to their side. A "shtibel" was rented for this goal, where young people could pray and learn together, and study the old Yiddish books. This "shtibel" was located in the market, inside the house of Moshe Mendel Friedman. A Sefer Torah (Torah scroll) was ordered from a Sofer (scribe), and was inaugurated with a great parade. In addition to the core members of the "Tiferet Bachurim" society, there was a greater circle of young men, sons of well to do parents. I remember its following members:

Itzik Leib Ajzner, Abraham Inglick (Now called Osher), Itzik Szperling, Abraham Inglick (Mordche Katzav), Eliahu Szperling, Aaron Niedzele, Abraham Risental, Aaron Weiss, Eliahu Friedman, Itzik Zacks, Itzik Gelbard, Avraham Asher Szmulewicz, Baruch Szimkowicz, Berl Szperling, Gershon Ajzner, Groynem Mass, David Besser, Mordechai Szperling, Henech Feige, Hertzl Goldberg,

[Page 90]

Leibele Gos, Wolf Szperling, Mordechai Gelbard, Yehoshua Inglick, Yaacov Granek, Yaacov Dawidowicz, Yaacov Zigelman, Yossef Mendelewicz, Yechiel Rosen. Of the entire group, the only ones who remained alive were: Baruch Szimkowicz and Abraham Osher (formerly Inglick) both in Israel. Also Yehoshua Unglick who lives in Canada.

The society "Tirefet Bachurim" was active until the independence of Poland after World War I. In 1920-1921 when many young men were taken into the Polish army to fight during the Polish-Soviet Union war, the shtetl was emptied of young men, and the society "Tiferet Bachurim" fell apart.

Translator Footnotes

Chaye Adam is the name of a book of Halacha (book of Jewish laws) written at the end of 18th century or beginning of 19th century by Rabbi Avraham Dantzig (Source Wikipedia)

Progress here means the Haskalah (Enlightenment) movement who propagated among Jews the European culture

[Page 91]

Jewish Conflict and the First Mizrachi Organization

by Yakov Szperling

Translated from Yiddish to English by Asher Szmulewicz

After WWI, as in other Jewish shtetls in Poland, a substantial (and organized) social movement started in Klobuck. The Y.L. Peretz library, which contained a large number of Yiddish books, was founded in Klobuck. On virtually every Shabbat afternoon, readers gathered in the library, and held discussions about writers and their works. There was also a theatrical club, under the direction of Shmuel Franck, which put on theatrical productions with local actors or actors from Czestochowa.

During these times, Zionist ideas were not wide spread. Some Jews knew about Drs. Hertzl, Sokolov and Weizmann. The well to do Jews used to say: a Jewish state, (but) with an English passport. That was how people viewed the Yishuv (the name of the Jewish installation in Israel before the State of Israel), which was being established in Eretz Israel. The fanatically observant Jews believed that Jews had to wait for the Messiah to come (before the State of Israel could be established) and the "final" (Biblical) war (Gog and Magog, the enemies of the Jewish people to be defeated in the "final battle" at the "end of days"). They saw in the revolution (Soviet Revolution), the coming of the Messiah's time. That was the way the Rabbis then interpreted the events, and at that time they still had spiritual influence over the majority of the shtetl Jews.

There were a few exceptions among several of the well to do Jews of Klobuck. Two Jews – Reb Itzik Chade and Reb Eliahu Friedman, the sugar manufacturer, both observant Jews, took the initiative to establish a "Mizrachi"* organization in Klobuck. For this purpose they rented a room

[Page 92]

from Yechiel Kraszewski, and there started a Minyan to pray each Shabbat. Reb Itzik Chade understood that a social movement required young members, so he started to spread the idea of "Shivat Zion" (return to Zion), among the youth. As a result of his efforts, a "Young Mizrachi" organization was established.

It is noteworthy to specifically write about Reb Itzik Chade, one of the wealthiest and important landlords from Klobuck. In those times he had the spirit of an idealist, and he spent a lot of his time and effort on the Zionist ideal. He owned and rented a sawmill; engaged in substantial trade transactions with Czestochowa merchants; and bought significant forest rights from the land owners in the Klobuck area. He was the only person in Klobuck to contribute very large sums of money to the "Keren HaYesod" (the United Jewish Appeal).

Why Reb Itzik Chade adopted Zionist thoughts, and became an enthusiastic leader for the "Return to Zion" movement is unknown. He studied Torah, and prayed with the Gerer and Alexander Chasidim, who fought against Zionism, and was a follower of the Rav Kook of blessed memory, but on all occasions he promoted the Zionist ideas. He became the spokesman of the Zionist Movement, and spread the "Return to Zion" ideas among the Jews of Klobuck.

In the orthodox and observant community, Reb Itzik was despised. It went so far that once, when he was in Czestochowa and went to pray in a Gerer shtibel, the Chasidim refused to start the prayers until Reb Itzik Chade agreed to leave. In Klobuck there also were opponents to Zionism, led by Rabbi Henech Goldberg, who fought a campaign against the observant Zionists. In spite of all of this opposition, Reb Itzik Chade established the "Young Mizrachi Movement" in Klobuck, provided the young Mizrachi members with literature, and a Zionist movement started in the shtetl.

Soon there were two groups of observant Jews in Klobuck: observant, orthodox, Jews against Zionism; and observant Jews, who supported the "Shivat Zion" ideas. Both sides competed with speakers, who

[Page 93]

spoke in the Beit-HaMidrash and the Shul (Synagogue). Mizrachi brought from Czestochowa the famous publicist and Mizrachi activist, Reb Moshe Halter. The orthodox (opposing Zionism) brought the Rabbi from Wielun, who was renowned as a good Baal Tefilah (Chazan), and a good preacher against assimilation. With his Kabbalat Shabbat (prayer on Shabbat's eve) and his Shabbat morning service he was winning over the congregation.

The Wieluner Rabbi spoke before the Torah reading. He didn't really speak that much against Zionism, but rather against the organization, where young men and young women were gathering: "Young women - the future Jewish mothers", with a crying pathos he finished his oration, : "Gewald (Emergency) Jews! There is a fire, help! There is not much time left."

Reb Itzik Chade directed his activism towards the young men. He spoke to them like a father, and convinced them to adopt the ideas of the Young Mizrachi Movement. He was so profoundly involved in his Zionist activities that he neglected his private business. Subsequently he lost his fortune and became poor. Later he moved to Czestochowa.

*

[Page 94]

The second Mizrachi activist – Reb Elyahu Friedman was a confectioner. In the shtetl he was named after his trade, because there was another Elyahu Friedman in Klobuck. Friedman Zuckerbecker (the confectioner) was originally from Rembielicz. His father, Reb Zalman Rembieliczer, lived his entire life in that village, traded with the peasants, and only for the day of Awe (Yom Kippur) did he come to pray in the Klobuck synagogue. He sent his son, Elyahu, to Lodz to learn the trade of manufacturing of sugar.

While in Lodz, Elyahu did not only learn a trade, but he also developed spiritually. He learned Hebrew and read modern Hebrew and Yiddish literature: Peretz, Shalom Aleichem, Asch, Mapu, Y. L. Gordon, Bialik, Smolenskin, etc. When he established himself in Klobuck, he was a spiritually mature person. He knew by heart chapters from Tanach (Bible). He loved philosophic questions and strategy. He was at home in politics. His political wisdom camefrom the Warsaw newspaper "Haynt" (Today), and from the articles of Grinbaum, Dr. Tean, Rotensztreich and Itshele Yojon.

The business of Reb Elyahu Zuckerbecker did not do well. He had his confectionery, and sold ice cream in the market in the summer, and thereby he made a scarce living. He never complained about his fate. He was enthusiastic about "Shivat Zion" (Love of Zion) ideas. As an observant Jew, he joined the Mizrachi Movement, and together with Reb Itzik Chade founded the "Young Mizrachi" movement. In public meetings and conferences Reb Elyahu gave enthusiastic speeches and commanded the audience with jokes and folk stories.

Today, I still remember Friedman's lectures about Zionist figures, people and religion, the sacred places in Eretz Israel, etc. He thought that without religion, a Jewish state could not exist. He had an enormous influence on the Klobucker youth.

Hitachdut, Gordonia and Other Zionist Organizations

by Yaakov Szperling

Translated from Yiddish to English by Asher Szmulewicz

Yaakov Chade, the son of the Mizrachi activist, Reb Itzik Chade, did not follow in his father's footsteps. He was caught up in the Communist ideology, and for a long time became involved in Communist illegal activities. Then a crisis occurred with respect to his convictions, and he began to adopt Zionist ideas. With the impetuosity of the youth, he started to organize the socialist–Zionist "Hitachdut" (Union).

The young Chade surpassed his father as a speaker. He successfully convinced the pro– Zionist youth of Klobuck of his views, and he became their spiritual leader. Shortly after Chade started the "Hitachdut", the "Gordonia" organization was established. The two organizations shared the same premises.

Many other Zionist youth movements arose. There were many active sections and commissions such as: a literature section, a dramatic art circle, the Keren Kayemet (Jewish National Fund) commission, and the Keren HaYesod (United Appeal Fund) commission, etc . Every year the remembrance day of Herzl and Gordon was celebrated. Yaacov Chade was active in virtually all of the sections and commissions. He was, in fact, the spiritual leader of the Zionist Youth Movement. Through his speeches, lectures and discussions he lit the flame of the Zionist ideal in the hearts of the young men and women of Klobuck.

[Page 95]

Itachdut

Gordonia

[Page 96]

Chade devoted a lot of his energy on the library: "The library must have more readers and more books," was his slogan. When extra money was made from the earnings of a theatrical production, Chade used the funds to buy books, mostly with national Zionist content. He recommended that all should read and study Herzl's book, "Alt Neu Land (Old New Land), Pinsker's, "Auto Emancipation", and the writings of A. D. Gordon, Echad HaAm, Bialik and Max Nordau.

Chade taught the young: take a moral lesson from A. D. Gordon. You should not wait until you become 50 years old to transform yourself from an office employee into a farmer. We have to become pioneers during our youth, and go to Eretz Israel.

Regarding the issue of buying books for the library, there was a heated debate among the members of the management. Several members demanded that only classical literature be bought: works from the classics, and works from Shalom Asch. Chade preferred books with Zionist content. After he did what he wanted, he told us: now you can buy beautiful literature novels, but the ones that are interesting to read.

Despite these controversies, we established a library containing several hundred books, which included works of our classical literature, novels, stories and writings on current public affairs.

The "Hitachdut" organization did not restrict itself to spiritual–educational activities. The organization also was active in the political and social life of Klobuck, participated in the election campaigns of the community council and the city council, and supported its representatives in these institutions. Thus, for the community council, as a community representative, was Pinchas Unglick, and in the city council, Itzik Leib Szperling.

[Page 97]

Preparation to Aliyah (Hachshara) and pioneers (Chalutzim)

On Yaacov Chade's initiative, the central branch of the pioneers in Warsaw agreed to open a pioneer branch in Klobuck. In a very short time, pioneers of men and women enrolled in the training center in our shtetl. Chade's first assignment for the pioneers was to work in his father's (grain) mill and in the sawmill. The pioneers worked together with Christian workers, carrying the long wooden blocks to the saw–machine, taking out the cut timber beams, and sorting them by length.

**On training (Hachshara) in
Klobuck**

Several of these pioneers are recorded in my memory. I remember Nachman, the oldest pioneer. He stood out for his work at the Kurland's mill, which operated all day long. In the mill he acted as a supervisor, and he saw to it that not a grain would be damaged, and that the tools remained intact. He encouraged the pioneers to perform their work consciously, and not to lag behind the Christian workers.

[Page 98]

On training (Hachshara) in Klobuck

In the Kurland house, Nachman was welcomed as if he was in his own home. During the winter when he was cold, he used to come into the Kurland's house and stand with his shoulders against the tile–oven in order to warm his bones. During the summer, when his throat was dry from the flour dust in the mill, he left work, and went to the Kurland's house, where Rivkele, the miller's wife, served him cold sour milk from a big earthenware pot. His soul was refreshed, and he went back to work.

Later he made Aliya to Eretz Israel. In 1946, during the events in Israel, he was killed by an Arab bullet. Silently, without close friends or family, his idealistic soul went to the Hadassah Hospital in Tel–Aviv.

[Page 99]

It was difficult for the pioneers to work outside the sawmill and the mill. The Jewish observant manufacturers argued that physical, difficult, work was possible for non–Jews, but not for Jews. With these arguments, and other reproaches, they declined to employ pioneers in their businesses. Nor was it easy for the pioneers to rent a room or an apartment. What Jewish landlord would agree to permit a pioneer in his house? What would the Rabbi say? What would be said in the Beit HaMidrash or in the Shtibel?

Yaacov Chade finally found an honorable Jew in Klobuck, who was a respectable landlord, and who agreed to accommodate the pioneers. This Jew, Reb Itzik Zeibel, deserved to receive a special mention in this Book of Remembrance.

Reb Itzik Zeibel was a Jew, and a hard worker. He, his wife and young girls worked from dawn to late in the evening at their new sewing machines, sewing clothes, and bedding for Klobuck's Chatanim and Kalot (fiancis about to get married). The hard work did not make him close minded. Reb Itzik was a learner. He lived close to the Shul (Synagogue), and although he was always busy, he found time to go the Beit HaMidrash, to read a book. When he finished a chapter, he made a bookmark, so that the next day he would not have to look for the place where he stopped his reading.

Besides sewing new clothes, Reb Itzik Zeibel also was busy with farming activities. He owned a field, which he cultivated alone, and he harvested and thrashed the grain in his own barn. He also raised pedigree poultry, in accordance with methods described in a manual he received from America. These farming activities aligned Reb Itzik with the pioneers' ideas. He sent his son, Moshe Mordechai, to Hachshara (preparation) in Tomaszow or Radomsk, and opened his house to the pioneers from Klobuck.

The Rabbi of Klobuck was profoundly saddened by this behavior, and summoned Reb Itzik (to a meeting), at which time Reb Itzik Zeibel and the Rabbi had the following conversation:

[Page 100]

"Good morning Rabbi, why did you ask me to come to see you in the middle of the day? It must be an important subject."

The Rabbi angrily answered Itzik:

"I will not allow Shikes and Shiskim (non–Jewsish women and men) to stay in your house."

Reb Itzik answered with good humor:

"Rabbi of Klobuck, these people are not Shikes and Shiskim, but only honest Jewish sons and daughters like your children."

Itzik Zeibel with his family - one daughter lives in Israel

Following that answer the conversation between the Rabbi and Reb Itzik Zeibel ended, and the pioneers stayed in his house.

[Page 101]

It was not easy to conduct Zionist work in Klobuck. Fanatically observant Jews and the Beit HaMidrash young men did not easily accept the precepts of "Shivat Zion" (return to Zion). They believed that they needed to wait for the Messiah (in order to return to Israel), and labeled the Zionists as heretics, who had to be cut (out of the community) from the roots. Often we endured a difficult struggle while conducting a Zionist gathering or a meeting in the Shul (Synagogue).

I remember in summer, 1930, I received a notification from the board of directors of the Keren Kayemet (United Appeal Fund) in Warsaw that Rabbi Jacobson from Eretz Israel was being sent to visit our shtetl by the Keren Kayemet. All of the Zionist organizations, "Hitachdut", "Gordonia" and the others made preparations to organize a great meeting for the Keren Kayemet. My uncle Reb Moshe Szperling, who was a community representative, was asked to arrange that the Shul would be made available for the purpose of the meeting. Special placards were posted to announce the great assembly.

On the designated day, between Mincha and Maariv, (afternoon and evening prayers), the Shul was full of people, who came to listen to Rabbi Jacobson from Eretz Israel. The dignity of the Rabbi, his being an emissary from Eretz Israel, and his speech, of rich content, which intertwined the citations of our Sages and pictures of the life in Eretz Israel, all captivated the public. Suddenly, a fire was seen from one window of the Shul, and immediately somebody shouted: "It's burning."

There was panic in the Shul. People pressed to get out through the exit door. Meanwhile, people standing outside of the Shul extinguished the fire, and the organizers, with difficulty, calmed down the public. The lecture of Rabbi Jacobson ended with the singing of "Hatikvah". The fire in the courtyard of the Shul, as it later turned out, was an irresponsible act by the opponents of Zionism.

The mock fire was set by "hot headed" young boys, who were students at the Beit HaMidrash. They prepared a haystack in the Shul courtyard, and they set fire to it, so as to trigger a panic among the public gathered in the Shul, who came to hear the Zionist emissary from Eretz Israel. The result of this infamous act had a contrary effect:

[Page 102]

The next day almost all the Klobuck Jewish families hung the white blue box of the Keren Kayemet (Jewish National Fund) (from their homes).

Following the appearance of Rabbi Jacobson, an intensive fund raising effort for the Zionist cause started. From the "Blimel Teg"[1] (Flowery Day) and other contributions, hundreds of zlotys were sent to the main branch of the Keren Kayemet.

Later, there was a greater scandal in the Shul during a fund raising gathering for the Keren Hayesod. While the emissary of the Keren HaYessod, Mr Azjner, was speaking about the Keren HaYessod to the public in the Shul, the Rabbi came in with several young men. He climbed on to the pulpit and shouted:" Shaigetz (impure), get out of the synagogue," and pushed the speaker. There was an uproar. Two camps were created. The meeting ended with the song "Hatikvah".

Due to all of the controversies that both sides instigated on behalf of "LeShem Shamaim" (For the sake of Heaven), the shtetl was shaken. People argued, and the Zionist ideas spread, and the movement found more supporters. During the early 1930's the following people went to various preparation centers: Yaacov Starzinski, Meir Rotbart, Shmuel Goldberg, Daniel Szperling, Rachel Chade, Batia Zeibel, Moshe Mordechai Zeibel, Kopel Mass, and the writer of these lines.

In 1932 there was the first attempt of illegal Aliyah, which did not succeed. The following friends left Klobuck to go to Eretz Israel: Menachem Chorzowski, Daniel Szperling and Leah Birenbaum. Their return to Klobuck had a negative influence on the shtetl. Shortly thereafter, all three received their certificates, and thus they were able to make Aliyah to Eretz Israel, legally. Menachem Chorzowski and Daniel Szperling got along and stayed in Israel. Their sons are already serving in Tsahal (Israel Defense Forces). Leah Birenbaum went to Paris in 1937 and remained there.

Translator's Footnote

Seems to be a special money raising day for Zionist purposes. See pictures on page 107 and 108.

[Page 103]

Zionist Activity After the First World War

by Shmuel Goldberg

Translated from Yiddish to English by Asher Szmulewicz

After the First World War, new winds started to blow in Klobuck. The Jewish youth became involved in several (social and political) movements: Zionism and Socialism. I came to the conclusion that the only solution for Jews (in Poland) was in Eretz Israel. I felt that in Poland the soil was "burning under our feet" (that there was no future). I was not the only one, as many Jews understood the situation and felt the same way.

The first religious Jew in Klobuck who wound up his businesses and left for Eretz Israel was Chaim Zeidman. The whole shtetl came to see him off.

Under the direction of Reb Itzik Chade, a society "Hachsharat HaYishouv" (Israel Land Development), to buy land in Eretz Israel, was established. Later the "Mizrachi" Organization was founded. In 1924, the first organized chapter of the Zionist worker party, "Hitachdut", was established in Klobuck. Its leader was the son of Itzik Chade, Yankel.

I went to the first (meetings) at the premises rented by "Hitachdut". There I learned Hebrew, listened to lectures about the history of the Zionism and learned how to implement the Zionist ideal. I was enlisted in the movement, and got involved in fund raising for the Eretz Israel, and participated in all of the tasks of the Zionist organization.

In 1925 the "Hitchadut" established its own "Hachsharah" (preparation for making Alyah to emigrate to Israel). The pioneers worked in the field of Reb

Itzik Chade. People worked all week, and on Fridays the crop was sold to Jewish households. The leaders of the "Hitchadut" organization were: Avraham Goldberg, Shmuel Gliksman, Shmuel Goldberg, Shlomo Zigelbaum, Rachel Chade, Zisser Lapides, Chaim Kurland Shlomo Reiber, Yaacov Szperling, Itzik Leib Birenbaum.

[Page 104]

Shmuel Gliksman, shot in Bavaria by the Germans on May 7th 1945

The "Tarbut Shul" (Cultural center) in Klobuck

In 1926 the "Gordonia" organization for the youth was established by the "Hitachdut". A significant number of young people were enlisted in its cultural activities. The young men and women were provided with a spiritual (and intellectual) environment, in which books were made available to read in Hebrew, Yiddish and Polish. The discussions on Friday evenings are still in my memory.

We took a bold step in our cultural activities, and opened a "Tarbut Shul" (Cultural center). We brought in a special Hebrew teacher. He came from Stryj in Galicia. It was not easy to operate the cultural center. We had problems from both the inside and outside of the community. The fanatically-observant Jews, and especially the Melamdim (Cheder teachers), were against us. They were afraid of losing their livelihood. They fought against us both with proper and improper means, including by drashot (harangues) in the Beit-Hamidrash and by making "reports" to the Polish Authorities. Parents did not permit their children to go to the cultural center.

[Page 105]

The center had very limited income. The teacher taught for almost no wages. He did not earn enough to feed himself, and his meals were provided by the following families: Asher Goldberg, Yossef Meir Kurland, Itzik Chade, Moshe Zigelbaum, Mendel Birenbaum, Itzik Leib Szperling. The steering committee of the cultural center was constituted by the following people: Yankel Chade, Shmuel Goldberg, Chaim Kurland, Shlomo Zigelbaum, Blume Unglick etc...

The first anniversary celebration of the cultural center was attended by people from Klobuck, who already had moved to France. Virtually the entire shtetl participated in the celebration, which was presided over by Shmuel Goldberg. The guests from France gave us hearty and warm greetings.

Cultural center in Klobuck, On the right stands the teacher, Gelber

[Page 106]

To the "Hitchadut" Conference in Warsaw on a Bicycle

In December 1931 we received an invitation to participate in the "Hitchadut" conference in Warsaw. We were confronted with a difficult problem: how would we get the money for the travel and lodging expenses in Warsaw. We decided to travel without money. Yankel Szperling and I took our bicycles and went on our way to Warsaw. It took us three days to get there (approx. 225 kilometers). We spend our nights in the offices of the "Hitchadut" in the cities we traveled through. We arrived just in time for the beginning of the conference in the Jewish Academic House, under the presidency of Avraham Levinson.

After the conference we met the famous journalist, Dr. Yehoshua Gottlieb, and consulted with him about illegal Aliyah to Eretz Israel. We proposed to rent a car and start the journey, and to smuggle ourselves through the borders (of the various countries), until we arrived in Eretz Israel. Dr. Gottlieb dissuaded us because it was too risky. When we returned to Klobuck we decided nevertheless to make illegal Aliyah to Eretz Israel. Three of our friends: Daniel Szperling, Mendel Charzewski, and Leah Birenbaum left Klobuck. After a long and difficult journey they reached the coast of the promised land. There, they were caught and sent back.

Thereafter those same people tried again, and successfully arrived in Eretz Israel. After them, Yaacov Szperling also made Aliyah. The following people went to the "Hachsharah" (preparation to Aliya): Yaacov Stajinski, Moshe Mordechai Zeibel, Shmuel Goldberg, Rachel Chade, Lifshe Unglick etc...

Thanks to the activities of the "Hitachdut" and "Gordonia", a significant number of young people from Klobuck made Aliyah to Eretz Israel.

[Page 107]

My Zionist Activities

by Yehuda Szperling

Translated from Yiddish to English by Asher Szmulewicz

When I was thirteen years old I left the Cheder, and I started to learn a trade. I went to the veteran tailor (ready to wear), Hersh Wolf Friedman. I apprenticed in the trade for three years. I accompanied my boss to the markets in Krzepice, Rudnike, Bjejnice and other shtetls. During the winter, in the coldest weather, we awoke at 2:00 am, and traveled with the coachman to the market to sell trousers and coats.

In winter of 1938, after the holidays (Christmas and New Year), we set up our stand, stocked with our goods, together with all of the other Jews. Suddenly, around midday, a pogrom started. The market was crowded with Christians. They looted all of the goods; Jews were beaten.

Money raising for Zionist purposes.

"Flowery Day" for the "HaChalutz" fund

[Page 108]

(Due to the chaos) it was impossible to get out of the market. Two police trucks arrived from Czestochowa and restored order. Finally, in the evening we were able to return home safely.

Such attacks on Jews were occurring often. When we travelled to the market, stones were thrown at us.

These events moved me towards the Zionist Worker Party, "Hitchadut". I became a member of the steering committee, and was involved in the "Keren Kayemet" (Jewish National Fund) commission.

[Page 109]

At that time there was a disagreement within the organization. The squabble, between the two leading members, Yankel Chade and Shmuel Gliksman, arose because of an Oleh Certificate, which authorized travel to Eretz Israel. There was a split in the party. I supported the Shmuel Gliksman group, along with the following people: Pinchas Klapek and Rivka Weichman, (and others). We established an organization of "Z. S." (Zionist Socialist) in Klobuck. The organization rented premises, where we gathered every evening for lectures and discussions. After a time we again reunited with "Hitachdut".

**"Flowery Day" for the "Keren Kayemet"
(Jewish National Fund), carried out by the "Hitachdut"**

[Page 109]

The Betar Organization

by Avraham Goldberg, Tel-Aviv

Translated from Yiddish to English by Asher Szmulewicz

Gathering of Betar from Klobuck and surroundings

Betar, Brit Yossef Trumpeldor (Alliance of Yossef Trumpeldor[1], was the newest organization in the shtetl of Klobuck. At the end of 1931 this new youth group was created, with the goal of establishing a new Zionist Youth Movement, and to set an example (for others) by its activities and its readiness to sacrifice. The new movement, like a (flowing) stream, attracted large contingents of Jewish youth, who were not (otherwise) connected to existing Jewish (Zionist) organizations, due to their religious or national affiliations.

The personality of the Betar leader, Zeev Jabotinski, and his thoughts and beliefs, expressed in words and writings, influenced everybody like the words of a prophet. The Betar-Youth started to demonstrate in streets of the Klobuck, and included the wearing uniforms, and marching with drums and trumpets. Before then, such demonstrations had been limited to the Polish "Sokol"[2].

[Page 110]

The entire shtetl, kith and kin, were on the streets. On Lag BaOmer, for the first time, we marched through the shtetl to the woods of Kamik.

The young members, intellectually gifted young men and women with the impetuosity of the youth, worked hard, and at the election of the 18th Zionist Congress, secured a victory. The Betar Organization then won an absolute majority.

We conducted a wide range of cultural activities. Every Friday evening there was a "box-evening," where each person wrote a question that puzzled him, and put it in a box. Lecturers answered the questions, or there was a discussion about the subject. In addition, articles from newspapers were read aloud, and there were discussions, until the middle of the night.

Every day, Jewish life in the shtetl became more difficult. The concerns about the future, the inherent anti-Semitism, the ascension of Hitler to the (height of) power in Germany, all together did not portend any good for Jews. It was as if we were locked in a cage. All of the emigration gateswere closed, and the gates to Eretz Israel were locked with seven keys. Everything was stacked against making Aliyah (moving to Eretz Israel) for the Betar members.

Day and night we thought about how we could escape this closed circle. In response to the committee, established in Warsaw, to help people make Aliyah, by any means, even by foot, we were all ready to go. Two of our best friends: Yaacov Moshe Weichman and David Diamand went to the "Hachsharah" (Preparation to Aliyah), in the agronomy school of the Betar Organization in Vilna. This required large sums of money for expenses, but our friends did not spare any energy or money to prepare themselves to reach the coast of Eretz Israel. Sadly, they did not arrive at their dreamed about land. Yaacov Moshe drowned during the "Hachsharah" in Vilna (more about his tragic death is written in another chapter). His death left a shocking impression on the shtetl. Diamand was murdered by the Germans during the war.

[Page 111]

The first Betar steering committee in Klobuck was constituted of the following people: Adele Unglick, Yaacov Moshe Weichman, David Diamand, Israel Reiber, and the writer of these lines. Former women students from the liquidated Beit Yaacov School took a prominent place in the organization.

[Page 112]

I will never forget the four friends: Mania Szperling, Chaya Rivka Weichman, Sarah Unglick and Chade. Their loyalty and devotion tor Eretz Israel was boundless.

In the beginning of March, 1934 I made Aliyah to Eretz Israel. In those days, Jews were attacked in Klobuck. Hooligans from all of the surrounding areas were enraged. It was dangerous to go outside in the streets.

Nevertheless, all of my friends, family, acquaintances, and strangers (Jews) came to say goodbye. Everybody kissed me warmly, and like helpless orphans they said with their eyes: "Take us with you to Eretz Israel."

Unhappily, only a few of my friends from Betar achieved their dream, and arrived in Eretz Israel. The large majority was murdered by the Germans.

A group of members of Betar from Klobuck during the "Hachsharah" in Vilna, among them Y. M. Weichman, second from left who passed away, during the "Hachsharah"

Translator's Footnotes

1. Joseph Trumpeldor (1880 – 1920), was an early Zionist activist. He helped organize the Zion Mule Corps to bring Jewish immigrants to Palestine. Trumpeldor died defending the settlement of Tel Hai in 1920, and subsequently became a Zionist national hero. (Source Wikipedia).

2. The Sokol movement (from the Slavic word for falcon) was a nationalistic youth sport movement. (Source Wikipedia).

[Page 112]

The *Yesodey HaTorah (Cheder)* School and the *Beis-Yakov* School

by Arieh Guterman

Translated from Yiddish to English by Asher Szmulewicz

After World War I, in 1920 when the "Agudat Israel"[1] was founded in Klobuck, it became clear that changes were necessary in the Cheder (Jewish) educational system. Changes were necessary both in the teaching methods, and in the hygienic conditions of the school premises. The "Haskalah" (Enlightenment) became a threat to the religious education institution.

With the initiative of Rabbi Yitshak Chanoch Goldberg, righteous of blessed memory, a committee was established among the following people: Moshe Zigelbaum, Moshe Reiber, Shmuel Friedman, Yossel Markowicz, Chaim Zeidman, Wolff Weiss, and Daniel Zeligowicz. The committee established the Cheder "Yesodey HaTorah". A large house with five large rooms was rented and the pupils' registration started.

At the beginning, the melamdim (teachers) of the shtetl were unhappy. But they had no choice and had to remain silent. A few melamdim were hired in Cheder "Yesodey HaTorah". Israel Lapides taught the youngest children; Yossef Buchwicz – Chumash and Rashi; Avraham Kanopnicki and Peretz Eliaszewicz – Gemara. In order to operate the school a manager, Zishe Barensztein, was hired from Warsaw. The teacher of the non-religious subjects was Fishel Banker from Sosnowiec.

The Cheder "Yesodey HaTorah" typified a religious school. There were no beds in the teachers' room, as had been the case in the old Chaderim (Plural of Cheder). The pupils were divided among different classrooms. There were examinations, and diplomas were issued.

The Cheder "Yesodey HaTorah" acquired many supporters and a favorable reputation. The number of pupils increased. The students' parents were pleased about the school's teaching program. Over time it became an exemplary Cheder. Pupils came from the surrounding shtetls.

***

[Page 113]

The "Beis-Yakov" school was established two years later, in the year 1922. The founders were Sarah Shnirer, who came from Krakow to establish the school, and Ms. Asher. This was a religious school for girls, which was modernly organized, and was located in the large hall at Eliya Weichman's premises. Yonatan Djalowski was the president of the "Beis-Yakov" school. The school developed well, and the girls received a religious education.

*****

The leader of the "Agudat Israel" was Reb Yossef Dudek, who was its president. A "Young Agudat Israel" organization was also established, which had its own library, "Akad HaSefarim" (Book Collection), and an "Evening Lectures Program", where young people attended religious and general lectures.

Translator's Footnote

1. Agudat Israel literally means, Association of Israel, but was the religious orthodox party.

[Page 114]

Cultural Activities Between the Two World Wars

Dramatic Circle and Library

by Sarah Brat, Paris

Translated from the Yiddish by Asher Szmulewicz

After World War I, the youth (of Klobuck) realized that they were living as if they were on a wild (deserted) island. The limited "entertainment" consisted of marriage, (on the one end), and a funeral on the opposite end, Those, were the (only) events that everyone participated in, like in a large family.

The scarcity of general culture in school motivated the majority of the youth to (explore new ideas and) learn by themselves. Young people yearned for a book; for a theatrical play; or a movie in the cinema. With youth's impetuosity, we organized cultural activities, in an attempt to create a new way of life. It started with announcements of general meetings. Out of the frequent gatherings, it evolved into a cultural circle. The first pioneers of the cultural circle in Klobuck were: Dvorah Jarzombek, Shlomo Rypsztein, Fishel Kleinberg, Leib and Berl Szmulewicz, Pinchas Niedjela, and Malka Szimkiewicz (and others). (All of them were murdered by the Germans).

Among the cultural activities, we started to explore our dramatic and performance abilities, as actors, and created an amateur theater company. We associated with (actors from) Czestochowa, and arranged to bring two professional actors to Klobuck: Lewenstein, from the Vilna troupe, and Franck. They came several times a month, and taught us how to produce plays.

Our theatrical activities started with the play, "Money, Love and Shame", from Lateiner. The two actors from Czestochowa were dedicated to our theatrical company, and were largely responsible for our success. Our

[Page 115]

performance was very well received, and it produced income. The net profits of the performance gave us the ability to rent premises, and to buy our first books in order to establish a library.

The first culture activists in the shtetl:

**From right standing: Libe Ajzner, Dvorah Jarzombek
Sitting: Malka Szimkewicz**

Fishel Kleinberg with his wife, killed

Berl and Chana Szmulewicz, killed

Page 117]

Shlomo Rypsztein killed in Auschwitz

Members from the Cultural Society

Over time, our performances became better. Our morale and financial success would have been even greater if not for the trouble caused by the religious fanatics of the shtetl. It became a stubborn and constant conflict between the older generation, and the younger one. The Rabbi, and the well to do Jews, wanted to stop us, but we didn't want to discontinue our gatherings, theatre plays, reading books and living (our lives) according to our desires.

[Page 118]

Despite (the opposition) and these conditions, we continued with our theatrical plays, and we directed the following works: "Broken Hearts" by Z. Libin; "The Young from the Village" by Leon Korbin; "The Yeshivah Student" and the "Jewish Hamlet" by Zolotorewski; "The Dibuk" by Anski ;and others.

We bought books, by paying on installments. On more than one occasion, we didn't have enough money to pay our debts for the books. (To raise more money) we then organized a lottery, and we sold the lottery tickets by ourselves. This was not an easy task. In order to sell a ticket we had to promise a golden future (a big prize). The buyers, of course, knew that the majority of the tickets were bound to lose.

Our library became more attractive and we increased the choice of books by Jewish and European writers; and it was named after Yitzhak Leibush Peretz, the famous Yiddish writer, whose picture was displayed in the place of honor. This beautiful picture of Peretz greatly irritated the religious people. "They hung a picture of some lord, with his uncovered head, and his big mustache", complained the religious Jewish householders, and they would not calm down because of the (so called) "heretic". One evening, a group of religious Jews broke into (the library) and violently tore the picture of Peretz (from the wall).

In our house the situation was terrible. Our parents believed that our dramatic circle was a center of debauchery, and worst of all they argued that (our activities) would result in apostasy. I was too intimidated and did not have sufficient arguments to refute my parents. I could not calm them down, and tell them that nothing was going to happen to me, and that I would not renounce my faith and would remain a Jewish daughter.

We were very poor. During the entire week we ate as if it was like the "nine days" (preceding Tisha be'Av), and ate only diary meals. However, on Shabbat eve my father became "extravagant", and permitted the ritual slaughter of a lamb in honor of the Shabbat. When the Shochet (ritual slaughterer) came to our house, he demanded that my father give him a "handshake" (a pledge), and assure him that his daughter would stop going to the "Poretz" library (changing Peretz to Poretz, which is a derogatory term and means licentious). This was a painful experience for my observant father.

[Page 119]

**The parents of Sarah Brat
and their grandchildren, killed**

Shlomo, the Shamash (caretaker of the synagogue), came to us from time to time and summoned my father: "Zalman, the Rabbi wants to see you".

The tense tone of the Shamash (communicated his anger), and the atmosphere already smelled like "gun powder". My father came home from the Rabbi's meetings depressed and irritated by the morality speeches. The Rabbi forbade him from giving the Kohens' benediction (the Priestly blessings) during public prayer services (my father was a Kohen). After a few such meetings with the Rabbi, my father directed his anger at me, (accusing me of causing shame) and a scandal. His wrath evoked pity on both of us.

Once my father caught me reading Maupassant's "Bel–Ami", a book from our library. He tore it up in small pieces. I had to work a whole week to repay (the library) for the damage.

The fanatically–observant Jews of our shtetl (also) reported the library to the police, (falsely) claiming that it was a Communist nest. During an exhibition, there was a police raid and they arrested three of our members: Benzion Szwierczewski, Shlomo Rypsztein and Berl Szmulewicz. They remained in the Pietrkow jail for three months, and finally they were freed because there was no proof of their (alleged) Communist activities.

[Page 120]

The exhibitions continued. We replaced our three friends with other actors, and went on with our work. After long and laborious effort, at a time when the library already contained two thousand books, our society split, due to conflicts about direction and different party thinking.

In 1928 I went to France. I maintained a correspondence with my family and friends until the war's outbreak.

During the war I received very bad news: my home was destroyed and my mother passed away tragically. This is how I was told it happened:

At the war's outbreak, when the Germans bombed Klobuck, the inhabitants fled in panic. Everybody took what they could from their homes, and ran onto the desolated roads.

My father stayed to pack the bedding. My mother, Gitel, and my sister, Reisel, left and went out onto the street. We had a cow, and my mother could not bring herself to abandon a living creature. She knew that the cow would be bloated by the milk, and there would be nobody to milk the cow, (causing the cow's death). So she took pity on the cow, and took it with her.

The airplanes were deafening, and brought deathly fear. People had to move faster, the cow slowed down (my mother's) pace. Suddenly my sister pulled harder on the cow, and my mother was able to catch up, but at that moment a bomb was dropped and my mother, together with twenty five other Jews were killed.

Jewish Klobuck disappeared with smoke and blood, and was razed, like many other Jewish communities. No longer were there an old generation and new generation; nor the Rabbi; nor a shochet (ritual slaughterer); nor Shlomo, the shamash (Shul caretaker). The ruthless Germans brought an end to the honest, hardworking Jews of the Klobuck community.

[Page 121]

May my memories be a remembrance for all of those killed and persecuted Jews from Klobuck. They stood up with self–denial for their ideas and thoughts, both the observant Jews, who held to their well–established ways of life, and the modern Jews, who wanted to break the chains of generations of conventional habits and traditions, in order to bring a new form of life for the Jews of Klobuck.

Shimon Rosental

[Page 122]

The Peretz Library and the Society "Bildung" (Culture)

by Moshe Wajnman, Paris

Translated from the Yiddish to English by Asher Szmulewicz

In Klobuck, like in the other shtetls in Poland, the establishment of a Jewish library developed at a later stage. Before the establishment of the library, people, of course, read books. From time to time a book seller came to Klobuck, and displayed his books on the table of the great "Beit HaMidrash" (House of study). Together with Havdalah (end of Shabbat) candles and other religious articles, the book seller displayed story books, which were usually intended for women. A few families also had books of classical Yiddish literature.

The first attempt to establish a library was made by Zale Lapidos, the son of Israel Lapidos, a popular melamed (teacher of religious study). He was held in very high esteem by his students, because of his beautiful Shanah Tovah (Jewish New Year) greeting cards, which were written so artistically. Zalman Lapidos was assisted in this venture by Shimon Rosental and the two Teper brothers (I forgot their first names).

This first attempt (to establish a library) did not succeed due to several reasons. This institution was backed by the "Bund" party, which did not have a strong presence in Klobuck, and thus, it did not attract a large number of readers. In addition, the influence of the religious Jews was still very strong, and to them these books were considered, "Terefa–Psul" (impure and unfit).

For a long time, a limited number of books could be found in Shlomo Rypsztein's house. Shlomo, the son of a coachman, helped his father, Berish, transport passengers from Klobuck to Czestochowa, so he read books during his free time, and he became an amateur critic of Yiddish literature. He demonstrated an exceptional initiative in the field of cultural activities.

A few youngsters used to borrow books from Shlomo Rypsztein for free. Shlomo did not wait for people to come to him to borrow books, but he went out of his way to find readers. It was more difficult when he tried to get his books back. On more than one occasion he discovered that a religious father (discovered his children reading), and tore the "Terefa–Psul" into small pieces.

[Page 123]

In the year of 1924 another attempt was made to establish a Yiddish library (in Klobuck). This time the initiative came from a group of young Jewish communists. Among them were: Benzion Szwierczewski, the two brothers, Berl and Leib Szmulewicz, Shlomo Rypsztein, Fishel Kleinberg, Dvorah Jarzombek and Malka Szimkowicz, (all killed).

The library was established under difficult conditions. The police were very well aware of the political activities of Benzion Szwierczewski. He already had been jailed in the Pietrikower prison, due to his communist activities[1], and his sister, Bronia, also had been imprisoned in many Polish jails over many years. Once, when she was being brought from the Pietrikower jail to the dentist, she successfully escaped, in spite of a heavy police guard. Later, she became a leader in the communist party in Berlin, and then later, she made her way to the Soviet Union. Hela and Meir Szwierczewski were active communists in Poland.

Because of the communist activities of the founders of the library, the police made it difficult to obtain the official authorization for a new cultural institution. In the end, after prolonged efforts, the library received the legal authorization to function as a library under the name of Y. L. Peretz.

After we received the legal authorization to function, we directed our efforts to the difficult task of obtaining money to buy books. The books we received as gifts, in the main, were not of great value, as literature. We bought the first books on installment terms, and the payments were made with great difficulty by the members. In addition, securing premises for the library was not easy.

Finally, we found a small room off Kaminer's way, on a back street, and with great joy we opened the library. Mordechai Glicksman, who was a member of the steering committee, and a carpenter's son, made a small bookcase, which we placed on a stool to make it look bigger. The walls of the library were decorated with pictures of Y. L. Peretz, Shalom Aleichem, S. Anski, and others.

[Page 124]

The number of readers increased, but the Y. L. Peretz library did not continue operating for long. As a result of the communist activities of its leaders, the repression against the library increased. Police raids and arrests were common–place in Klobuck, Czestochowa and the surrounding areas. As a result of this repression, the library was (forced) to close.

The loss of this cultural institution was dearly felt. The youth yearned to read a Yiddish book. At that point, Dr. Kruk (today living in Israel), the former leader of the "Independent Socialist Party", offered his assistance, and due to his efforts, together with Hershele Erlich, who came from neighboring Kamyk, they successfully obtained legal authorization to function as a cultural society, under the name of "Bildung".

The solemn opening of the "Bildung" society took place in the Fire Station hall. Many people came, including many guests from the nearby cities and villages. There were delegations from Czestochowa: Dudek Szlezinger, Shmuel Franck and Moshele Levenson, and twenty people came from Krzepice. Then, for each cultural event in a shtetl within the surroundings of Czestochowa the Jewish youth came and were present. The solemn opening of the new culture society ended with a banquet that lasted the whole night.

The ideological conflict between the young and the old generation.

The elected steering committee of the society "Bildung" was composed of: Aaron Szmulewicz, Yankel Moshe Unglick, Moshe Weinman, and other active young people, who engaged in intensive activities. Every Shabbat, in the afternoon, local and non–local speakers gave lectures about literature themes. We had "box–evenings" (evenings where people put questions in a box). Literature "trials", and a dramatic circle were established. There was an active reading room to browse newspapers and periodicals. Also, various committees were organized and met often.

[Page 125]

A group of members of the society "Bildung"

The number of readers in the library increased. Well to do and even Chassidic youngsters attended the library, first secretly and later openly; thus it can be said that (the library) caused a "revolution" in Jewish Klobuck. The society "Bildung" was not the only Jewish cultural institution in Klobuck. The Zionist youth movement also had a library, which had a significant number of books and a dramatic circle. The two dramatic circles often organized a joint theatre performance. Also, a sports group, that played soccer, was created.

The continual expansion (and popularity) of the cultural society activities were despised by the observant, religious, Jews, since they viewed the secular books and the theatrical productions as threats to the old Jewish way of life. And indeed "Jewish Klobuck", during these times, became more secular. The number of young people that studied in the Beit–HaMidrash decreased, and the new modern life captured the youth. The religious Jews measured (and tried to maintain) themselves by reacting against the "Progress".

[Page 126]

The reaction of the religious Jews took various forms. Following the example of other cities, The Jews, Chassidei Gerer of Klobuck, established their own political religious party, the "Aguda", and a religious youth movement, "Young Believers Israel", which erected its own library of Jewish books, namely those that would not "steer people from the right way". The writing of Peretz, Mendele, Shalom Aleichem, etc. were declared as impure, and because those books were forbidden, several yeshiva students came to our library secretly, in order to read these impure books. Among this group were: Elie Rosental (who lives today in Poland), Benyamin Dudek, Arie Guterman and Leibel, the Rabbi's (student). They even read books about communist literature, political economics, the history of Socialism, and the like.

The orthodox also established a religious school for girls, "Beit Yaacov", where daughters of religious families were taught.

These cultural alternatives, which were meant to overcome the "heresy", apparently did not have the expected result (of diminishing or eliminating the non–religious influences). Thus, a few fanatics came up with a plan to denounce (the leaders). It was reported (to the authorities) that the leaders of the library were communists. As a result, the police raided (the library) again, and placed people under arrest. Yet, the library did not close. The youth embraced the society "Bildung" with its warmest sympathy (and support). Among the well to do families, the situation was bad. The rift between children and their parents widened. Parents did not permit their sons and daughters to go to the library. The books they brought home were torn and burned.

A special "Holy War" (Milchemet mitzvah) was initiated by the religious Jews against theatrical presentations. They convinced the management (of the theater hall) not to rent the premises for a theater hall. They also requested that the Starost[2] revoke the license to permit plays in the theater. Since the theatrical presentations were conducted on Saturday nights, the Rabbi on Shabbat morning before the Musaf prayers (additional prayers on Shabbat and festive days) gave a fiery address, during which he banged on the table, and quoted verses from the Torah (Pentateuch), which attested that, God forbid, in Klobuck, like in the biblical text, for Jews who let their children go to "Triater"[3] or to the library, all of the children would die in the "Gehinom" (hell).

[Page 127]

In light of such sermons, parents convinced their children, by persuasion or by threat, not to go to the theater or to the library.

I remember how difficult the conflict was with my observant mother (my father already passed away). My religious mother honestly believed that because of my participation in the theater plays and my activities in the library, our household would suffer and become poorer as a punishment from God. I suffered worst morally from her silent crying. My poor mother did not "have a chance" with her children. My elder brother was one of the founders of the library, he belonged to the communist party, he acted in the theater and he had a lot of success.

The fight in Klobuck between the fanatic religious Jews against the secular youth came to a sad end.

One evening on Hoshanah Raba in year 1928, while young people were sitting in the reading room and reading books and newspapers, suddenly the door opened, and a group of Chasidim, headed by the Rabbi, burst in violently. They removed the pictures of Y. L. Peretz, Shalom Aleichem, Anski and others from the walls and tore them into small pieces. The young people, out of respect for the grown–ups did not put up any resistance, and thus prevented a bloody fight.

However, on the next morning, on Simchat Torah, angry youngsters threw stones at the windows of the Rabbi's house and (at the homes) of the other religious Jews.

These painful incidents diminished the anger of the people who had become worked up. Such events no longer occurred. The society "Bildung" went on with its cultural activities and political work of enlightenment. In the year 1928 in the municipal elections, the society "Bildung" put up and ran its own "progressive" list, out of which two candidates were elected as council members: Moshe Szmulewicz and Leibke Unglick. Szmulewicz already had been a Klobuck council member in prior years. The candidacy of Leibke Unglick, who came from a poor family, aroused an understandable interest among the poorer Jewish population in Klobuck. The list of candidates from "Bildung" indeed received the largest number of Jewish votes.

[Page 128]

During year 1929 I had to leave Poland. The leadership of the library was then taken by Aaron Szmulewicz, Zelik Berkowicz and later on by Yankel (Yaacov) Szmulewicz.

The library later had to change its name because of the repression of the police, and in the end had to close completely. The books, numbering a few thousands, were saved by the last steering committee, but later were destroyed, together with the Jews of Klobuck, together with the whole of Polish Jewry, who were persecuted by the Germans.

Members of the society "Bildung" giving respect to their young deceased friend Levi Brat at his Matzevah (tombal stone) inauguration.

Translator's Footnotes:

1. Between the two World Wars, being a member of the communist party in Poland was forbidden by law, and punishable by imprisonment.

2. Starost is a title for an official or unofficial position of leadership that has been used in various contexts through most of Slavic history. It can be translated as "elder". The territory administered by a starosta was called starostwo. Wikipedia

3. Deforming the name on purpose is very derogatory in Yiddish.

[Page 129]

Cultural Activities in the Years on the Eve of the Second World War

by Yaacov Szmulewicz

Translated from the Yiddish by his nephew Asher Szmulewicz

During the years before the outbreak of World War II, the library was located in the center of the town, in a house that belonged to Chaim Mass. The cultural institution was comprised of three rooms on the first floor:

– A reading room;
– A library lending room, where books were lent up to three times a week; and
– A room for the free discussion club.

Close to the library were located:

– A cultural club that organized conferences, "crossword" evenings and various social events;

– A dramatic club that gave theatrical performances and poem recitals in the evenings; and

– A teaching – tutoring group that gave evening courses dedicated to most neediest learners among workers and people who did not have the opportunity to learn during their childhood at school.

The teachers were close friends:

Aaron Szmulewicz and Zelda Berkowicz – Yiddish;
Shlomit Marder – Polish;

and Yaacov Szmulewicz – arithmetic.

The same friends were also active in the cultural club and they organized lectures on Friday's evenings about literature and political themes. After the lectures there were discussions. The lectures were lead by Dr. Yossef Kruk, and they were very successful (and popular).

That is how the cultural activities were conducted in Klobuck until the beginning of the World War II.

The Klobuck Jewish youth, most of whom were from poor families, living in poverty, found consolation from their hardship in the books and cultural activities. The young people lived with the illusion of a free and happy life that could be brought to the world by culture and enlightenment. But instead of the dreamed liberty there was bloodshed brought by the German hordes who put an end to the most beautiful illusions.

[Page 130]

Types and Images

Reb Yossef Buchwicz and his Melody

by Borukh Szimkowicz

Translated from Yiddish to English by Asher Szmulewicz

In the shtetl, Reb Yossef Szames was known by the name of his father in law. His mere appearance drew respect. He was a tall man, his face was full of dignity, and he had a black beard. He was a faithful Alexander Chasid, and he traveled to (and studied with) the Rabbi Reb Israel Yitzhak, the "Baal Yismach Israel"[1] (The one who rejoices Israel).

Reb Yossef Buchwicz was one of the Torah scholars. He was also an expert in the Aggadot, Midrashim and Mussar. As a teacher, he taught Chumash and Rashi, and even Tanach, with all of the Perushim (commentaries). He taught with a special nigun (melody). None of the other Klobucker Chadarim (elementary religious school students) could sing the verses of the Songs of Songs, the Ecclesiastes and the book of Ruth as well as Reb Yossef's students.

During the week of Shavuot, from Reb Yossef's Cheder, people could hear the beautiful songs of "Akdamot" and "Yetziv Pitgam" (liturgical hymns sung during Shavuot). Also at the time of the weekly Torah portion, "Vayechi", the shtetl could hear the song: "And I when I came back from Padan Aram ..."(Mesopotamia), and also "Shimon and Levi brothers". Everything was sung with the appropriate trope (Torah melody). Because of these songs, no other Cheder could compete with Reb Yossef's Cheder.

Reb Yossef was also a great specialist of reading Tehilim (Psalms) aloud in public. By saying Tehilim, he was the prayer leader for all the sick people in the shtetl. Everybody was sure that with his wailing song of Tehilim, he obtained, by persuasion, a full recovery for the sick people from God. When an epidemic (God forbid) broke out in the shtetl, and later it stopped, everybody was sure that Reb Yossef with his Tehilim songs, as a prayer leader, canceled the bitter decree.

[Page 131]

**Reb Yossef Buchwicz,
murdered by the Germans**

Reb Yossef took care of the poor people. Himself, he had nothing to give. He was a very poor man. Often he used to go to the important landlords, and walk from house to house to ask (wealthy) Jews for charity --"Anonymous Charity" – (the highest form of charity) to give to a respectable poor family. He used to say in the Beit HaMidrash, during the prayers to one of the assembly: "You should know that if God allows, for Chanukah or Purim, the shtetl will gather a few gilden (coins) for a respectable poor family". The well to do Jews, from whom he requested (contributions), never asked to whom the money would be given, because if Reb Yossef raised money for the poor, they knew that he would give it to those who needed help.

It was said about him in the shtetl that he is a man of God and of the people.

Translator's Footnote

1. "Yismach Israel" is the name of a book written by Rabbi Israel Yitzhak. It is usual to refer to a Rabbi by the name of his main book.

[Page 132]

My Grandfather - the Pious, Believing Tailor

by Moshe Goldberg

Translated from Yiddish to English by Asher Szmulewicz

The lives of my grandfather, Chaim Moshe, and my grandmother, Fromet Goldberg, were typical of the lives of the large majority of Jews (in Klobuck at that time). The inclusion of my grandfather's and grandmother's (experiences) in the Yizkor book will perpetuate the lives of the courteous, observant Jews from the Klobuck community, whose life descriptions are unknown.

My grandfather lived close to the Zavade (name of a pond), opposite the watermill with the enormous wooden wheel, which was constantly spinning day and night. I often visited my grandfather and grandmother. Each one nurtured me in their own (special) manner: my grandmother made my present world better, by giving me good cheese and egg cookies she always kept hidden for me; and my grandfather focused on the future world, by reading to me aloud the Torah weekly portion, and the Rashi commentary every Shabbat.

My grandfather was very concerned that the laws of (religious) observance be continued by his grandchildren. He saw to it that I could davenen all the prayers over time, and that I should answer "Amen" when people said Kaddish, because if I did not, (the belief was that) one could become, God forbid, orphaned. My grandfather made sure that I made my best efforts to be observant, (and to such a degree), by always keeping an eye on me, that I became jealous of the boys who were able to play around freely in the yard, like throwing a bucket down the well or doing other silly things.

Each festival my grandfather adhered to all of the divine instructions, which were mandated in the Holiday observance (rituals), like Pesach, the Exodus from Egypt in which all the Jews, even nowadays, participate; the "Tal" (dew) bentshen (benediction), which is a prayer for good livelihood, during the whole year; Shavuot, the receiving of the Torah, which was given (to the Jewish people) for all generations and for all times, and every year it is renewed as if we were standing before Mount Sinai. Then there was the teachings about Succoth, and Simchas Torah, when we rejoice again with the Torah, at the time of the harvest Festival, and the remembrance of Eretz Israel, where every Jew sat "under his vine and under his fig tree" and went to Jerusalem for the Festivals, with the belief that this will happen again in the future, when we (Jews) deserve it. These were the thoughts with which my grandfather welcomed the Festivals.

For my grandfather every event in the world was linked to the coming of the Messiah. Every day he really hoped that the Messiah would come. That is why he did not worry about furniture or the apartment. "For what do we need to buy furniture?" he would say. "Everything is waiting for us over there. Any day the Messiah may come. In order to be able to welcome the Messiah, we need to be clean (pure) of all impurity." He indeed kept himself clean, without any sin, and every day, summer or winter, he used to go to the Mikveh (ritual bath house): "When you dive into the water you feel like it was before the Creation, before the "Original Sin" when everything was Tohu Bohu".

Chaim Moshe Goldberg with his wife, Frimet

My grandfather was also knowledgeable about secular events. He was an assiduous reader of the "Haynt" (Yiddish newspaper), and was delighted to read Itshe's political letters, which were part of his rejoicing during Shabbat. The letters of Itshe (Yojanes) were explained and interpreted by my observant grandfather in his own manner. Regarding all of the political events of his time, he saw the anticipated coming of the "Gog and Magog war" (between good and evil), and the "Righteous Liberator".

[Page 134]

From each wrong doing in domestic life, my grandfather saw the impurity, which was the greatest enemy of man. A blow, an abscess on the body, a meal that was burnt, the dough that did not leavened properly, everything, according to my grandfather, came from impurity, from not washing hands. My grandfather also strongly believed that the deceased had a great influence on the living. "If it were not for the deceased (good deeds), he would say, the world would have stopped to exist a long time ago". That is why he prayed with great fervor in the Shemonah Essere (prayer), where the "Techiyat HaMetim" (Resurrection of the dead) is recalled.

On every Rosh Chodesh (new moon: beginning of Jewish month) eve, for many years I found him in the cemetery. My grandfather was convinced that on Rosh Chodesh eve the souls came down from the World of Truth and hovered above the tombstones. Then they were ready to listen to the prayers of their relatives and bring them to the higher worlds in the heaven. He was never short of requests from the dead: livelihood, health, marriage of a daughter, free a son from non-Jewish hands (military service) and the general liberation of Jews that would come from the "Righteous Liberator".

In particular, for a long time my grandfather prayed over the tombstone of his grandfather, Shmuel, who was, according to the family tradition, a miracle worker. Among the family it was said that the ancestor, Shmuel, saved Klobuck from a fire. Once a house was burning, and the wind was blowing the flames in the shtetl's direction. The well to do Jews came to Reb Shmuel to pray. He took his stick and an old book and went to the fire. After a short prayer he raised his hands to the heavens, as if he was pointing to the wind (and directing) where it should go. After a moment the wind changed its direction and the shtetl was saved.

The tombstone of my ancestor, Reb Shmuel, was made of wood and it was very old, and it was covered by gray-green moss. Each time my grandfather came to the cemetery he removed the moss from the tombstone and read aloud the date (of Reb's Shmuel passing away). During my time, in the 1920's, according to my grandfather, the tombstone was already 119 years old from "the day he passed away". By his side was the tombstone of my ancestor's wife, Chava. When coming back from the cemetery, Jews used to greet my grandfather (by saying): "May this be of good fortune for you".

[Page 135]

My grandfather had a hard life. He made a living as a tailor. He worked hard, day and night with the needle, the scissors and the sewing machine, producing "ready to wear clothes" to sell in the market. Whether in the summer's heat, or winter's frost, he used to work half a night in order to be ready to go to the market at dawn with his goods. He had to provide food for his large family of sons and daughters. One bill of exchange pushed another one. When his sons grew up, he taught them to be tailors. In his apartment the sewing machines buzzed from the morning until late in the night and it was also financially difficult to marry off his daughters.

Slowly by slowly the family emigrated. Four sons went to England. The large table, where on Shabbat (the family) used to sing Zemirot (Shabbat songs), became deserted. My grandfather envied the families that were able to keep their "nests" full.

Once when my grandfather received a photograph from his sons, he looked at it attentively and told me: "Do you know the meaning of the verse 'your life will hang in front of you'? I will explain it to you". My grandfather said: "Your children who are as dear to you as your own life will hang in front of you on photographs on the wall. You will see their images, but you will not (really) see them. This is my fate."

Later his sons sent photographs of themselves in tuxedos and top hats, and their wives, his daughters-in-law, dressed in low-cut evening dresses. My grandfather wondered and in his manner asked: "Is this Naomi? Are these my children." Then came pictures of growing grandchildren and my grandfather had a new worry: he asked his sons when their sons will start learning Chumash and to which Cheder they went. They answered that they went to "school" where they also learned "Hebrew". So as to please their old father and mother, the sons from England sent their children's school assignments in Hebrew.

My grandfather took great satisfaction (nachas) from his grandchildren in London. He went going around with their essays, showing them (to all) and said: "You certainly thought that there (in London) our children become Goyim (non-Jews). But look at this, written in the Holy Language. Try to write such a letter yourself in the Holy Language, with vowels. No, the Torah will not be forgotten by my sons and sons' sons."

[Page 136]

With these words he wanted to reassure himself. But silently the doubt gave him anxiety. Once on Shabbat after studying Pirke Avot (Ethics of the Fathers) he told me, in a broken voice:

"Avraham, I hoped that one of my children would study Torah, and continue the legacy of the past generations. Unfortunately, it did not happen, so at least I would like that one of my grandchildren will continue this legacy. You have a good head for learning. If you wanted you could become a Rabbi."

From his words I felt his supplication. I did not become a Rabbi, but I studied with great devotion. When I excelled in an examination of Gemara and Commentaries that troubled Torah scholars, I felt that I provided my grandfather with a great satisfaction. My father, agreeing with my grandfather, wanted to send me to a Yeshiva, but by then, at that time I already was caught up with Zionist ideas, and I had no desire to sit for years crumpling on the bench and wasting days ...

When my grandfather was in his seventies, his situation changed completely. His sons in England became wealthy, but they did not forget their parents. They instituted a lifetime pension for their old father and mother. My grandfather did not need to work anymore. In his old age he could afford to live comfortably, and give generously to charity ("with a large hand"). Even so, he could not free himself from his work, and he often picked up the scissors and the needle, simply out of habit. Their kindness did not go un-noticed. The old couple became sick. My grandfather did not complain about this new worries and explained his present situation with a Rashi commentary: Rashi says: " Yaakov requested to live in peace but he had to worry about Yossef." What happened to Yaakov Avinu (our forefather) whose image is engraved in the Throne of Glory, who could not get (to live in peace) in this world and in the world to come? My grandfather learned the literal meaning: how can I, as such a simple human being, live in this world without any sufferings. I can obviously, God forbid, waste in this world all that I prepared for in the world to come. My grandfather justified the judgment and calmly bore his sufferings that came with his old age.

[Page 137]

The old couple loved each other very much. Their entire lives were in harmony, with common work and helping each other. When he was tailoring, she sewed, with extraordinary dexterity, buttonholes and buttons in clothing. She ran the household. The cleanness in her house was renowned, although in her house there were wooden floors. My grandmother was also very observant like my grandfather, and wept in supplications while blessing the Shabbat candles. Like my grandfather, she prayed to God for the family: for the sons to be freed from non-Jews hands (military service), for livelihood, for the daughters to have a righteous husbands, etc.

My grandmother and grandfather also prepared for the world to come in their old age. In addition to their efforts to prepare themselves with good deeds, they worried that they should not to be separated after death.

The old couple had great satisfaction from their son, Shmuel, who came for a visit from England. The whole shtetl was stirred. During the reading of the Torah, Shmuel pledged to donate generously to all of the charity institutions, and also made contributions to the charities. My grandfather, as usual, brought his wealthy son to the ancestors' tombstones, and he requested that a plot be bought, where he and his wife could rest in peace together.

Shmuel wanted to reassure his old father, and told him that it was too early to think about the world to come. My grandfather answered him with a verse: "At all times your clothes should be white" an allusion to be ready to die at any time. The son surrendered to his father will. The transaction was made. The "Chevra Kadisha" (Jewish burial society) charged a lot of money, and my grandmother and grandfather received their plots to be buried, while they were still alive.

*

[Page 138]

About the passing away of my grandmother, my father told me that he used to visit my grandfather in the morning. One morning, my father found my grandfather saying Psalms and Maamadot (prayers) as always. My grandmother was still lying in bed. She suddenly asked my grandfather to read her the letter of Leibele, their son. During the reading she asked for water, she dipped her hands in water and said: "now I am finished". She died painlessly, being 69 old.

My grandfather was very grieved after his friend, as he called his wife, died. He did not let himself stop grieving, and expressed his mourning with a verse like Yaakov Avinu mourned about Rachel: "Rachel died by me". The fact that his daughter, Yochebed, came to him and treated him like a king did not help. My grandfather did not stop mourning. He immersed himself in books of ethics, and always spoke about the lives of the souls in the other world. He longed for the day when he would meet his friend in the other world in (Gan Eden) paradise.

The last requests of my grandfather to his grandchildren were: study the Torah, keep the Jewish Laws and traditions, and when my time will come to go from the "world of life" to the "world of truth" I should not be left lying in my apartment during the Shabbat.

His very last wish was fulfilled completely. After a long disease he passed away on Shabbat eve, Zayn beAdar (7th of Adar). His agony lasted for a long time. His soul did not want to leave his body. We feared that his last wish could not be fulfilled. But suddenly two hours before candle lighting his soul was elevated to Heaven. It caused a lot of effort to deal with all of the (funeral) formalities in such a short time. (Jews must be buried as soon as possible and cannot be buried on Shabbat). We had to "grease" all sides (all those involved). Fifteen minutes before candle lighting, he was buried in the Jewish cemetery close to his "friend", as he used to call my grandmother, when she was alive.

He lived seventy-two years as an honest, God-fearing, hardworking man. No one else had as strong an influence on me as did my grandfather. May these remembrances be a tombstone on his tomb, and on all of the tombs of all of the other observant Jews from the old generation, whose tombstones were torn out and desecrated by non-Jewish hands.

[Page 139]

The Child Prodigy of Klobuck

by Moshe Goldberg

Translated from Yiddish to English by Asher Szmulewicz

Avraham Naphtali Hertzke Goldberg, my brother, was born in Klobuck in the year 1896. When he was one year old, my father was drafted in to the military service by Czarist Russia. My father served the Czar for five years, and our mother, Blume, suffered alone with the little Avraham and raised him. When my father returned from military service, there was great rejoicing, and the neighbors came to tell him the good news: "Reb Yaakov, your growing son is a genius." Avraham was an exceptional student.

When he was nine years old his teacher came to my parents and told them that he was embarrassed because Avraham already was a scholar in all the subjects that he could teach him. Avraham needed a teacher who was a great Torah Scholar. "Our son can already study with the older students (who studied) with the Rabbi."

So, indeed Avraham Hertzke went to study with the Klobuck Rabbi. After two years of studying he was admitted to the Czestochowa Yeshiva. In Czestochowa he was famous among the other students. He was called the young prodigy.

Not long later Avraham Hertzke went to study at the Ostrow Yeshiva, with the famous genius, Meir Yechiel Halevi. The Ostrow Rabbi wrote to my father (and told him) not to worry about his son, because he learned very well, and that he would become a "Gadol be Israel" (Famous in the Jewish People).

My brother came back to Klobuck to celebrate his Bar Mitzvah (religious majority). My parents prepared a beautiful Mitzvah meal. My brother held a long oration, full of profound pilpul (argumentation). He spoke in "Lashon HaKodesh" (Hebrew). The whole shtetl then came to see the rising great prodigy.

Avraham Hertzke went away again. He came back twice a year for Pesach and for the days of Awe (Rosh Hashanah &Yom Kippur).

[Page 140]

ב"ה

ס פ ר

מעשה זית

כולל חידושים ודרושים על מדרז"ל על

סדר הפרשיות

גם דרושים **עץ חיים** על החזקת עמלי

התורה מסודרים על סדר הפרשיות

גם נלוה בסופו חי' והערות בהלכה

בעזהשי"ת אברהם נפתלי הירצקע ,ב"ר יעקב ז"ל

גאלדבערג מילידי ק"ק קלאבוצק וכעת פה וויעלון מחוז

לאדזי (פולניא)

ש נ ת ג ר ת צ

Ułożył Rabin Abram Hercka Goldberg, Wieluń

נסדר בדפוס של ר' בנימין ליבעסקינד, ווארשא, וואלאוו 6

„ספר מעשה זית" פון אברהם הערצקע גאלדבערג

Cover page of book "Maase Zeit" (Action of the Olive) by Avraham Hertzke Goldberg (commentaries about the Torah weekly portion published in year 1933 in Wielun)

[Page 141]

הקדמה

אודה לה' בפי ובתוך רבים אהללנו, על הטוב אשר גמלנו, ועשנו שאינו זוכה כוזכה, שהחיינו והגיענו לזמן הזה, להוציא לאור מחי'. חי' אגדה, על מדרז״ל, על סדר הפרשיות, וגם דרושים, עץ חיים, אודות החזקת עמלי התורה תלמידי הישיבות נר״ו מסודרים על סדר הפרשיות, אשר אמרנו ב״ה במקהלות, מדי שבת בשבתו, בדעתי הי' להוציא לאור, חי' בהלכה, ספר יד לקידושין חי' על מסכ' קידושין, אך מפני הוצאת הדפוס כי רבה, בחרתי להדפיס חי' באגדה, שהוא שוה לכל נפש, וגם באגדה יש לסלסל ולפלפל, כמו שאנו רואים בחי' אגדה מקדמונינו ז״ל, שהי' מפלפלים באגדה, בדברים חריפים ונחמדים, והי' מוצאי' בה חידושים, כמו בהלכה, כמו דאיתא בירושלמי פ״ב דסנהדרין, ה' ד', ר' לוי הוה עבר פרשתא, והוה ר' זעירא מפקד לחברייא, עלין, ושמעין קלי' דר' לוי דרש, דלית איפשר לי', דהוא מפקא פרשתא, דלא ריבון (הוה עבר פרשתא הי' דורש את הפרשה, ואמר רבי זעירא להחבירים, שיכנסו לשמוע קולו דר' לוי דורש, שאי אפשר שהוא מוציא הפרשה, בלא ריבון בלא חידוש) עאל ומר לין לא, (נכנס אחד, ושמע שהוא עוסק בפ' זו, ואמר להם לא, יש חידוש בדברים, שאילו דברי אגדה הן) ושמע ר' זעירא, ומר אוף באגדתי, אית ריבון (דאף באגדתי' יש לדרוש כמה חידושים) עי״ש ובספרי פ' עקב ד״א כי אם שמור תשמרון את כל המצוה הזאת וגו', שלא תאמר למדתי הלכות די לי, ת״ל כי אם שמור תשמרון את כל המצוה הזאת, כל המצוה, למוד מדרש הלכות ואגדות וכו' עי״ש, וגם כי הדרושים, עץ חיים, המה דבר בעתו, להחזיק ידים רפות, עמלי התורה, מתוך הרחק, תלמידי הישיבות נר״ו וכדי להעיר לבב התלמידי', דפסתי בסוף' מחי' בהלכה, ודפסתי מעט דפסתי, מצד הוצאת הדפוס כי רבה, והנה פעמים באי דברי' בארוכה, ופעמים בקצרה, היות כי חי' וסידור הדברים, הי' עת היתי מתגורר במקומות שונים בטרד' ולימוד הישיבה, ומנשים באוהל תבונך אמי' מורתי מר' בלומה תחי' אשר הרבה השתדלה עבורי, לגדלנו לתורה, עוד בהיותי ילד, אמרה נפשי להיות חלקי, עם עמלי התורה, אך רבות צרריינו מנעורי, ובעוה״ר התלאות והעניות, אשר עברה עלי, יכלו לי, מלעלות על במתי התורה והיראה, כאשר אמרה נפשי, וחסדי הד' כי לא תמנו, שלא שם חלקי מיושבי קרנות, וב״ה שהגיענו לזמן הזה, להוציא לאור, מחי', חי' אגדה, וגם מחי', מעט בהלכה, כן יעצרנו השי״ת ללמוד וללמד, ולא ימיש התורה מפי, וזרעי עד עולם ונזכה לחזות בשוב ה' שבות עמי אשר כהיום הזה, גזירות קשות, מתחדשי' עלינו במדינות שינות, השי״ת ירחם עלינו, ויקבץ נדחי שה פזורה ישראל לארצינו בב״א :

הכו״ח יום ה' פ' תו״מ א' אייר תרצ״ג פה ק״ק וויעלון יע״א

אברהם נפתלי הירצקע ב״ר יעקב ז״ל

די הקדמה פון ספר ״מעשה זיט״

141

Foreword of the book "Maase Zeit".G

[Page 142]

At 16 years old, he received the authorization to teach, and he graduated as a Rabbi, and his diploma was signed by forty famous Rabbis. He married when he turned 17 years old, to a daughter of a wealthy family from a village close to Wielun. The Rabbi of Wielun invited him to study with him. Indeed he studied there for two years. He became famous in Poland among the Torah scholars and he was renowned.

Once he received a letter from Warsaw. He was invited to become Rosh Yeshiva (Head of the Yeshiva) of the Lubavitcher Yeshiva in Warsaw. After three years of teaching in the Lubavitcher Yeshiva, he was contacted by the Warsaw "Metivta" (Rabbinical College) Yeshiva and was offered a better salary. He taught there as Rosh Yeshiva until the beginning of year 1939. Afterwards he went to Lublin to teach in the "Chachmei Lublin Yeshiva". A short time before the outbreak of the war, his wife summoned him to come home, and indeed the war broke out afterwards.

At the beginning of the war he sent me a parcel with several books he wrote, and added that for Heaven's sake, I should keep the books (safe) because his books were dearer to him than his own life.

During fifteen years my brother, Avraham Naphtali, worked on his dear books until he published them. His dear books received the (praise and) approval of the greatest Rabbis of his generation. Then came the cursed murderers, the Germans, and together with millions of other Jews and thousands sacred books, my brother Avraham Hertzke was murdered in martyrdom, and his books destroyed.

One book, "Maase Zeit", remains and can be found in Israel.

Reb Israel Eliyahu Dudek

by Moshe Dudek

Translated from Yiddish to English by Asher Szmulewicz

The name of my grandfather, Reb Israel Eliyahu Dudek of blessed memory (Israel Elie), was renowned in Klobuck. He was revered by both the Chasidim and the common well to do Jews. He was a Gerer Chasid. He sat at the table of the "Sfat Emet"[1], and was a great Torah scholar, well versed in Talmud and Poskim (Interpreters of the Law). He knew the Bible by heart. When the Rabbi had to leave the shtetl for a while, before his travel he announced that Reb Israel Eliyahu would represent the Rabbi for all of the questions about the law and in the "exorcise" of the "Evil Eye".

Every day, at 11:00AM Reb Israel Eliyahu could be seen going with his Talit (Prayer Shawl) and Tefilin (Phylacteries) to the Beit HaMidrash (House of Study). The piety was shining shining on his face. Until 11:00AM he studied Torah in his house. He made his living from a dry goods store that was managed by his wife, my grandmother, Esther, the daughter of Reb Chaim Leibish Dudek.

[Page 143]

Esther was a woman of valor. In the shtetl it was said that she was a born handler (businesswoman). Both non-Jews and Jews liked to buy goods in her shop. Reb Israel Eliyahu used to come to the shop when there were many shoppers and there was a need to look after them. Later (in the day) he helped to tidy up the overturned goods, and then right afterwards he went back home and studied in a book. Day and night he studied Torah or worked.

*

My grandfather was born in Woldowa. His father, Shmuel, the shochet (ritual slaughterer) of Woldowa, was a Kotzker Chasid. His son, Eliyahu Israel, learned shechita (ritual slaughtering) from his father, but he never wanted to become a shochet. (He was the best student) of all of the other boys, and he was a genius and very studious. People from Woldowa used to say that often he studied and stayed so long in the Beit HaMidrash that he fainted.

When he was 16 years old he married Esther, the daughter of his uncle, Chaim Leibush Dudek, who managed a dry goods store in the Klobuck market. Thus, Reb Eliyahu Israel became a Klobuck citizen. Reb Chaim Leibush committed himself to give 14 years of Kest (board and lodging to a student to enable the study of the Torah). Indeed, Reb Israel Eliyahu also sat and learned.

After a few years Reb Shmuel came to Klobuck to visit his son, the prodigy with the Kest. A sharp controversy started between the two brothers, who were also in-laws, about the behavior of Reb Israel Eliyahu, the son-in-law with the Kest. Reb Chaim Leibish told his brother: "I have a complaint for to you. You gave me a young man, a prodigy, a scholar, but he only studies mystic books and Kabbalah. This is not the way of Kotzk Chasidism. In Kotzk we study Gemara and commentaries, and not Kabbalah."

Reb Shmuel listened to the argument (of his brother) and conferred with his son for a few hours. A harsh conversation took place between the father and son.

[Page 144]

Reb Shmuel said: "My son, what happened to you? You are only studying Kabbalah books and mysticism, and you are only about twenty years old. In an effort to turn his son away from Kabbalah, he asked him to write "Chidushei Torah" (new commentaries about the Torah)." In order to honor his father, the son promised to write them.

Reb Israel Eliyahu fulfilled the promise he made to his father, and wrote three thick books, commentaries about the Torah and Kabbalah. But he never published them. The margins of all of the books in which Reb Israel Eliyahu studied, were full of handwritten remarks.

When Rabbi Yankele came to Klobuck and established a Yeshiva, my grandfather, then a young man, became an accomplished student of the Yeshiva. Very often they argued about a Torah issue. When my grandfather raised his son, Yossef, my father took him to Rabbi Yankele and to his Yeshiva. My father studied there until the Rabbi passed away.

Rabbi Yankele persuaded my grandfather to pass the graduation examination to become a Rabbi and thus to be able to answer halachic (Jewish Law) questions. Then Rabbi Yankele wrote to the "Sfat Emet", the Gerer Rebbe, to influence his great Chasiddic scholar, Reb Israel Elie, to help the Rabbi of Klobuck answer halachic questions. The letter was later found by Machel Dudek.

The "Sfat Emet" influenced my grandfather, to become involved in answering halachic (religious law) questions. Later like two "Princes of the Torah", the "Sfat Emet" and Rabbi Yankele "Baal Emet Yaakov" (name of the main book written by Rabbi Yankele), ordained my grandfather with his Rabbi graduation. My grandfather then started to participate in Halachic Responsa in Klobuck, but he did not want to make profit from his Torah knowledge, like an "adze used to dig with". He did not want to become a shochet or a Rabbi, although when Rabbi Yankele passed away, the shtetl leaders, and the Jewish representatives asked my grandfather to become the Rabbi of Klobuck. He did not want to accept and only agreed to answer halachic questions until there was a new Rabbi in the shtetl.

[Page 145]

When he reached 64 years of age my grandfather passed away in Czestochowa. His funeral was attended by numerous Rabbis, and a great number of people. His funeral was conducted with great honors.

Translator's Footnote

1. Yehudah Aryeh Leib Alter (1847–1905), also known by the title of his main work, the *Sfat Emet*, was a Gerer Rebbe.

Yaakov Moshe Weichman and his Tragic Death

by Avraham Goldberg

Translated from Yiddish to English by Asher Szmulewicz

My friend, Yaakov Moshe Weichman, was not murdered by the Germans, but his unnatural death reminds me, even now, of profound tragic thoughts.

After making Aliyah to Eretz Israel, I left numerous close friends behind, but with no one did I have such a close and heartfelt feeling as I did with Yaakov Moshe. He possessed all the qualities to be a happy man.

He was handsome, healthy, a well to do man and was a leader in all the fields whether in sports, organizational activities and business. He had an open hand (was generous) to the organization and to his friends. He bailed out all of the deficits of the organization (Beitar). All his aptitudes were dedicated to the "Return to Zion" ideas.

During the years of 1933-1934 the gates of Eretz Israel were already locked. But the thought that they would open again was raised by Yaakov Moshe in the Agronomical School of the Beitar Movement in Vilna. He was there with his close friend, from the school bench, David Diamand. They wanted to undergo the "Hachsharah" (preparation to Aliya) and be ready to make Aliyah (emigration to Israel) (when the opportunity arose) .

The letters I received from him were full of longing for the Land of our Forefathers. His writings described his knowledge about agronomy, and stated: "in another year, (or) half a year we will be together in Eretz-Israel".

His parents left no stone unturned to convince him to leave the "Hachsharah" of the "Beitar" and return home to manage the business,of which Moshe Yaakov was the "soul". The devoted idealist to Zionism did not want to listen to his parents, and tried to console them by saying that in the "Galut Poland" (Exile in Poland) the Jews will not have any existence. That is why it was a waste of time to spend effort to establish businesses in Poland that will ultimately be destroyed. The strong Anti-Semitism, and the slogan of "swoj do swego"[1] would surely only result in an outbreak of pogroms against Jews. That is why it was better for ourselves to establish beforehand a home in Eretz-Israel. Management of an iron business was also possible in Eretz-Israel. That is what Yaakov Moshe wrote to his parents.

[Page 146]

Yaakov Moshe did not succeed in (his dream) to arrive in the promised land. Cruel fate caught him bitterly. On a hot day he went to bathe in the Wilenka (Vilna River), and he drowned there. His tragic death put an end to all of his beautiful expectations.

When I received the letter with the news of his death, a black vision appeared in front of my eyes. Common sense could not grasp the event: The ebullient, full of life Yaakov Moshe is dead?! Is this possible? His death left a profound wound in my heart. And when the Chazan (Prayer leader and Cantor) remembers in The "Yizkor" prayer all the people that fell for the land and for the people, the shape of the dear, young man, who remained in his far away tomb and for whom nobody will come anymore to lay flowers, appears before me.

Writer's Footnote

1. " swoj do swego" (the same ones to the alike ones) which means that the Poles should buy only in Polish shops and boycott the Jewish shops.

Reb Moshe[1] Zander, Shochet, Prayer Leader and Mohel

by Yitzhak Zander

Translated from Yiddish to English by Asher Szmulewicz

Reb Moshe, of blessed memory, was born on Tav Resh Mem Tet (5649/1889), to his father, Reb Zeev, of blessed memory, in the town of Gorzkowice, near Piotrkow. He was a student of the genius Rabbi, the President of the Jewish Tribunal of Plawno, who wrote the book "Yad HaLevi" (Hand of the Levi). He learned Shechita and Bedika (ritual slaughtering and ritual inspection) with Reb Leibele Shochat, of blessed memory, from Belchatow. He was ordained and graduated in Shechita and Bedika by famous Rabbis, such as Rabbi, the genius, Reb Issachar Dov Grubard, righteous of blessed memory, the Rabbi of Bedzin. He became one of the most expert Shochatim (plural of Shochet) and was an "artist" with an exceptional hand. He served as a Shochet and Bodek (ritual slaughterer and inspector) in Klobuck with devotion, and his melodies, some of them he composed by himself, were pleasant. His prayers, as a prayer leader, were pleasant, and he was accompanied by his sons' choir for seventeen years, from Tav Resh Ayin Gimmel (5673/1913) to Tav Resh Peh Tet (5689/1929).

[Page 147]

Reb Moshe was beloved and esteemed by all of the people. His heart and house were open to everyone, and he welcomed everybody with a smiling face. To the many who came to speak with him, he helped either by giving good advice or by writing a note "kwittel" for an Admor (Master, Teacher and Rabbi), and sometimes he went along on the journey to the Rabbi, in order to speak on his neighbor's behalf, or to receive advice or instructions on various subjects. For himself he traveled to the Admor of Radomsk, righteous of blessed memory. He was one of his Chasidim and admirers. When he went there, he was the prayer leader, and the Rabbi honored him by allowing him to lead and sing the religious songs during the "Shulchanot" (while sitting at the Rabbi's table).

He always found the right words to compliment people. For a long time he also taught "GePet" (Gemara Poskim Teshuvot, Gemara and Halachic Answers).

People that studied with him are now in Israel: Mr. Baruch Szimkowicz and others, still remember the courses he taught "with good taste" (well argued) and with common sense. During his years in Klobuck he was also taught "Midrash Shmuel" during the summer on Shabbat in the Radomsk Chasidim house. When he was young, he spent many years with his older brother, the Rabbi genius, Reb Shlomo David, of righteous memory, (afterwards the Rabbi of the city of Stshemishitz (phonetical spelling), who served as a Posek she'elot (Halachic decision maker), and thus helped the famous great Rabbi, Reb Yaakov Yossef (Rabbi of Klobuck), who wrote the book "Emet LeYaakov", to free of the community halachic questions responsibility so he could study Torah with (greater) diligence.

His Public Activist Actions

There was no public institution in the shtetl that Reb Moshe Shochat either did not manage or was not actively involved in. Whether it was for the "Cheder" (religious school for boys), or "Beit Yaakov" (religious school for girls), or for any good deed, or choosing an appropriate teacher for the higher classes from outside the shtetl (because there was not always an adequate teacher in Klobuck), he did it with his heart and soul, full of devotion.

I remember his efforts to establish an "Eruvin" (Eruv is an area where Jews can carry items on Shabbat, usually enclosed by a wire) in the year Tav Resh Vav-Tav Resh Zain (5686-5687/1926-1927), which did not exist in this religious shtetl. Reb Moshe arranged the plan of the town like an architect, and he measured the streets and the alleys, the ups and downs, where there was a need for an "Eruvin". He received help from his younger sons, especially in the streets where Poles also lived, so as not to stir up curiosity and anger, as had been the case before, when an earlier, unsuccessful attempt was made, and when the Poles intentionally interfered and it was then a failure.

The designation of the Eruv were initially made with ropes, and then inside the rope was a marker, and to avoid interference (by non-Jews), sometimes it was necessary to install a post during the night and used tar or nails to fix the post, so that people would not notice the markings, and to make it more difficult to spoil.

After much effort and toil, and mainly after the installation of the electric line, of course a special line in a special manner, (the Eruv was established) . The electricity come from the "mill" of the Kurland and Ziegelbaum, and the electric lines

[Page 148]

were used as a cover up for the "Eruvin", that finally succeeded. You could not describe the joy of the Charedim (the very observant Jews) that there was an "Eruvin", which meant that people would not break Jewish Law by carrying things in the streets during Shabbat, so that there no longer was any reason for angry people to be always angry. (Before the Eruv, when someone saw a person carrying an item on Shabbat, a very observant person would become angry, and occasionally cause a confrontation).

The establishment of the "Eruvin" was made possible by devoted people. I especially remember Reb Baruch Zeidman, of blessed memory, son of Reb Aaaron, who was most devoted. You could not describe the joy of these people after their "underground" operations ended very successfully.

Charity Funds

Among the charity funds (loans made without interest) established by the "American Joint", there was also the charity fund number 155 of the Klobuck shtetl. The books of accounts were managed in an exemplary manner by Reb Moshe Shochat, of blessed memory. After receiving a few hours of instructions by Shlomo Ziegelbaum, the accountant of the "Mill" Reb Moshe managed the books of account like an expert. During a regional inspection meeting in Bedzin, he was congratulated by Mr. Giterman, the national manager. The charity fund was then managed by Reb Moshe Ziegelbaum, as Chairman; Reb Zalman Weichman, as Treasurer; Reb Yossef Markowicz, and others. In order to increase the income, the Chazan (Cantor) Badash, from Czestochowa, was invited to perform in Klobuck. The Chazan, accompanied by his conductor, prayed Maariv (the evening prayer), and sang various songs in the Synagogue. The price of the ticket was affordable, and the Synagogue was packed with people, and this was an important event for the community.

Public activities in Klobuck

I was eleven years old when I left Klobuck, and thus I don't very well remember the public activities in Klobuck. However, the Cheder "Yesodey HaTorah" (school) is still engraved in my memory. It was established by the "Agudat Israel" (Religious political party). The "Cheder" was located at the end of large rooms in the house of Feichel. The teachers of the higher classes and the manager came from outside of Klobuck. There were special teachers for the general education classes, and for teaching the Polish language.

For the girls, there was the school, "Beit Yaakov", also established by the "Agudat Israel", which was attended by almost all of the girls of the shtetl. The teachers (women) were from the Krakow Seminary. Once even the famous Mrs. Sarah Shnirer, the founder of the "Beit Yaakov" network of School for girls and of the Seminary (school for women teachers), came to visit Klobuck. Among the other political parties were the "Young Agudat Israel" and "Poalei Agudat Israel" (Agudat Israel Workers), to which most of the young, observant, people of the shtetl belonged. They had a library with several hundred books in Hebrew and Yiddish pertaining to Jewish religious themes.

During the Purim festival, there was a performance called "David and Goliath", which was performed for the Rabbi, and to us, and of course, to all of the town; all of the men, women and children came to see the performance.

[Page 149]

I have to recall an unfortunate incident engraved in my memory since my childhood. For some reason Jewish Klobucker bullies, young men from the "Cultural Association", decided that they would teach a lesson to "HaKli Kodesh" (literally the sacred utensil, but here means the religious representatives), and the best time to do so was on Simchat Torah, and so it was.

During Simchat Torah, while being in the Synagogue dancing with the Torah (Hakafot), they broke our window panes and those of the Rabbi. The other shochet, Reb David Dawidowicz, who lived close to the synagogue was more fortunate, and he was left untouched. For a long time this incident left a deplorable effect on the Jews, and even on the neighboring Poles.

I remember that the Polish Notary expressed his (disappointment and) regrets in front of us about this shameful incident (although I am not sure and I don't remember if he was a friend of the Jews). This incident also left a profound wound on my mother's health, since she was alone at home during the incident.

In 1929 (Tav Resh Peh Tet 5689) Reb Moshe was accepted as shochet and second Chazan (prayer leader, cantor) in the great Synagogue of Czestochowa. He was nominated almost unanimously, with no opposition from any political parties or from any Chassidut, which was exceptional. Also I can say that the former Klobuckers, then living in Czestochowa, were very vocal (in their support) (of Reb Moshe), and, in particular, Reb Wolf Szperling, who was a former Klobuck community leader. Reb Wolf, of blessed memory, even made a special trip to Klobuck, on behalf of the Czestochowa community, to help with the relocation.

Reb Moshe Shochat gave his sons a very religious and traditional education. Nevertheless, he provided a private general education to his sons in Klobuck and in Czestochowa.

Reb Moshe Shochat and his wife, Sarah Krasel, and his younger son, Yaakov, were deported to Treblinka on the eve of Sukkot 5703/1942 (Tav Shin Gimmel), when he was 53 years old, and there he died as a martyr.

Of his seven children, only two remained alive, his son, Yitzhak, and his daughter, Zissel-Naomi, who live in Israel.

Translator's Footnote

1. Sometimes Reb Moshe is called Reb Moshe Zander, sometimes Reb Moshe Shochat (his craftsmanship)

Reb Zelikl

by Gitl Goldberg

Translated from Yiddish to English by Asher Szmulewicz

Each time I think about the Lamed Vav Tzadikim (36 Righteous), the hidden, God fearing and observant Jews, whose merit allows the world to exist and continue, I remember Reb Zelikl from Klobuck, a God fearing Jew who sat and studied Torah throughout the entire night. The shtetl knew very little about him. His way of life was completely reminiscent of the way of life of the 36 Righteous. He was very humble, lived in poverty, and had a bad (unhappy) life because of his wife.

He lived in a low house opposite the "church".

[Page 150]

In Klobuck, people said (that the church was) the opposite (of righteousness), it was the"impurity". A narrow and dark corridor led to his apartment, in which there was a dark room, used to store various things. This room was used by Reb Zelikl as a repository for his goods, which he, or more precisely his wife, sold, which included, limes, fruit in summer and other things. During a certain period Reb Zelikl (also) had a small shop of dry goods; yet from all of these activities there was no real livelihood.

Reb Zelikl's wife, Dobre Rachel, had a bad nature, and her observant husband had substantial problems with her. In his old age he lived in great poverty. His body consisted of only skin and bones. He never complained to anyone; he never requested anything from anyone; and he just sat and studied. There were Jews in Klobuck who knew about the situation of the righteous, God fearing, Reb Zelikl, and used to help him out with some money. But Reb Zelikl did want to benefit from the gifts of human beings, so the good people put money in his apartment and left.

The righteous, observant Jew never let anybody say a bad word about his wife. He always defended her because she had a difficult life because of him. Reb Zelikl accepted his wife's anger towards him with love. Reb Zelikl cited proofs from great, righteous (Rabbis), and even from Tanaim (Rabbinic sages whose views are recorded in the Mishnah - Wikipedia), who also had bad wives. " We have to suffer in this world anyway", he consoled himself.

The depth of the empathy for Reb Zelikl from people of Klobuck can be seen from the story that was told in shtetl:

And the story is as follows: Reb Zelikl's wife, Dobra Rachel, once asked her husband to go to Czestochowa to bring back limes. When a woman "asks" it is not worth arguing; the husband has to obey. So Reb Zelikl woke up early and went to the coachman to start his journey. This was noticed by the Klobucker coachman, Reb Beinish Horowicz, who had a restaurant in the old city.

[Page 151]

Reb Beinish called his wife, Chanele, and told her that Reb Zelikl was standing close to a carriage and bargaining with the coachman. They both went to the righteous, and when they found out what it was all about they invited Reb Zelikl into their restaurant. They did not let him go on the journey, but instead sent a non-Jew to buy lime in Czestochowa and to bring it back to Reb Beinish's restaurant.

So it was, Reb Zelikl stayed the entire day, studying his book. Reb Beinish gave him something to eat and to drink. In the evening, the non-Jew brought the limes from Czestochowa. Reb Beinish requested that Reb Zelikl keep their activity secret, and that he not tell his wife, Dobra Rachel, what happened. He sent the righteous back home with the limes.

It is noteworthy to remark that Reb Beinish and his wife, Chanale, were good hearted people. There was no institution in Klobuck that the Horowicz family did not support and participate in.

Reb Meir Sofer (Scribe)

by Baruch Szimkowicz

Translated from Yiddish to English by Asher Szmulewicz

Reb Meir was the "Hidden" (Righteous) man of Klobuck. He was almost never seen in the shtetl. He did not know (how to travel through) the streets of Klobuck and seldom spoke with anyone of the well to do Jews. He was a scribe "STAM" (acronym for Sefer Torah, Tefilin, Mezuzot), and he made his living from his trade. Observant Jews, fearing God, considered it to be a privilege to pray with tefilins with "parashiot" (scrolls of parchment inscribed with verses from the Torah) written by Reb Meir or checked by him.

Reb Meir Sofer lived in the Shul Street. He was always busy with his sacred work. Jews from Klobuck and the surrounding areas used to wait for a few months until Reb Meir had time to write a few "parashiot" for them. Before he had to write God's name he went to the Mikveh (ritual bath). He prayed in the Beit-HaMidrash (House of Study), and during the prayers he stood near and was inspired by the "Aron HaKodesh" (Holy Ark).

Once an incident involved Reb Meir, which stirred the whole shtetl. Here is how it occurred:

Reb Meir's neighbor was Pinchas Brat, the cattle driver. In the middle of the night to prepare himself for a journey, he went to the building attic to fetch his big boots. With a candle in one hand, Brat looked for his boots, and suddenly he noticed that a man was standing covered in a talit (prayer shawl), shaking and moaning. Brat was very afraid, and while he was going down the ladder, he fell.

[Page 152]

The frightened Jew screamed. Neighbors awoke, gathered around, and with fear heard what Pinchas Brat told them. Nobody believed him, but because he was shaking so much while telling the truth of his story, the most audacious of his neighbors, Yechiel Ber, Yakil Rypsztein and Reb Yossef Buchwicz went up to the attic with a lit lantern, and there they indeed found Reb Meir Sofer, wrapped in a talit. The observant Jew was praying Tikun Chatzot (the prayer to be said in the middle of the night). He asked his neighbors to go back to sleep, and not to make any more noise.

Since then it was known that Reb Meir is one of the hidden (Righteous), observant Jews, and people paid a lot of money for a pair of his tefilins.

Reb Shmuel Friedman

by Yaakov Friedman

Translated from Yiddish to English by Asher Szmulewicz

It is not usual for sons to write about their fathers. It is better that outsiders should write about the goodness of a person, and such writings should not come from close family members, especially from a son. But since there is no one alive from my father's generation, it seems to me that I can write about him. Thus, I have given myself the permission to undertake the sacred mission to record my father in the Yiskor Book, as he, Reb Shmuel, deserves .

For many years my father undertook the management of the Talmud-Torah of Klobuck, and provided the means for the existence of this religious institution. Reb Shmuel was well known in the shtetl as a unpaid volunteer community activist. He held an honorable position in most of the Jewish institutions, and strived to help Jews as best he could. I will recount a few facts of his activities that are engraved in my memory:

One evening, between Mincha (late afternoon prayer) and Maariv (evening prayer at nightfall) when my father, together with other Jews, were studying in the Beit HaMidrash (House of Study), he suddenly closed the Gemara, and went out into the street. Later that night, when everyone was at home, we were all very nervous due to his delay.

[Page 153]

My father showed up suddenly, and he was very happy because of what he did for the poor people of Klobuck.

Recently he had been informed that the city council appropriated a certain amount of money to be shared among the needy. The political activism of my father was aroused, and he went to the city mayor and requested that the Jewish needy should also benefit from the authorized money. After negotiating with the city mayor he succeeded in receiving an endorsed sum of money for the Jewish needy of Klobuck.

My father was Gabai (trustee) of the "Bikur Cholim" (Visiting the Sick) institution, which distributed medicine mainly to the sick and needy people. The institution got by on small contributions given by Jews from Klobuck. These small contributions were insufficient to pay for a doctor to visit the Jewish, needy sick people. There was only enough money to receive subsidies at the pharmacy, when buying medicine. But the expensive medicines were very difficult to obtain.

Reb Shmuel, who was a member of the city council and a representative in the budget commission, was well aware of the difficulties of the "Bikur Cholim" institution to provide medicine to the Jewish needy sick people. When the question of medicine assistance arose in the budget commission, he requested that the medicine assistance should also apply to Jewish needy sick people. Reb Shmuel succeeded in providing help to the Jewish needy people with free medicine.

Also in the struggle to revoke various decrees and anti-Semitic "szykanes" (harassment) against Jewish handlers, my father was always ready to get involved. I remember once on a Thursday, a baker with a broken heart came to us and told us that the police closed his bakery.

It was during the period when the ministry of Health Skladkowski[1] conducted an economic extermination against the Jews. The police and the health authorities complained about the smallest of details, and demanded improvements in the bakeries that were impossible to implement for the Jewish bakers.

[Page 154]

The Jew, who came to complain to Reb Shmuel, was one of the non-wealthy bakers. His bakery was closed a whole week and now on Thursday, when he could earn something for the Shabbat, the police did not let him work.

My father went right away to the police commander. He did not want to yield until the police commander went with him to the bakery and removed the seals from the closed doors of the bakery. The baker's wife thanked the police commander with tears in her eyes. She wanted to kiss his hand, but he did not accept and said: "you have to thank Mister Shmuel Friedman, who would not yield until I accepted his request."

My father made his livelihood from the "Tartak" (sawmill). Also in his work he demonstrated his human attitude towards poor people. Often poor women came to the sawmill to pick up wood chips, which were used to warm their poor homes in winter. My father always helped the women fill their sacks. He also sent me to help them carry the heavy sacks.

My mother, Esther Chaya, was the same way as my father. She always thought about the poor and sick people, exactly like my father. She provided sick people with appropriate supervision, and with meals feeding the sick people. On Fridays she sent her children with meal parcels to people (God may have pity on them), because she knew that they did not have enough food for Shabbat. Esther Chaya, exactly like her husband, was involved in activities for the benefit of all. She participated in all of the Jewish women's institutions that existed in Klobuck.

Translator's Footnote

1. Felicjan Slawoj Skladkowski was a Polish physician, general and politician who served as Polish Minister of Internal Affairs, and was the last Prime Minister of Poland before World War II. He issued many decrees about sanitation. (From Wikipedia)

[Page 155]

Reb Shlomo Rosenthal (Oleyaj)

by Batya Izraelewicz Zajbel

Translated from Yiddish to English by Asher Szmulewicz

My memory is engraved with the vision (memory) of Reb Shlomo Rosenthal, Oleyaj (Oil maker), as he was called, by reason of his craft. He was a Jew of the old generation, with large shoulders and a dense black beard. He was a good man. Calmly and quietly he performed good deeds for people. He did not want people to know what he did.

He lived in a small house at the beginning of the "Zavades". His trade was the "Alearnia" (Oil Press). The peasants from the surrounding villages brought him "rzepak" (to be pronounced jepak: rapeseed), from which he made oil, by primitive means. The high season was during the "Fast" (Lent, the period starting 40 days before Easter) when Catholics do not eat meat. Then the customers waited in line at Shlomo's oil mill.

In the small house, there were three rooms. One room was the oil mill, the second room was his apartment and the third was given as a good deed to the "Chaye Adam" institution, and used for prayer on Shabbat and Holidays. He did not charge any rent for this room. In Autumn and in the Winter, on cold market days, Reb Shlomo went to the market and distributed cookies and hot tea from a jug to outside Jewish merchants, who came to Klobuck from the entire region, in order to sell their goods.

When Reb Shlomo knew that a Jew was short of money, he went to the person's home and gave him money and told him: "I am lending you this as a "Gemilut Chasadim" (without interest), until such time as you will have the means to give it back to me.

In the same manner as Reb Shlomo was good to people, ready to help and do a good deed, he was equally irritable towards non-observant, non-religious and anti-religious Jews, who did wrong doings to their fellow human beings. In such cases it was difficult to temper his anger.

Reb Shlomo's brother, Reb Yaakov Fishel, was a community activist, an observant Jew and a Radomsker Chasid. Reb Shlomo used to joke: "I am better off than my brother because when I will do a match (Shiduch) for my children, I will be able to claim my brother, Yaakov Fishel, from my lineage. Is this a small thing? But my brother, when doing a match, will not have anybody (from his family) to refer to. When he will be asked who is your brother, he rather should not say: "Shlomo Oleyaj", the fool.

With this kind of humility he looked at himself. He was a dear Jew from the old generation.

[Page 156]

Reb Borukh Szperling

by Yakov Szperling

Translated by Gloria Berkenstat Freund

My uncle, Borukh Szperling, was an artisan, a tinsmith by trade. He lived in Czenstochow, where he occupied two rooms for his entire life. In one room was the tinsmith shop and the other one served as a reception room, a salon, an eating room.

Reb Borukh always was seen going with a pail packed with tools, blackened with soot, his hands scorched. He added gutters to the roofs or smeared them with pitch. My uncle Borukh was never embittered by his labor. He greeted everyone with a bright *sholem aleykhem* [Yiddish expression – peace to you – used as a greeting], asking about everything, about the entire family. For his entire life he did not stop banging with his hammer. He loved his trade. He did not mix in *kehile* [organized Jewish community] matters but he and his three sons, who were able to study as a result of his "toil," were well known in Czenstochow.

The oldest son, Yantshke (Jan), graduated as a lawyer and after several years became a judge in the Czenstochow appeals court until anti–Semitism grew sharper in Poland (1936–37). During the course of anti–Semitism, it was proposed that he convert; then he would be able to continue in his office, as a Jew, [he could] not. Jan resigned from his post, opened his own office and prospered.

The second son, Groinem, graduated as an engineer and, the third son, Yitzhak – a doctor–surgeon. It should be understood that the simple Jew, the artisan had great satisfaction from his three sons and daughter. The educated sons with academic professions were bound to their parents, to their father, the tinsmith and to their mother who wore a *sheytl* [wig worn by pious women]. The oldest son often was seen with his parents in the synagogue. This was Borukh's delight and pride. He prided himself that with his banging with his hammer in his tinsmith shop he had given his sons the opportunity to study and to graduate from three different university divisions.

None of the sons survived. Two were murdered by the Germans. The doctor, Ignac [Yitzhak] Szperling, was the chief doctor in the HASAG–factory [Hugo Schneider AG – a German metal goods manufacturer that ran a forced labor ammunitions factory] in Czenstochow during the German occupation and survived the war. After the liberation, he and his wife were murdered by Polish Fascist bands.

[Page 157]

Reb Hershl Szperling

by Yakov Szperling

Translated by Gloria Berkenstat Freund

When I start to write, or more correctly said – to say *Kaddish* [prayer recited for the deceased] for my father, mother, brother and sisters and their families, the images of my large, many–branched family who were mercilessly tortured, float before me eyes. Here I see them all: my father and my mother, my brother Mordekhai and my sister–in–law Hinda and their four children; my sister Chana and her husband Berl Szmulewicz and their only daughter Tsesha; my sister Rywka and her husband Shlomo Unglik and their two sons – Moshele and Itshele; my sister Tseril and her husband Yerakhmial Markowicz and their child, whose name I have forgotten. It was born at the outbreak of the war. And, finally, my youngest sister Manya, who was barely 14 years old when the war began.

My father, the sixth of his brothers, was the liveliest child, the most ingenious in his family. He had an example, an aphorism for everything. He always boiled over with humor even at the saddest moments that often happen in a family. He found the necessary sayings that brought out happiness and cheering up.

It seems that all of his undertakings succeeded because of his constant optimism. There was no lack of income. Before the First World War my father tore down a small house and built a large house in which he occupied four rooms.

We moved into the house in 1914, shortly before the outbreak of the First World War. When the war broke out, we left everything and ran because the first confrontation between the Germans and the Russians was in our *shtetl* [town].

[Page 158]

Several days later, the Jews began to return to their apartments and their houses. Most of the windowpanes were knocked out, the goods in the stores – looted. However, life again calmed down. There were other ways of earning a living. Reb Hershl Szperling again did not lose courage. He adjusted to the new situation and continued to live.

Hershl Szperling and his family
One son lives in Israel
Except for him, all were tortured by the Germans

In independent Poland, my father resumed his earlier line of business [making] cheap clothing and remained with it until the end. He went to fairs where he sold his goods. He never made out any promissory notes and if it rained or snowed, he left the fair. "The promissory notes would lead to not being paid," he would say.

[Page 159]

After the new year, when the season ended and there was little work, that was the time for communal matters. Reb Hershl was the treasurer of the Artisans Bank, Eliayhu Wajchman – chairman, Yitzhak Zajbel – vice chairman, Avraham Asher Szmulewicz – secretary.

Deliberations took place in our house, both about hiring a *Khazan–Shoykhet* [cantor–ritual slaughterer] and about designating a chairman of the kehile [organized Jewish community]. When it was necessary to unseat the mayor of the city managing committee and to choose another one – the decision was made in our house.

My father was the *gabbai* [sexton] at the large house of prayer, where the "common people" prayed through all the years. The money from the contributions was combined to make *Kiddush* [prayer recited over wine before a Sabbath or holiday meal] on *Shimkhas Torah* [autumn holiday celebrating the completion of the annual cycle of Torah readings and the start of the next cycle]. This continued year in and year out. It is worth describing a characteristic *shidikh* [matchmaking] story in our family that illustrates the relationship of the artisan parents to their children.

My father and Reb Moshe Szmulewicz arranged a marriage. My sister Chana was to be the bride of Berl Szmulewicz, who was captivated by the communist ideology. When it came time to discuss the terms of the wedding, Reb Szmulewicz requested a dowry of 10,000 *zlotes* for his son. Then a conversation between my father and his son–in–law's father took place:

– Perhaps it is better that your son should wait for his inheritance. It is not nice that a communist is involved with commerce.

– My son is not even an artisan; he must have money to open a small shop.

My father laughed hard at this. At Reb Moshe Szmulewicz's question as to why he was laughing, my father answered:

– I am laughing at this, that you have raised strange communists that have not even learned a trade. But you want them to do business and I, who have worked all my life, am a bourgeois...

All of this was said in good humor. Reb Hershl Szperling did not permit the marriage to be broken off because of a dowry. He gave the appropriate dowry and, with luck, the time of the wedding was decided.

On the 1st of May, when all of the communists in Klobuck were arrested, my brother–in–law also was not treated with respect. [His father] came to us with a complaint, "How could it be that they can let them sit [in prison]. We need to free him. For money, he can be freed." My father answered: "It is your son, so you give money." Nothing helped. Moshe Szmulewicz gave ransom money and his son was freed.

[Page 160]

My Brother–in–Law, the Communist, "Travels" to Birobidzhan and I Emigrate to *Eretz–Yisroel*

Once Berl said that he had received a post in Katowice. He barely said goodbye before leaving. And two weeks later, we learned that the son–in–law Berl had traveled to Birobidzhan.

My father sent for my sister, Chana, and asked her: "What does this mean? Berl has traveled to Birobidzhan; did you find it necessary to be quiet so that strangers had to tell me?"

My sister disagreed and assured [my father] that he [Berl] had received a post. It seems that she had received a strong message to keep the matter a secret so that the regime would not learn of it.

Several weeks later, when I was waiting at the main train station, I was surprised to notice my brother–in–law Berl. It turned out that he actually did travel to Birobidzhan, but the Soviets sent him back. He asked me to keep this matter "secret" because he easily could be arrested.

When I already was on the way to *Eretz–Yisroel*, the Polish police arrested him for crossing the Soviet border illegally. Later, he was freed.

[Page 161]

I emigrated to *Eretz–Yisroel* on the 28th of August 1934. Accompanying me to my departure were my parents, my sisters, my wife's family, all of my comrades from the party, my brothers–in–law and sisters–in–law.

It was not easy to leave the house. A strange distress enveloped me when I looked around the four walls among which I grew up and was raised. Every item in the house, the bed, the closet, the pictures on the walls, the brass candlesticks, over which my mother blessed the candles every *Shabbos* [Sabbath], everything, everything was beloved and dear to me! Today, a chill goes through my entire body when I remember the moment of parting from my home.

We already were at the Polish cemetery. The chairman of the *HaHistadrut* [labor Zionists] organization gave a farewell speech that moved [me] to tears. Everyone began to say goodbye to me. Everyone wished me the best. It was very difficult for me to approach the separation from my sisters and brother and from my father. He was never so moved by an experience in his life, so sentimental as to shed tears. I do not remember ever before seeing my father cry. When I heartily said goodbye to him and both our lips began to move, he simultaneously broke out in a moaning cry. I also cried.

With tears in his eyes, my father said as follows: "I already am old and broken, already in the 70s. I can no longer work. Everyone has gone. Your mother and I remain in our old age and who will help? We remain alone!" In the end, he added: "Who knows if I will have the good fortune to see you again..."

I do not remember what I answered to this. I only know that I cried intensely.

[Page 162]

The parting with my mother was a little easier. She cried loudly because a mother always cries at every opportunity, particularly when separating from a child and she does not know if she will see him again. With tears in her eyes, my mother asked me to write at once, not to just think about it...

Thus, I parted with my family and with the *shtetl*, Klobuck.

*

A new chapter began for me and for all of those closest to me. My leaving for *Eretz–Yizroel* with still other travelers stirred the world at that time. We wandered for weeks and months on a Greek freighter on the waters of the Mediterranean Sea. All ports were closed to us. We had left lightly dressed, in the summer. We continued to wander aimlessly on the water during the months of January and February. We suffered from hunger, cold and various illnesses. Three Jews [fell into the water] trying to disembark; one died. Our leaders were the comrades from *Mapai* [acronym for *Mifleget Poalei Eretz Yisroel* – Worker's Party of the Land of Israel] – Swerdlow and Tsbik. Our hardships and suffering were terrible. We had our first opportunity to write home from a city in Greece.

The Yiddish newspapers in Poland had reported about the disappearance of the ship Vallos that was carrying 400 pioneers, and all signs indicated that it had sunk. One report ran counter to another. My mother did everything she could; she could not sleep entire nights. Later, she wrote to me that they did not want to tell her the truth. My mother was relieved when my first letter arrived.

I received many letters from my comrades: Asher Wajchman, Shmuel Glikman, Ayzyk Leib Birnbaum – all consoled me and expressed sympathy for my suffering. My sister and brother wrote to me that I should hold up because I have a great purpose in my life – to arrive in the land of the Patriarchs.

My father had complaints in his letters to me! Why does it happen to him that his children have to endure immense problems? "Berl went to Birobidzhan and returned; Shlomo returned from Sosnowiec drained, but the worst would be if you have to return. What will the gentiles say? I wish for you that you will quickly arrive on the shores of *Eretz–Yisroel* and our hearts, which are broken by your troubles and have bled so much, will rejoice and the true redemption will come."

[Page 163]

We returned from Greece to Poland, to Zaleszczyki [Zalischyky, Ukraine] through Constanza [Romania]. We waited there for two to three months for the legal emigration.

I endured and did not return to Klobuck. My father had advised me that I not come home. "It is not fitting" – he wrote to me – "to say goodbye twice, to break our hearts twice." He did everything so that my wife could come to me.

He wrote to me in 1938 that black clouds were drawing near the skies of Poland and the scapegoat would be the Jews. He expressed the idea that he would sell everything and come here.

In 1939, when trenches already had been dug in Klobuck, he wrote that the Jews already had missed the train. The end of Polish Jewry draws near. And I received the last letter in 1940, sent through America. All of my sisters wrote; my father added, in short, about all of the cruelty of the Germans and that "now everything is lost." We received no further information. The end had come.

When the *Judenrat* [Jewish council created by and beholden to the Germans] began to be administered by the Klobuck *kehile*, they started to persecute the former, honest communal workers. So I was told by eyewitnesses, who felt the affects of the *Judenrat* on their own skins. Borukh Szperling, the pre–war chairman of the *kehile*, was persecuted by the *Judenrat*. My brother, Mordekhai, who was a *dozor* [member of the synagogue council], had to hide with gentiles in the villages, in Lobodno, Kolaczkowice and Wilkowiecko. My father was thrown out of his house, everything was broken and with my mother, he was chased far away to the factories. There they lived in a broken up, wet cell. That is how the members of the Judenrat treated the

[Page 164]

honest, communal workers who did not want to serve the Germans and help in the extermination of the Jews in Klobuck.

None of my closest relatives survived, only I who has lived in *Eretz–Yisroel* since 1934.

Reb Moshe Szperling

by Dora Wajs

Translated by Gloria Berkenstat Freund

My uncle, Moshe Szperling, lived in Klobuck for all his years and was an esteemed businessman in the *shtetl*. He was elected as a *dozor* during the German occupation in the First World War. Later, the *kehile* elected him as chairman of the Jewish *gmina* [municipality]. When Reb Dovid Hersh the *shoykhet* [ritual slaughterer] died and the majority of Klobuck Jews asked that his son, Reb Shlomo, succeed him, Reb Henekh Goldberg and all of the Gerer Hasidim were against this because Reb Shlomo was an Aleksander Hasid. A bitter clash flared in the *kehile* that lasted for months. It even came to blows and to trials. Until Reb Moshe Szperling, who had a decided influence as chairman, stood up on the side of the "common people" and Reb Shlomo was appointed as *shoykhet*.

After being *shoykhet* in Klobuck for several years, Reb Shlomo the *shoykhet* could not overcome the difficult struggle that the Gerer Hasidim had carried out against him and he left the *shtetl*.

In 1934, when I already was on the way to *Eretz–Yisroel*, they wrote to me that my uncle Moshe had become ill. He was taken to the Jewish Hospital in Czenstochow. On the second day, he asked to be taken home. He thought that he would die. He wanted to die in his own bed. He breathed out his soul on the way home.

At the funeral, the entire *shtetl* cried over the death of Reb Moshe Szperling, who had been chairman for about 30 years of the Jewish *kehile* in Klobuck, which he had served greatly.

Six sons survived Reb Moshe Szperling: Ayzyk, Elihu, Yosef, Berl, Yakov, Wolf and one daughter, Basya. All perished with their mother Hena. They ended their painful lives – some in German camps and some at Treblinka. No trace of their children remains. Only a son of Ayzyk Szperling remains. He is in Glasgow (Scotland).

[Page 165]

Types of Klobuck Jews of the Past

Reb Shmuel Dawidowicz, the Rozprza Rabbi
– the son of Dovid Hersh the *shoykhet*

[Page 166]

On the right, Khulka Wajsfelner and his wife; on the left, Chaim Mendl Mas and his wife. Perished in Treblinka

Yehuda and Miriam Cyncynates

[Page 167]

**Berish Rypsztajn and wife Yakhet
with grandchildren – perished**

Hershl Ratchart with his wife and family

[Page 168]

Yakov Dawidowicz in Paris

[Page 169]

**The headstone of Rayzl Laya Dawidowicz.
Standing next to it is her son, Chaim Dawidowicz,
who with his family, was tortured by the Germans.**

[Page 170]

The Last Community of Klobuck

by Dora Wajs

Translated from Yiddish to English by Asher Szmulewicz

My uncle, Reb Moshe Szperling, was the president of the community of Klobuck for many years. Before his passing away he left a will, in which he requested that his brother's son, my father, Baruch Szperling would become the president of the community, when he, Moshe Szperling, went to the world of truth (pass away).

Reb Moshe Szperling passed away, and the community accepted his will and elected my father as the community president. This happened in year 1934. I was then 9 years old.

My family was very happy with the election results, because being the president of the community was a family heritage. In my home I was always told that my grandfather, Reb Shmuel Szperling, was the president of the community and that he had a respectful relationship, until his passing away, with the Rabbi of Klobuck, Reb Henech Goldberg.

When my father, Reb Baruch Szperling, took his office as the president of the community, he implemented improvements in all of the institutions of the community. In the synagogue, which was one of the historical worship places in Poland, he introduced crystal chandeliers and electric lighting. The walls were recovered with mahogany veneer, according to the pattern of the synagogue in Czestochowa.

The interior painting of the synagogue was restored. The (scheme) was a remnant of my uncle, Moshe Szperling, who brought the best artist painters to paint the ceiling like the sky, with stars, and the walls with the zodiac signs and the emblems of the (Hebrew) tribes.

Despite all of the economic difficulties, Reb Baruch Szperling provided that a tin cover (was installed) on the roof of the synagogue. The work was shared by all of the tinsmiths of Klobuck, so as to not offend anybody. The Jews of Klobuck understood how to appreciate (the costs of the improvements), and they did not complain about at all of the taxes they had to pay the Polish Government. Each one contributed from his savings to the community's

[Page 171]

needs. Therefore, each Jew took great satisfaction when sitting in the Klobuck holy place. During the later elections of the community leaders, my father was re-elected as the president of the community with a larger majority of votes.

In addition to being the president of the Klobuck community, Reb Baruch Szperling was also the president of the "TOZ"[1] institution, which played a great role in providing health care to the Jewish population. TOZ used to send children with lung disease to Otwock for treatment. The Jewish women of Klobuck also participated in the TOZ institution. I remember the following names of TOZ women activists: Mrs. Lapides, Tova Unglick (who lives in Israel), Mrs. Mass, Paula Lubiczki, Bela Kurland Zigelbaum (who lives in Israel) and my mother, Sarah. The TOZ institution provided medical help to poor people, and created camps for children. One of these camps was in Klobuck, and was managed by Helka Weinreich, a teacher, who installed various games and entertainments for the children.

As president of the Jewish community, Reb Baruch Szperling took full responsibility for the life and welfare of the Jewish Klobuck population. He did not pay attention to personal threats when he had to help and protect the community from a danger.

The Thirties were a difficult period (for Jews), because the Endenkes-Fascists started Anti-Semitic actions, in the form of pogroms, including in Klobuck. My father did not spare any effort, and risked his life to protect the life and welfare of the Jewish population in Klobuck. (In other chapters of the

Yiskor book there is muchwritten about the Anti-Semitism in Klobuck during the Thirties).

Thus, Reb Szperling led the community until the murderous Germans came.

[Page 172]

At the outbreak of the war, when the desperate flight from the Germans started, we also, together with our father, fled through side country paths. The Germans met the fleeing refugees and arrested all of the men, and let the women and children go. Large groups of men were dragged by foot in the direction of Wolczszawe.

My father successfully escaped from the Germans. He came back home. When he returned home, he found our apartment empty. Everything had been looted, partly by the Germans and partly by the Poles.

Two weeks after returning home, the Germans arrested my father, together with the other representatives of the community, including the Rabbi, Reb Henech Goldberg. They were locked in the synagogue, and the Germans demanded a large sum of money, as ransom, to release the prisoners. If the German conditions were not met, the prisoners would be shot.

My mother did everything she could (to raise the funds), running to everyone she knew, but did not receive any money. My father stayed calm during this danger, and he came up with the idea to ask the Germans to free him, so he could raise the requested ransom. The Germans agreed, and let him go.

As soon as he was liberated Baruch Szperling started to gather money. Everybody understood the danger confronting the community representatives if the demands were not to be met. There were people who were ready to give their last penny to free a Jew. These were people that were not asked to give money. These people brought their jewelry because they did not have any money left. I will cite the Jews who in such a troubled period fulfilled the duty of freeing the prisoners: the widow, Perel Israelowicz from the market, brought a gold chain, an heirloom from her late husband. Reb Yechielke Israelowicz, and the orphans of Marek Rosenthal gave their last little means and gold. The daughter of Reb Shlomo Weiss, Pesele, gave gold belongings of great value. Thus, the demanded sum of money was raised, and all of the prisoners were freed.

[Page 173]

A short time after their liberation, the Gestapo came from Czestochowa, and looked for the president of the Jewish community. They were told to go to Reb Baruch Szperling. The Gestapo people came to him and demanded that he hand over a list of the Jews of Klobuck, by a deadline. The list had to be given to the commandant of the Gestapo in Czestochowa before the deadline. If not, he, the president of the Jewish community, would be shot.

Walking in the streets at that time exposed people to great dangers. Reb Baruch Szperling had to go from house to house to register the inhabitants. A military unit arrested him in the street and brought him to the "Kommandantur" (Headquarters). There he was sadistically tortured. They hanged him from his feet and gave him murderous blows. When our family was informed of his arrest, all of his close relatives went to the Kommandantur shouting and crying until the Germans opened the door and threw my father out, beaten, covered in blood and unconscious.

He was taken home. There was no doctor available to give him first aid. Someone ran by foot to Czestochowa, and no doctor there wanted to risk his life to come to Klobuck.

At that time I was very young and I was in Czestochowa. When I learned about the situation I immediately took a carriage and went to Klobuck, and brought my father to Czestochowa to my uncle, Itzek Leib Szperling's, house.

There was no functioning hospital. My cousin, Dr. Szperling, took charge of caring for my father. The convalescing took six weeks. When he returned the German military no longer was present. They were replaced by the German police, who did not have any hatred of Jews; they just required loyalty (to the German power). The police established three Jewish shops, which were supplied with food for Jews. One shop was managed by my aunt Feigel. The second one by the daughter of Mantshe Unglick, whose husband was shot by the Germans. The third one was managed by Aizik Weissfelner, the son in law of Meir Spiegler. At that time the situation for the Jews was not that bad. They handled and earned money and could travel.

[Page 174]

This "good" time lasted until the arrival of the "good Jews" from the Sosnowiec Judenrat: Jasne, Wiener and Merin. They wanted to impress the Germans by sending the largest possible number of Jews to work camps in Germany, and levy for the Germans monthly payment from the Jews. My father opposed sending Jews to work, and also was against constantly extracting money. He told them that he did not have anybody to send (to the camps), and that the Jews were poor (and had no money to give).

The commissioners from the Sosnowiec Judenrat understood that they could not get my father to collaborate, so they found other people who were ready to advance their private interests to collaborate with the Sosnowiec Judenrat.

Soon the Police staff was changed. A new police force came in. The Sosnowiec members of the Judenrat immediately took the opportunity to report that the president of the community, Baruch Szperling, was a wealthy Jew, a crook and that he sabotaged the German decrees.

The police arrested my father and confiscated all his belongings. It took three days to take everything out of our house. The Germans planned to burn the house and send my father to a camp.

The Libidzer Lord (estate owner) was then the mayor of Klobuck. He did a lot for the Jews. Although he was of German origin and was a brother- in- law of the sadly famous Governor Franck, he was, the estate owner and a Polish patriot. The landowner was sent to an extermination camp, because he would not sign the German Folks list (list of people of German origin). In the beginning when he was mayor of Klobuck, he intervened with the Germans on behalf of my father, and after great efforts and the payment of a large ransom, he succeeded in gaining my father's freedom.

After his liberation, Reb Baruch Szperling no longer was the president

[Page 175]

of the community. The community had other leaders, who were nominated by the Sosnowiec Judenrat. My father no longer was involved in the community matters. Therefore, he was sent to hard work outside of Klobuck. The Polish supervisors took good care of him and sent him back home. They did the same for my brother, Aaron David Szperling, who was sixteen years old. Usually only people above eighteen years old were sent to work. But this was an act of retaliation against my father and his family.

When the Germans started to requisition the Jewish houses, ours was among the first that was requisitioned. The whole family was sent to Krzepice. My father was able to return to Klobuck after difficult endeavors, and lived in his mother's home close to the market.

In the first months of 1942 , the Jews in the Klobuck ghetto already lived in fear. People waited for the final liquidation. In June 1942, people knew for sure that it was the end of the ghetto. We communicated with relatives and close friends and we left Klobuck through the fields and the forest that stretched in lengths like stripes. My father, with Groynem Weinfelner, knew a Goy (non-Jew) who lived on the "border" between the Reich and the "General Government".

In exchange for a very large amount of money the peasant smuggled a group of about 30 Jews through the border, which was a crime punishable by the death penalty. Everybody arrived safely in Czestochowa. After 3 months, during Yom Kippur, 1942 the general deportation of the Czestochowa Jews to Treblinka started.

Page 176]

My parents were sent, together with the Jews of Czestochowa and the surroundings, to a death camp. I remained alone without any family or friends. My brother was sent somewhere to a work camp, and I did not receive any news from (or about) him.

About three months later, a Jew who escaped from Treblinka, brought me greetings from my father, that he lived and was employed in a worker commando in the death camp.

After the war, Yeshayahu Lachman from Dzaloszyn, one of the seven Jews who survived Treblinka, told me that my father lived together with him and participated in the Treblinka uprising against the camp tormentors. The large majority of the rebels died during the uneven battle and among them was the last president of the Klobuck community: my father, Reb Baruch Szperling, of blessed memory.

Translator's footnote

1. The Towarzystwo Ochrony Zdrowia Ludno ci ydowskiej (Society for Safeguarding the Health of the Jewish Population, TOZ) was established in Warsaw in 1921 (Source Yivo Encyclopedia)

[Page 177]

Jewish Doctors

by Fishl Fajga

Translated from Yiddish to English by Asher Szmulewicz

In Klobuck we had three Jewish doctors: Yitzhak Djalowski, Aaron Maas and Rodel Mantshe. Each of these doctors had a special role.

Yitzhak Djalowski was a specialist for the "mild" diseases: a cold, a flu, a sore throat or if someone had fever, then people called Yitzhak Djalowski. If the sick person did not feel better, God forbid, people then called Aaron Mass.

Aaron Mass used to walk slowly leaning on his cane. He knew his importance. The cane was a sign for the entire household of the sick person of his diagnosis. If the doctor left and forgot to take his cane, people knew that the sick person was in a critical state.

Rodel Mantshe was a woman pediatrician. When a child was ill, people ran to Rodel. She was always ready to make any call. Her mere presence brought calmness in the house of the sick child. Just with her greetings to the people in the house she already brought healing.

Mothers used to complain to the doctor wringing their hands: "Oy my child is moribund". Rodel used to stretch the child's feet and hands and smacked her lips to the child. The child started to laugh, the mother was happy and said to the doctor: "You came at a fortunate hour".

Rodel explained that it was not serious. The child had a cold, or a sore throat, (and instructed), take some warm sand, put it in a small bag and place it on his throat.

The doctor left the apartment and the mother of the sick child gave her hearty greetings.

[Page 178]

Jewish Women Community Workers

by Borukh Szimkowicz

Translated from Yiddish to English by Asher Szmulewicz

There were Jewish women in Klobuck who did a lot in the shtetl through various charity organizations to help the poor people and bankrupt handlers. I would like to remember three of these women here.

Sheindel Broches (from Bracha: benediction)

Sheindel Azjner, or as she was called, Sheindel Broches, was my grandmother, and one of the oldest inhabitants of Klobuck.

When I was young she already was more than seventy years old. Her husband, Baruch, my grandfather, was killed in a sad accident on the road to Zagorz. While he was in a carriage on the road, his horses became startled by something, and they bolted away (out of control). The carriage turned over, and my grandfather did not jump off in time, and he was killed.

After his death my grandmother lived in poverty. She lived in a small room in Shmuel Leib Fajga's yard. She made a living from "small handling". She sold raisins, dried plums, onions, and garlic. During Pesach she provided the weathy Klobucker Jews with kosher for Pesach beet root borsht and matzah flour, which she made from her own small mill.

The small mill was constructed with two round shaped stones, fastened together with four long wooden beams. Between the stones was a kind of funnel into which the broken matzot pieces, which were brought by the well to do Jews, were deposited. In the front of the mill there was a handle. When the handle was turned, the stones moved and ground the matzot into flour. Before putting the matzot in the small mill we had to crush them in a "stempe", as the wooden mortar was called.

[Page 179]

The work at Sheindel Broches' mill was part of celebrating Pesach for the Jewish children of Klobuck. Almost all of the children of Klobuck came to grind matzah flour. My grandmother did not allow the childrento participate in the festivities of the mill just like that. In front of the apartment there was a jug of water, and each child had to wash his hands before being able to help with the Pesach work of grinding the matzot into flour.

In addition, my grandmother sold homemade wine for making Kiddush.

Chayele Weiss

Chayele Weiss was a Chasidic woman with a kind face. She was affiliated with the Raspjer Rabbi court, and was always ready to do a good deed. She knew all of the people who had difficulties, and all of those who did not have enough food for Shabbat or Festivals.

Chayele had an agreement with the state doctor: he would not charge the poor people for his visits, but afterwards he was directed to send her a note with instructions as to (the doctor's) payment terms. The doctor honored the agreement, and Chayele paid the bills. She was very involved in "Hachnassat Orchim" (hospitality), and thereby provided the poor people, who stayed in Klobuck overnight, with a clean bed and with a meal.

There were three blind lonely women in the shtetl. Chayele Weiss took care of them. She provided them with food, a room in which to live and a clean bed. Chayele was also active in the "Bikur Cholim" (visit to the sick people) institution.

Hinde Miriam

Hinde Miriam was a woman of the people. She took care mainly of poor fiancées (Kalot), and women in childbirth. When she knew that a poor family had a young woman about to get married, and there was no money to do so, she came to the family's apartment, and simply asked what was needed for the young woman. She did the same for women in childbirth. People told her everything.

When she had a list of all of the needs, she went to Wolf Weiss' drugstore, and selected linen and trimmings, which she then sewed by herself into what was needed, or she cut diapers for the women in childbirth. She provided the poor kalot with linen and bedding, and even, on one occasion, with the wedding dress.

Hinde Miriam received the money to pay for the expenses in the same manner as the community activist noted above: she went to the well to do Jews and she gathered money.

The women community activists often gathered together in Chayele Weiss' apartment, and discussed how to help the poor, needy, Jewish families of Klobuck. The women community activists always had a group of women who helped them in their charity activities: Freidel Aaron, Freidel Hartze, Rachel Ziegelman, Sarah Itshe, Freidel Meir, Chana Beinish, Beindel Liberman, Chanele Zeidman, the cook, my mother, Libe Yossel, and Leitshe Itshe Yankel.

It was said by Klobuckers that Hinde Miriam Green was shot dead by the Germans in front of her door.

[Page 181]

Rivkele Kurland

Rivka Kurland was a partner in the Klobucker mill. Her heart and pocketbook were always ready to help Jews who needed help. When any of the bagel bakers in Klobuck did not have money to buy a sack of flour, Rivka sent them a sack of flour and told them: "when you have the money, pay me back".

Rivka always took the time to help the poor and sick people, by providing them with a doctor, an old time barber (surgeon) and also medicine. When she knew that a household had nothing for the Festivals, she immediately asked a well to do Jew for help, and both of us went through the shtetl to collect some money for the poor family. Chanukah, Purim and Hoshana Raba were her "seasons". Then she went to the rich houses and collected larger sums of money for the needy. The Klobucker scoffers nicknamed her "the purse knocker".

After the liberation, a tombstone was put on the tomb of Rivka Kurland. Her daughter and son-in-law, who stand by the tombstone, found the tomb

[Page 182]

Pictures of the Old Time Jewish Women of Klobuck

Sheindel Aznjer (Sheindel Broches)

Rivka, the wife of Hirsh Shochat

[Page 183]

Perel Diaman, the wife of Pinchas Diaman

Feigel Fagja, the wife of Daniel Fajga

[Page 184]

Klobucker Righteous Gentiles

Dr. Brzozowski, a Pole
Who Saved Jews During a Pogrom

by Borukh Szimkowicz

Translated from the Yiddish to English by Asher Szmulewicz

Among all of the personalities and figures of the former Jewish [town of] Klobuck, I would like to include a clever Pole, a socialist, and a real humanist, who risked his life for Jews and saved them from a pogrom. I think of the well-known Dr. Brzozowski.

In addition to his qualifications as a good medical doctor, he was known as being a good man. He did not charge poor sick people for their medical examinations. He showed his friendship for Jews at every opportunity. He really fought against the anti-Semitism of the Klobucker priests, and against the boycott of the Jews that anti-Semitic people wanted to enforce in Klobuck.

Even [his appearance] and his face seemingly brought him closer to Jews. [He looked like a Jew.] He had a small stature, and a long satin beard. Even in the Czarist period, Dr. Brzozowski was known as a socialist. Due to his membership in the P.P.S[1] he was jailed in the Pietrikower prison. Also arrested with him was the Jewish barber (old time surgeon), Shlomo Bams.

*

[Page 185]

I remember from my youth the story about the pogrom in Klobuck, that was avoided thanks to Dr. Brzozowski.

As it was told then, the hatred against Jews in Klobuck started in the nineties (1890-99). This was linked to an event that occurred in year 1890. In that year, during Purim, the Klobucker, Reb Moshe Zalman, a Jew, and a Torah scholar, who liked to drink, wanted to get joyful about Haman's[2] (hanging). When Reb Moshe Zalman drank alcoholic beverages he made a doll and hanged it on a hook, like the one used to get water with a bucket from a well.

With the hook and the doll, the drunk Jew, Reb Zalman Moshe, strolled through the streets and shouted: "Patrzeæ jak Haman wiszy" (Look how Haman is hanging). The Gentiles went to the priests in the church, and reported that the Jews were [making fun of] and laughing at Jesus.

At that time there were three priests in Klobuck, two of whom were nicknamed "the big one and the red one," because of their physical appearance, and they were the avowed enemy of the Jews. They took advantage of the event with the hanged Haman, and with the help of secular anti-Semites, and with the Endeke[3] Witmeinski, as the leader, started to incite against Jews, who they claimed were laughing at the persecuted Jesus. As it was written in another chapter, a pogrom almost took place then. Although the anti-Semites did not succeed at that time, they did not give up, and they sought to take advantage of this event later.

In year 1906, throughout Russia there was a wave of pogroms, and the priests in Klobuck, with their followers, also prepared for a "settling of account" with the Jews. In the church, on every Sunday, the peasants from the surroundings towns gathered, and the priests often called for a pogrom. One was announced to happen on a designated Sunday. The peasants were told to come with sticks, hatchets and iron bars to attack the Jewish shops, and make a "real" looting.

Dr. Brzozowski was informed about the preparations against the Jews, and he went to the priests and advised them not to tarnish the Poles with hooligan murders. His warning did not help. The news spread amongst the Jews.

[Page 186]

There was turmoil. Jews knew that they didn't have anyone to rely on. At that time in Klobuck there were six Russian policemen and a sergeant, who also was a great anti-Semite. In such occasions, Jews usually looked for some miracle.

On the announced Sunday, the peasants came to the church, prepared to carry out a pogrom on the Jews. Dr. Brzozowski also went to the church. During the priest's harangue, the "praying" people grabbed the Doctor. They all shouted from all sides: "Kill the servant of the Jews". The Doctor barely escaped. Shots were fired at him. He left his fur coat (it was winter time), and ran to tell the Jews what to expect.

Dr. Brzozowski went home and invited the following Jews to his home: Moshe Szmulewicz, Shmuel Szperling and David Zigelman. He pointed out to them the danger that threatened the Jews. A pogrom against the Jews was going to start in approximately two hours, when the "looting" would start. The Doctor advised the men to find two riders with agile horses, and ride to the county representative in Czestochowa, who was one of his good acquaintances, and let him know what was happening in Klobuck.

Three Jewish riders were dispatched immediately: Abraham, Michael and Aaron Mass. The Doctor gave them two letters, one for the county representative, and one for the military commander. Approximately two hours later, a few hundred Cossacks arrived in Klobuck, and they spread out throughout the shtetl. The Gentiles stayed in the church for the entire day. A few of the Endekes leaders, who also hated Israel Witmeinsky, were arrested by the Authorities. Klobuck was spared from a pogrom, thanks to the humanity of Dr. Brzozowski.

After this event, Dr. Brzozowski advised the Jews to join, in the greatest possible number, the "Stra¿ak Ogniowa" (Firemen Society), and thereby create an organized force, able to resist anti-Semitic attacks on Jews. Klobuck Jews followed his advice, and enrolled in the Firemen Society. The leader of the Firemen Society was actually Dr. Brzozowski. Drzemba, his deputy, also was not an anti-Semite.

[Page 187]

Hartzke Feige was the commander of the Jewish Firemen.

Through the pogrom that didn't happen, the observant Jews saw a miracle. The Jews were saved thanks to the merit of the saintly, righteous, Rabbi Yankele, who they said protected the Jewish Klobuck community.

Translator's Footnotes:

1. P.P.S Should be something that would translate in English Socialist Polish Party.

2. The Jewish holiday of Purim relates the story about Haman (an adviser to the king), who instigated a plot to kill all of the Jews of ancient Persia. The plot was foiled by Mordechai and Ester (a Jew and the king's wife). Haman was hanged and the Jews celebrated the saving of the Jews.

3. "Endeke" From the initials N. D. (pronounced ende) in Polish (Narodowa Demokratia) National Democrats: reactionary Polish party, who like the German Hitlerist "National Socialist" party, based its program on the extermination of Jews.

The Libidzer Estate Owner Who Saved Jews
from Danger During the First World War

by Fishl Fajga

Translated from the Yiddish to English by Asher Szmulewicz

I don't remember his name. In Klobuck he was called the Libidzer good owner. He had German origins. During World War I he saved the lives of scores of Jews and Poles. This happened as follows:

In August 1914, when the German Army invaded Poland there was a great battle in Klobuck. The majority of inhabitants, both Jews and Poles, fled away from the shtetl, and went to the nearby villages. Meanwhile, a German officer was killed on the road between Kamyk and Klobuck. The corpse was put in the cellar of a Christian old age home.

The German military leadership was notified about the death of the officer, and the surrounding inhabitants of the house were accused of the murder. Fifty people, Jews and Poles, were arrested. Among the arrested Jews were: Chaim Leibish and Eliyahu Dudek; David Hersz Shochat; the lame man, Israel Meir Blau, and his father; Leibele, Lipman Bielas, Birenbaum, Asher Goldberg and others.

[Page 188]

All of the arrested people were assembled with their hands up in the church. The Germans wanted to shoot them, and burn Klobuck in retaliation for the killed officer. The Libiczer good owner was informed of the Germans' intention. He immediately came to Klobuck, and intervened with the German Commander. He proved that none of the civilians took part in the killing of the German officer. He vouched for the civilians with his life, and signed (an oath) that he was responsible for the Jews, and for keeping the peace in the village. At that time, the Germans acted with some restraint in regard to their mass murders; they let themselves be convinced (of facts), and did not act out with their wild acts of retaliation. The arrested people were freed.

Much later when the Libiczer good owner died, representatives of the Jewish community, led by the Rabbi, participated in the funeral ceremony. Flowers were laid on his tomb. Jews from Klobuck always had good memories of the "Administrator".

Also, his son followed in his father's footsteps. During the first week of World War II, when the Germans ruled with barbarity in Poland, the good owner's son was the mayor of Klobuck. His attitude towards the persecuted Jews was very good. There was a rumor that he opposed Hitler. He indeed proved his opposition.

The German Authorities requested that he sign the list of "Volks Deutschen" (Polish people of German origins), and that he send his son to Hitler's army. The good owner declared that he was a Pole, and would remain a Pole.

One day he was arrested and sent to Auschwitz. Ten days later, his family received a box full of ashes with the inscription that he died in the camp.

[Page 189]

The Jewish Mill That Provided Klobuck with Electricity
by Chaim Kurland
Translated from the Yiddish to English by Asher Szmulewicz

The Klobuck mill, our mill, where I was born and where I was raised. Each pebble, and each screw still are very well preserved in my memory. We had good times and bad times in that mill. I will recite some of my memories about the mill.

In those years there were two mills in Klobuck, both old fashioned mills, from the old days, which were operated by the water from the stream. One was at the Zagorz pond, with a big wheel, which always rotated slowly. The second mill was at the Zakszewer pond, and that one was always rented by my grandfather, Zisskind. He leased it for many years.

Yossef Meir Kurland and his family

[Page 190]

Over time, as the new, modern, mills were built, the old ones slowly disappeared. My father, Yossef Meir, a flour merchant, who lived in Czestochowa, often came to Klobuck. He saw that Klobuck was an appropriate location to build a new, modern, mill. At the same time my uncle, Moshe Zigelbaum, my grandfather Zisskind's son, rented a mill in a village called Dambie, near Czestochowa. My father proposed a plan to build a modern mill in Klobuck, and presented him with the prospect that in the future it could provide a nice livelihood.

In 1905 the work commenced to build a large mill in Klobuck on the Grodziker road. In 1906 the mill was finished. It had two pairs of rolling mills and two pairs of grindstones. One "Perlak"[1] to grind barley, and one "Jagielnik"[1] to grind millet.

In the beginning the mill was operated by a diesel-motor, and the neighbors often complained that it bothered them and prevented them from sleeping, because the motor was very noisy. So we bought a steam engine, which operated with coal, and it was a quiet engine.

In the mill, flour was being ground. In the past, the bakers bought flour from Czestochowa, and from the Kowalsk mill in the nearby shtetl of Krzepice. The bakers indeed were relieved. They no longer had to go through a flour broker, or wait until the flour sacks arrived from Czestochowa. Similarly in the past, the bakers of Klobuck could not store and preserve large quantities of flour, because they could not afford to appropriate the necessary sums of money to buy standby reserves of flour. (As a result of the mill), the bakers (in Klobuck) became prosperous.

The Jewish mill, which was managed by my father, became a popular institution. When a baker needed a half sack of flour to bake bread or rolls, he came to the mill and took a sack of flour. Even when the baker did not have enough money to pay for it, he never left empty handed. The peasants from the surroundings brought their grain and wheat from their harvest to have it ground, and they went back home happy.

[Page 191]

The Mill that Lit up Klobuck

Like in all of the shtetls, at that time in Klobuck there was no electric lighting. During the evening people assembled around night lamps. Since the mill had a large dynamo engine, the owners of the mill, my father and my uncle, Moshe Zigelbaum, decided to provide electric lighting in the shtetl.

In 1918 we delivered electric lighting to the Klobuck population. Everywhere wooden poles were erected, and electric wires were pulled to connect all of the houses. At once, on a summer evening after sunset, suddenly all of the houses were illuminated. There were no electric switches in the houses. Switching the lights on and off occurred in the mill. The mill became the electricity provider, and it was nice and good.

The Fire

In 1920 a fire suddenly broke out in the mill, and all of the flour was burned with the smoke. The fire lasted three days, because the mill's warehouse was full of grain. We were left without a groschen (penny). Moreover, the mill was under insured; the insurance recovery barely was enough to buy the stones and nails. We did not have any ability to rebuild the mill. Since my parents and uncle Moshe were held in high regard, and were loved by all Klobuck inhabitants, both Jews and non-Jews alike, people came forward and offered to help to rebuild the mill. Also, the Libidczer land owner contributed front money to help rebuild the mill.

The work started, and in 1922 the mill was rebuilt and again started to grind grain. Because of technical problems we could not immediately restore the electric lightning of the shtetl. In 1925 the electric lightning of the shtetl was resumed.

My father and my uncle, Moshe Zigelbaum, committed to provide electricity for the Synagogue and the Batei-Midrash for free, and they honored their promise. I became the collector of the electricity fees. Each month I went from apartment to apartment to collect what was called "electric money". It was duly conducted. In 1933 I made my Aliyah to Eretz Israel, and my father came to visit me in Israel.

[Page 192]

The End of the Jewish Mill

When the Germans invaded Klobuck, the destruction came. They immediately confiscated the mill, and they put a German in charge, and left my father as a supervisor of the mill. That situation lasted until the Germans implemented the final liquidation of the Klobucker Jews.

A camp was established in Zagorz, and my father and sisters were sent to the camp. My uncle Moshe and his wife went to Czestochowa and hid themselves. They died from hunger and cold.

After the war, my surviving sister, Rachel, returned to Klobuck. Understandably, the mill was taken over by foreign people. The owner was one of our former workers, called Matinski. Rachel requested that the mill be given back. The new "owner" said that the mill was owned by him. My sister filed a complaint in the Czestochowa court, and after many difficulties, she received her share of the mill. She sold her share to another non-Jew, and barely escaped after receiving death threats from Matinski.

Translator's Footnote:

1. Perlak and Jagielnik are the names of the types of grindstone used by the mill. It could be the name of the grindstone brand, or of the name of the town of provenance.

[Page 193]

Anti-Semitism in Klobuck

Murderous Attacks on Jews

By Fishel Feige

Translated from Yiddish to English by Asher Szmulewicz

From my earliest years in the shtetl I remember that people talked about thieves and murderers who attacked Jews from Klobuck on the roads. As frightened children we listened to these stories. Later we realized that they were not stories, but real accounts of murders, perpetrated by gentiles (goyim) against Jews. I will recall below a few murders, that are fixed in my memory.

In our house, close to the mill, lived a Jew, Yaacov Chode. Since he did not have a job, he moved to another village, Borowe, with his family, where his father had a (grain) mill and a saw mill.

During the First World War, in a dark night, a band of thieves attacked the Chode family house, and killed Yaacov Chode and his father, and seriously wounded Yaacov Zuckerman, who was formerly in charge of the mikveh (ritual bath).

*

Yitzchak Tshochne, an elderly Jew, went to the village to buy a carpet of skin animal, a calf, a few eggs and a hen. Two gentiles (Shiktsim) from Klobuck followed him until they arrived the forest, which was called "Makom-Wald" (The forest place) or "Mokra Wald"(The damp forest). In the forest the two gentiles attacked the Jew, killed him, and stole the few kerblech (roubles – Russian money), he had with him, and ripped off his boots.

The murder was discovered. The murderers, Karkotek and Albert, were tried in court. After they were sentenced and served their prison term, they returned to the town.

[Page 194]

Albert became a policeman in the independent (country of) Poland (after WW I). A guardian of the Justice ...

*

A few Klobuck horse merchants were returning from the market in Czestochowa. On the bridge between Grabuwke and Lgota, their carts were stopped by two Poles, who ransacked everything. One of the merchants, Yitzhak Zachs, was late, and when his cart arrived it was the last one. By the time the cart arrived it was already night, and the two murderers had shot Zachs. None of his money was taken by the murderers, and the cart with his dead body was driven into the city.

*

Wolf Eizner lived in the village of Ostrow. He was born in Klobuck. Murderers attacked him in his house and killed him.

*

A weird story happened to Yaacov Reiber, the cattle merchant, who lived in Kamyk. He bought and sold cattle amongst the villages, so that most of the time he was on the road.

One time while traveling through the forest, he met the well-known highway man Slomtshinsky, who was wanted and hunted by the police for a long time. The police could not catch him, because it was said that he hid in a cave deep underground. From time to time he sent threatening letters to rich merchants and landowners with the following demand: bring a large sum of money to a designated place in the forest, or he would shoot them.

When Slomtshinsky saw the Jew (Reiber), he stopped him and asked where he was going. Reiber answered that he was on his way to a village to meet a peasant who asked him to come to sell a calf. Instinctively the frightened Jew took out his insubstantial amount of money and presented it to the thief. Slomtshinsky asked him if he had any more money.

[Page 195]

Upon hearing a negative answer, the thief took out enough money from his own pocket to buy a cow, and gave it to the Jew, because not much of a living could be made from selling a calf.

It was said that the thief Slomtshinsky only robbed rich people. When he came across a poor Jew walking to a village, he gave him some money, in order to meek out a living.

Finally, Yaacov Reiber, the cattle merchant, was assassinated by murderers. About his death it was said:

One day he went away and did not return when he was supposed to. His wife and children kept weeping and lamenting. We looked for him on all the roads, but could not find a trace of him.

One day, the Rabbi of Klobuck, HaRav Yitzchak Chanoch, righteous of blessed memory, called a meeting of a few Jews from his closest circle. When they came in, the Rabbi told them that he had a dream: Yaacov Reiber was killed and was laying in the forest at a specific place, covered by twigs. The Rabbi asked his followers to summon more Jews and go to the forest to the specific place, where they would find the dead man.

The Rabbi never went to the forest, but because his word was revered by everyone, the Jews went to the place identified by the Rabbi, and sure enough, found Yaacov Reiber's corpse.

*

Close to Hersh Szperling lived a Jew. He was called The Big Eliyahu. He was not rich. He made a living from trading in the villages, had a lame, sick wife and young children. He was a native of Miedzne where he was trading.

Once he went to the village and never came back. After a few days he was found dead. Later the lame widow made a living by selling vegetables in front of her apartment.

[Page 196]

In the village named Fasseidowke lived a rich and powerful Jewish man named Shidlowski. One night burglars attacked his house. The burglars did not occupy all of the rooms. Family members started to yell. The attackers became frightened and ran away. Nevertheless they had managed to stab Shidlowski.

The rich and powerful Jewish man left the village the next day and moved to Klobuck. He lived near us in a house close to the mill.

*

Thus the Jews in our region were constantly exposed to life threatening dangers. In the last years before the War, all of the Jews living in the surrounding villages left and settled in Klobuck. Only in the village of Miedzne did Jews still live.

All the victims remembered above were laid to rest in the Jewish cemetery of Klobuck.

Endek [Polish National Party] Terror
and Boycott of the Jews

by Yaacov Szperling

Translated from Yiddish to English by Asher Szmulewicz

In the 1930's, when the anti-semitism increased in Poland, Klobuck was not spared. In Klobuck, the leaders of the "Endek" anti-semitic movement[1] were among the local Polish "intelligentsia": the notary Boganski; the pharmacist; a Polish doctor; and the priests. The Endek members, as everywhere in Poland, had a special group of hooligans and pugnacious gentiles (shiksim) called "Boyuwke", who organized hooligan attacks on Jews. The leader of this group was a limp and fat Pole who worked in the mill.

During Purim 1933, the hooligans attacked a group of Jewish young people. The young Jewish people were leaving Moshe Szmulewicz' house, where they had spent the evening. Three Jews: Aaron Szmulewicz, David Tzigelman and Wolf Kirtzbart were seriously injured. (Other) Jews came to help them and to save the injured, who were between life and death.

The wounded were taken to the state hospital, which was located close to the site of the attack. The Christian hospital attendant did not want to admit the injured Jews, without an order from the doctor, who lived near the hospital. Doctor Woytshick, an "Endek" member, did not want to open his door (it happened in the middle of the night). Nothing helped, despite knocking on the door, or shouting for help; the doctor remained "deaf".

There was no other alternative but to call Czestochowa (by phone) for help. Dr Geisler came immediately from Czestochowa, and after administering first aid, he ordered that the wounded be transported to the Czestochowa hospital. For two of the wounded it took many weeks to heal. David Tsigelman recovered, but Aaron Szmulewicz became an invalid.

[Page 197]

I wrote a letter to the editor of the Czestochowa newspaper, "Die Zeit" (The Time), about the hooligan attack and the anti-semitic doctor, and his unethical attitude. I described the attitude of the doctor, whose behavior contradicted everyone's humanity and medical ethics. Doctor Woytshick was very upset by the publication of my letter and he "left no stone unturned" to have the newspaper publish a denial. Since I refused to retract my account of the true events, Mr. Moshe Zigelbaum, a member of the Klobuck city council (ratman), came to the help of the doctor.

Mr. Moshe Zigelbaum, a friend of my father, who was also a member of the Klobuck city council, asked my father to influence his son to write a retraction to the Czestochowa Jewish newspaper. But my father could not influence me to publish such a letter. Consequently, Mr. Moshe Zigelbaum published a letter of denial in his own name, and thus exonerated the anti-semitic doctor.

The Jewish member of the city council (Zigelbaum), by doing so, intented not to exasperate and incite the gentiles (goyim). But it did not help. The terror and the boycott against Jews spread to our shtetl.

Memories

Shlomo Birenbaum, who was present at this hooligan attack, wrote in his memoirs:

I was a member of the Zionist Young Organization, "Gordonia". I left that organization with a group of friends to participate in the "Hitachdut" (Union), which conducted a wide range of Zionist activities and owned a library with a few thousand books. I was elected to the "Hitachdut" committee.

[Page 198]

In October 1938,[2] on Friday night, there was a important meeting, which lasted until midnight. When we came out to the street from the meeting, we were attacked by gentiles (shiksim), and beaten up mercilessly. We had wounded people: Aaron Szmulewicz, Aaron Tsigelman, David Rypstein, David Yossef Zeibel, Shimshe Zeidman and myself – Shlomo Birenbaum - the writer of these lines. Aaron Szmulewicz suffered the most, and became an invalid

This hooligan attack created turmoil among the Jews in the shtetl. The next morning, on Shabbat (Saturday), the atmosphere was like Tishe B' Av (the day of mourning for the ancient Temple's destruction). The wounded were in the hospital. As soon as we recovered, we renewed the activities of the "Hitachdut" (Union) and directed the organization until September 1939[3], when the German armies attacked Poland.

Translator Footnotes

1. "Endekes" From the initials N. D. (pronounced ende) in Polish (Narodowa Demokratia) National Democrats: reactionary Polish party who like the German Hitlerist "National Socialist" party, based its program on the extermination of Jews.

2. The authors Szperling and Birenbaum obviously recounted the same incident, but their recollection of dates and certain other details are inconsistent.

3. In the book it says 1938 it is obviously a typo it should be 1939.

4.   Sk□adkowski spoke out against physical violence against Jews, adding, however, "but yes to the economic struggle" (against Jews). "Yes (Owszem)" became the symbol of the economic competition against Jews in Poland at that time.

From translation excerpt of the following Wikipedia Polish page http://pl.wikipedia.org/wiki/Felicjan_S□awoj_Sk□adkowski

[Page 199]

Fear of a Pogrom in Klobuck

by Yaacov Szperling

Translated from Yiddish to English by Asher Szmulewicz

It was well known that during the years 1936-37 the pogroms against Jews increased. These attacks were provoked by the pretext of brawls between Jews and Poles. The anti-semitic hooligans in Klobuck engineered a pogrom on a wider scale by using, as a pretext, the scuffle between a Jewish butcher and a policeman in Brisk, during which the policeman was killed. As it happened, the policeman was from Klobuck, and from a well known anti-semitic family, by the name of the "Kendjares".

Immediately after the "Brisk affair", on Friday night the hooligans began attacking the Jews. The hooligans (first) broke the windows of Jewish houses. The next morning, on Shabbat (Saturday) when the Jews were praying in the shule (synagogue) and in the "shtiblech" (small prayer house), the Endekes (Polish national anti-semitic party) members gathered close to the "Kosciol" (church), and from there with the Gentiles (Shiksim) and the "Kendjares" at the lead, armed with knives, marched towards the shule. The Jews, aware of the danger, fled to their homes. The hooligans were able to hit a few Jews with stones. The Jews hid in their homes, and did not return to the streets for the remainder of the Shabbat.

[Page 200]

The leader of the community, was my father, Mr. Baruch Szperling, (read page 170-176 about his activities). Ignoring the danger, he went to the police station and asked that the Jewish population be protected.

The police refused to help, using the pretext that they were not capable of subduing the seditious bands. However, the police commander did not find it necessary to ask for help from the police of the town of Czestochowa, which was close by.

Mr. Baruch Szperling assumed responsibility for protecting the Jewish community, and he drove to Czestochowa in his own car, and went directly to the county police. Once there he emphatically demanded protection for the Jewish population of Klobuck from the pogroms and attacks. His intervention was successful. The commander of the county police sent several squads of policemen, armed with steel helmets. They patrolled the streets day and night and re-established order. The leaders of the gang were arrested and the Jews again were able to return to the streets.

The police from Czestochowa left. But the Jewish community remained afraid of new attacks. They did not repair their broken glass windows. Instead they nailed them shut with wooden planks. The broken windows gave the town a frightful feeling. It looked like a silent protest against the Polish power. The burmistrz (mayor) called the leader of the community, Mr. Baruch Szperling, and demanded that he use his influence to instruct the Jews to remove the wooden planks from their windows and to re-glaze the windows with glass. The leader of the community promised to influence the Jews in that direction, but as a condition, the police behavior had to change, and the police needed to protect the Jewish population. The police commander refused to give a clear response.

My father, together with the Rabbi, travelled to Warsaw, and with the help of the Jewish members of parliament, the two representatives of the Jews from Klobuck, met the Prime Minister of the Polish government, Slawoj Skladkowski, who was known for his "Owszem Polityk"[4] (Yes Policy) towards the Jews. That policy segregated Jewish economic life (from the greater Polish population and economy). It prevented Jews from prospering, and sought to interfere with their means of subsistence. "Owszem" was permissible; but not pogroms. Sk adkowski was not really motivated to protect the Jews; rather he feared that the unrest would spread and his government would be jeopardized.

[Page 201]

For whatever reason, the intervention of the Rabbi and the community leader with Sk adkowski brought good results: the commander of the Klobuck police was replaced. The new police commander was a more liberal person. As soon as he arrived, he reassured the Jewish representatives that came to welcome him that the Jewish population would be protected against hooligan attacks. At his request, the Jews assembled in the shule, and the police commander comforted them and told them that as long as he remained in Klobuck calm and order would be enforced.

The new police commander kept his word. He initiated police night patrols, which protected the shtetl during the night. The situation again became calm. The leader of the community, Mr. Baruch Szperling, then asked the Jews to remove the wooden planks from their windows and replace the broken glass panes. The Jews obeyed and the shtetl got back its normal appearance.

*

After the pogrom the "Endekes" from Klobuck started to implement the "Owszem Polityk" of Sk adkowski. They started by encouraging the Poles not to buy from Jews. Then Jewish shops were picketed, "Piketnikes". The same activities occurred on market days. The "Piketnikes" did not allow the peasants and the Christians to go into a Jewish shop, or to have any contacts with Jewish merchants. On market days the "Piketnikes" stood on the roads from early in the morning and shouted to the peasants: "nie kupuj u ̄ydów" (don't buy from Jews).

[Page 202]

The Jews from Klobuck who went to the market to trade were beaten and stones were thrown at them.

For this kind of anti-semitic behavior there was no solution. The economic boycott of Jews was also combined with "mild" hooligan attacks, and they were not stopped by the Sk adkowski government. There was a need to find another way to help the Jews avoid losing their means of making a living.

Mr. Baruch Szperling, the community leader, devised the following plan: he knew the leader of these anti-semitic acts and decided to bribe him. The leader was the Polish employee of the Jewish mill: Meyer, a limp and fat gentile. He was a blood thirsty anti-semite, who became a "Volks Deutsch" (German people) during the German occupation.

Mr. Baruch Szperling took advantage of an opportune time and met with this person, who accepted a determined sum of money to leave the shtetl, and the boycott actions against Jews stopped.

[Page 203]

A Summary of the Jewish Life in Klobuck between the Two World Wars

by Moshe Wajnman

Translated from Yiddish to English by Asher Szmulewicz

During the first election of the Sejm (Polish Parliament) in 1922, the Jews of Klobuck were greatly divided. Influenced by the publication of the Balfour Declaration, which recognized the right of Jews to have a national homeland in Israel, Zionist ideas found support in Klobuck. Abraham Yakubowicz announced and advocated his candidacy as the Zionist candidate for election to the Sejm. This represented the first time that a large segment of the Jewish population of Klobuck "rebelled" against the Rabbi.

At an election meeting of the religious block, which was held in the great shule (synagogue), the Rabbi called Yakubowicz a "Sheigetz" (gentile). Yakubowicz confronted (the Rabbi), and answered him back. A great scandal ensued. The respected iron merchant, David Zigelman, who had always remained silent and had his permanent seat close to the mizrach[1] wall in the great shule, together with his seven sons, started to express their public opposition to the Rabbi and the frume (religious) supporters. David Zigelman and his friends, Moshe Szmulewicz, Shlomo Mordechai Green, Itzik Djalowski and Shime (Simon) Lichter, started to influence the simple craftsmen, who did not really like the frume tradesmen, who were part of the religious block. In that way a political war flared up during the first Sejm election between the religious block and the Zionists.

*

The educational activities of the progressive secular Jewish parties and their cultural activities had an influence on the small Klobuck Jewish community after the First World War. The Jewish community of nearby Czestochowa also had a strong influence. The thinking and mindset of the Jews from Klobuck underwent a revolution.

[Page 204]

People no longer were ashamed of being craftsman, and the craftsmen stopped aspiring for their daughters to marry Beit Midrash Bachurim (Beit Midrash students). In addition, Chasidim parents approved and encouraged their teenage children to learn a profession.

The number of Beit Midrash Bachurim (young men) decreased, and those who still engaged in religious learning started to "smuggle in" secular Jewish books, which were first read in secret, but later these Bachurim read books in the reading rooms.

But the new way of life for the Jews from Klobuck, and their thirst for enlightenment and science, did not bring any economic improvement to their lives. On the contrary, after the First World War the economic condition of the Jews from Klobuck worsened. First, there was inflation, which lowered the value of money. Later, the Grabski[2] tax system, which was largely a way of confiscating the hard earned Jewish possessions, greatly impoverished the Jews of Klobuck. The small shops and the little merchants lost their bank credit. The market sellers: tailors (ready-made), cutters, milliners, shoemakers lost business.

The anti-Semitic propaganda spread across the villages and reached Klobuck. The Endekes (Polish National Party) slogan "swoj do swego" (the same ones to the alike ones), which meant that Polish villages buy and sell only to Poles, reinforced the boycott of Jewish trade. The good relationship between the Polish peasants and the Jews from Klobuck and its surroundings, which had lasted for decades, deteriorated. The local peasants, who always had a difficult and poor life, were incited against Jews during the 1920's and 1930's, by the propaganda that the Jews were the only reason for their poverty.

Jewish young people, who belonged to the Communist Organization, advocated Communist propaganda in the villages, but they risked their lives. The Polish reactionary regime vigorously persecuted them, and there was a great Jewish emigration from Klobuck.

The first Jewish emigration started with the failed 1905 Revolution.

[Page 205]

Later there was another emigration during the years 1912-1913, before the First World War. The last flow of emigration occurred during the 1930's, when anti-Semitism became stronger. At the end was the German extermination of the Jews from the grounds of Klobuck and other Polish shtelech (villages). The Jews of Klobuck were persecuted and the community was wiped out.

Translator Footnotes

1. Mizrach wall is pointing to the east, the closest wall to Jerusalem, usually a reserved place to most respected people in a synagogue

2. The authors Szperling and Birenbaum obviously recounted the same incident, but their recollection of dates and certain other details are inconsistent.

[Page 209]

The German Extermination of Jewish Klobuck

The First Months under the German Occupation

by Berl Yakubowicz, Israel

Translated from the Yiddish to English by Asher Szmulewicz

The Wandering Path between Death and Extermination

When the war broke out, we were the last Jews to leave Klobuck.

In our apartment we packed our luggage in the morning, and we were ready to carry it on our shoulders. We were ready to leave. Our family had four members: our father and mother, my brother and I. We remained confined in our house. My father, an old soldier from 1914-1918, told us that it was better to stay inside the house than in the fields. He believed that there were Polish soldiers in the fields and the forests around Klobuck. He was certain that there would be a battle around the city.

It was calm, almost four o'clock. Suddenly, we heard a loud explosion. The window glass broke and fell down. We all were afraid. My mother cried "Gevalt" (For Heaven's Sake), and asked if we should take our bags and flee like the other town's people. The explosion was from the railway bridge, which was blown up by the Polish military. Without thinking, all four of us took our packages and left the house. My father kissed the mezuzah several times with tears in his eyes, saying the prayer "Yehe Ratzsone" (Beginning of the traveler's prayer, meaning "May we would"). We were the only people in the streets.

While walking through the streets, I looked carefully at every house separately. The glass windows were broken; the rooms were empty; there was dead silence.

[Page 210]

At the same time I noticed that the Polish "Obrona Narodowa" (National Defense Force)[1] was looting the Jewish shops. They used the long French rifle with bayonet. Many of the "Obrona Narodowa" armed Polish National Defense men were drunk, and they were lying stretched out in the ditches, sleeping with their rifles thrown aside. Others of the "Obrona Narodowa" were busy tearing apart the Jewish shops and carrying off sacks, full of Jewish goods.

We ran in the direction of Kamyk[1], where everybody else was running. We passed in front of the Jewish cemetery. My father, pointing to the cemetery with his hand said: "There will come a time when we'll envy the dead. They have already reached the tomb of Israel, but we, are now just starting our suffering."

While running on the sandy roads, we were all together and we joined with the Polish military and the Polish population, all with packages on their shoulders, and many with young children. Many could no longer walk anymore, because they did not have the strength to go on.

We kept running, and we arrived in Kamyk. The Germans had already dropped bombs there. Wounded people and dead military horses were lying on the ground. We ran further in the direction of Kocin[2]. When we arrived in Kocin it was Friday evening, and my mother had tears in her eyes, because she wanted to bless the (Shabbat) candles, but unfortunately it was impossible. She told us that it is the first time that she was unable to light the Shabbat candles and say the blessings. My father welcomed the Shabbat and we ate something. It was already dark. We sat on the ground in Kocin for half an hour. People continued to walk in the direction of the village of Klomnice[3].

At 7:00PM we lifted our packages on our shoulders, and again started walking with the stream of people, among their horses, cattle, pigs, goats and dogs. In that way we walked the entire night. Jews with beards and sidelocks (payes) were very frightened. A few covered their beards with a handkerchief, as if they had a toothache.

On Shabbat, around 6:00AM, we arrived in Klomnice.

[Page 211]

Around midday the turmoil intensified. People fled into the fields. There was a rumor that the Germans are closer. We again took our packages and fled into the fields. Then there were rumors that the Germans went past Klomnice, so people were going back into the streets. We took our packages and returned to the village.

Tanks with the German swastika drove fast on the roads; full squadrons of airplanes flew in the sky. The approaching of the German military ground forces was imminent.

Not long afterwards, we decided again to take our packages on our shoulders, and to go back. Many people were on the road. The roads were also full with German armored military vehicles. We were searched every few kilometers; they looked for weapons. They either searched us or told us: "Anybody with a weapon, knife, or razor blade should turn it over to us and no harm will happen to him; anybody found with a weapon will be shot."

We walked until 3:00AM until we (again) reached Klobuck. Close to the big elementary school we were stopped by German military. We were told to stand against the wall, and the soldiers threatened to shoot us. They accused us of firing at German soldiers. With tears in our eyes we explained that we knew nothing about that. They locked the men in the dark cellar of the school and the women upstairs. In the cellar there were already several Jews and they welcomed us. While being pushed inside the cellar, I received a blow on the head from a rifle. The Germans told us that at dawn they would shoot all of us, because all the Jews fired on the German military.

German Soldiers Set Klobuck on Fire.

Meanwhile, more Jews, who had come back "home" to Klobuck, were pushed to the cellar. The cellar was full, and Jews were detained outside. Daylight came, and we sat there full with anxiety and fright. Soon we expected to be shot. It was Sunday, September 3rd. It was already 9:00AM. The door was opened, and we were ordered to go back home. We were searched, and we were ordered to leave as fast as possible, with our hands on our heads. We did not know where the women were.

[Page 212]

We went out onto the street and saw German soldiers throw hand grenades into houses that exploded with a big noise. Houses were burning. The German military watched as the fires burned to assure that the civilian population did not remove anything, or tried to extinguish the fire.

We returned home safely. Our arms and hands hurt from being on our heads. My mother arrived home before us and she impatiently waited for us. .

We were at home for about an hour. Suddenly the German soldiers came and shouted: "Everybody should get outside and go to the church".

Once again we ran with our hands on our heads to the church. People gathered outside the church, and then an old German in a uniform with medals came out, and climbed up on a table, watched by the assembled German military. He started to speak in German; a Pole translated his words, simultaneously, to Polish.

The German said that from now on we were under his rule. He was our provisional ruler. People should stay calm and welcome the German military. Those who possessed weapons should turn them in immediately and nothing will happen to them.

The shtetl was burning. The old German ordered the women, the elderly and the children go back home. He ordered the young people to bring buckets of water tools from the fire department, and to extinguish the fire as soon as possible.

The young Jews, including myself, stood in rows of five. Watched by the German military, we marched to the firefighter station. During the walk the Germans caught a few more Jews. We were about thirty young men. The warden of the firefighter station opened the gate. We harnessed ourselves like horses with the buckets and all of the tools and we went to extinguish the fire.

At 5:00PM the Germans ordered us to return all of the firefighters' tools, because there was a state of war and we were allowed to stay outside only until 6:00PM. We, the young ones, who were exhausted from the walking, thanked God that we were free from this difficult work. The fire burned our eyes; we had gone several days without sleep and had little or nothing to eat.

[Page 213]

The next morning German soldiers caught more Jews for work. The Polish children showed the Germans where the Jews lived, and Jews were forced out of their houses and were ordered to work in various tasks. Some of the Jews did not have a place to live, because their homes were destroyed by fire. They and their young children remained without clothes and shoes. A Jewish committee was formed, with the responsibility to assure that everyone has a place to live.

Every day the Germans ordered the Jews to go out to work. Then the committee ruled that every Jew should work only three or four days per week. We worked like this for six weeks.

It now was after Sukkot holiday, and it was raining. The work became harder and harder because the soil was mostly clay. When winter came, the Jews were forced to clean the roads and remove the snow. Jews were forbidden to travel by train. There were no buses, and the Jews were deprived of their cars and horses. Klobucker Jews remained without a livelihood.

Forced Labor and German Cruelty

After several months of German rule, the German cruelty came to a higher pick. The German military took out the Torah Scrolls from the synagogue (Shul) and used them to pad their boots. Jews were abandoned. Nobody was interested in their fate. The Cultural Center building, which housed the Jewish organizations and their comprehensive and valuable library, was burnt down. All of the Jewish organizations disappeared. The Jewish youth no longer were permitted to meet. It was forbidden for more than a few people to gather in one apartment. The Jews could no longer go to pray (davenen) in the synagogue. Immediately after taking over Klobuck, the Germans transformed the synagogue into a horse stable. The windows were broken. The military stole goods and food from Jewish shops.

A decree was issued that Jews who possessed a bicycle, a radio, razor blades, or a camera were required to turn them to the German authority, otherwise they would be severely punished. When winter approached, Jews were required to surrender their fur coats to the Germans.

[Page 214]

Every few days a new decree was issued against the Jews: brass door handles, candlesticks, copper dishes, lead, and tin were required to be handed over to the German Authority. If a prohibited item was found in a house, the oldest person in the house would be shot. Silver coins from before the war, in all denominations, must also be turned in.

Poverty spread among the Jews. Winter was very cold. Jews could not get any coal to heat their homes. An announcement was made that Jews could exchange their silver coins and obtain wood from the forest. Day in and day out we were required to work (for the Germans). We worked repairing the roads, cutting down trees, removing whole forests. The wood was brought to the train station and sent to Germany.

Then summer came, and Jews were forced to continue to work. We suffered from hunger and beatings. The Poles rejoiced that the Jews were forced to work hard.

On one occasion we loaded big trucks with straw in the Zagorz courtyard. There were about forty men. When four trucks were full of straw, the Germans brought ropes and harnessed ten men to each truck. We were forced to pull the big trucks uphill, between Zagorz and Klobuck. When we could no longer drag the trucks (from exhaustion) we were beaten with rifles until we arrived to Klobuck.

During the entire summer we worked non-stop in every tough job. Every Jew was required to wear on his chest the yellow Magen David sign, with black letters "Jude" in the middle.

Throughout the shtetl rumors started to spread that all of the Jews will be expelled from Klobuck. The Day of Awe (Yom Kippur) was approaching, but Jews no longer prayed together. Every one prayed alone at home. When my father prayed and wore a prayer shawl (tallit) or put on the phylacteries (tefilins), I would stand close to the door and watched to see that no German was approaching the house. Thus, all the Jews prayed in their houses with tears in their eyes.

Suddenly there was a new decree: Every house must send one or two members to work in Germany for two to six months.

[Page 215]

We understood that there would be no return from Germany. But the Germans with their language of flattery convinced the Jews that they would return after two months and that they would be replaced by others. The method was effective and soon many joined of their own will.

Along with the decree the Germans ordered that the Jewish Committee gather 140 Jews between ages of 18 to 30 years old. If the quota of people was not met, the Germans threatened to expel all of the Jews to the "General

Government". Klobuck was part of the Third Reich. We already knew the consequences of what it meant to expel all of the Jews from the ghetto. In Klobuck we had already received the very bad news from the Lodz ghetto. Although the situation was difficult and cold in Klobuck, people had a Jewish heart. We gathered food and clothes and sent to Lodz. But we never knew if the Jews in Lodz received our food and clothes.

My Father Wanted to Sacrifice Himself for the Whole Family

We sat in our apartment for evening after evening thinking what we can do. My father said that he will go to fulfill the German labor quota, and he will sacrifice himself for the whole family, thereby enabling the rest of our family to remain at home. My father was then 52 years old and was torn between the two choices. He believed that the Germans would send him back, but my young brother, who was then 17 years old, argued that he should sacrifice himself for the family. He thought that they would send him back home because he was not yet 18 years old. I was then 20 years old.

My mother heard the argument between our father and the children and could not stop crying, because she had to watch one child go away, without knowing whether he would come back. For myself, as an adult and a physically strong man, after listening to my father and brother, I said that the decision was with me: I would go and I will not let anyone else go other than me. I wanted that everybody else could stay home, and if we lived, we would meet again at home.

We received a notice that on 11.11.1940 one male per family had to be prepared to go to Germany for six weeks or two months.

[Page 216]

Those people had to bring warm clothes, shoes and a razor. I duly presented myself to the place that was given. We were about 140 men, mostly unmarried young men. From the meeting place, we were sent to the synagogue. There, the ground was covered with straw as if prepared for cattle. It was difficult to leave home; we couldn't separate ourselves from our parents, from our families, and also from the whole shtetl, where we spent our youth and from where we built our culture. We had to leave everything all at once.

The whole night we stay dressed and couldn't sleep because of the cold and anxiety.

The next morning, around 10 o'clock, the Germans came in uniforms and with their weapons, and escorted us to the train. Our parents accompanied us with tears in their eyes, unable to get close enough to give us a father-mother kiss.

We were heavily guarded by the Germans. In the train station, empty train carriages were waiting for us. Along with the shouting of the Germans, we were pushed inside the carriages, a few German guards per carriage. We looked at our shtetl, Klobuck, and everyone thought: who knows whether we would survive and come back home, to our wives, and our parents. Among us a few of the men were already married, and they left their wives and children. The locomotive whistled it's sad signal, and we left the shtetl Klobuck.

Writer's Footnote

i. "Obrona Narodowa", the National Defense, was a half civilian, half military organization formed to protect the military targets from destruction.

Translator's Footnotes

1. Kamyk located 6 kilometers east of Klobuck

2. Kocin to be pronounced Kotshin probably the reference is to Kocin Stary, 17 km north east of Klobuck

3. Klomnice to be pronounced Klomnitsh 35 kilometers east of Klobuck Re

[Page 217]

In the Chase with Death and the German Torture

by Yitzhak Szperling

Translated from Yiddish to English by Asher Szmulewicz

In Klobuck, like throughout Poland, people prepared for the war, although we did not believe that the war would occur. Nevertheless, a general mobilization was implemented. The entire shtetl commenced digging trenches (in anticipation) of the coming of the enemy.

On Friday morning, September 1st, the village did not appear as usual. In the streets, groups of Jews were saying that the war had already started. People spoke about the war with great despair. Jews from Klobuck knew that in a war with the pro-Hitler Germany, they would be the first victims. People anticipated that at any time the town would come under Germans occupation, because Klobuck was located so very close to the German border. People started panicking. Jews left everything behind, and started to run away to save their lives. But no one knew where we could run.

Within our family we also prepared to leave. My mother had passed away three months before the war started. My elder brother, Yehudah, was in the army; my elder sister, Chaya, was in Czestochowa. My father; my sister, Leah; my two brothers, Aaron-Meir and Pinchas-Menachem; and myself remained in our home. We abandoned everything in our apartment, taking only some food and we left the shtetl. We went to Lobodno, and from there even further. At 2:00 PM we arrived in Kocin (Kotshin), where a few Jewish families lived.

In that shtetl many Jews had already arrived from the other surrounding villages. We arrived there on Friday and remained until nightfall; we prayed Mincha (the late afternoon prayer); we prayed Kabbalat Shabbat (the prayer to welcome the Shabbat); we ate something; and then we walked farther. Thousands of people were walking, including women with their small children holding their hands. It was a dark night, and the fog covered everything, but we could still see one another. We wandered the whole night, without knowing where to go.

[Page 218]

On Shabbat at 10:00AM we arrived in the shtetl of Plawno on Gidzel. We stopped and remained there because we did not have enough strength to go on. Around 12:00AM we saw a tank in the village. There was a rumor that the French or the English entered the war to help Poland. Two hours later the shtetl was completely occupied with the German military. There was nowhere else to flee.

We stayed in a Jewish house until the end of Shabbat. On Motzei Shabbat (Saturday night), during the night, the village was awakened and shaken by gun fire. By dawn, it had calmed down. On Sunday morning we left Plawno, and started to return to Klobuck. The road-way was jammed with German military, and they detained the hundreds of refugees, mostly Jews. All of the detained refugees were gathered in the square, and were guarded by the German soldiers. We stayed there frightened to death. There was a rumor that we were going to be shot. Other people consoled themselves by saying that we were only going to be deported to a camp.

Finally at the end of the day, in the evening, when the roads were free of military traffic, the Germans let us go, and we were ordered to go back to our homes.

We walked through the entire night. The next morning, on Monday, we arrived back in Klobuck and discovered that half of the shtetl was destroyed and burned. Many people were left without a roof over their heads and without any food. Many of the small Jewish properties were burnt, and what was not destroyed by the fire was stolen by non-Jews.

We had to start our lives anew. Every day there was a new decree against the Jews. The Germans forced the Jews to work, and persecuted them and beat them. Observant Jews were taken to work at the Zagorz camp close to Klobuck. There they were forced to eat treife (non-kosher) food from the military kitchen. The Germans ridiculed them and persecuted them by various bestial means.

I was ordered to work in the mill with a group of well to do Jews. We were guarded by Germans from the so called "work troop". They were rabidly anti-Semitic, and took every opportunity to persecute us and to belittle our humanity and our Jewish dignity.

[Page 219]

Close to our workplace we found a dead dog. The Germans became excited and ordered us to hold a "funeral" for the dog. One of the workers, an old well to do Jew, was sent home to bring a white kittel (man's solemn white linen robe used on Yom Kippur and for his burial). Others were ordered to nail a cross. The dog was laid in a wheelbarrow, which was preceded by a Jew with the cross, and flanked on the side by another Jew, wearing a kittel. Behind them the dog was carried in the wheelbarrow, and the remainder of the Jews followed in procession, like in a "Levayah" (Jewish funeral). Thus the bestial Germans, all the while provoking us with their joyful laughter, marched us around the shtetl.

A few months later a Judenrat was established with a Jewish police force. Jews were forced to leave the central part of Klobuck and move to the ghetto. The Judenrat had to implement the decrees of the Germans and were ordered to provide Jewish workers.

I worked in Klobuck until April 1942. One day, the Gestapo people came to our workplace and took all of the people who were present. We were ordered to go to a room in the firefighter station. We were brought in front of a commission and the next morning we were taken to the train station and sent away to the NiederKirchen camp (in Upper Silesia). My brother Aaron-Meir was sent away with me. We were torn away from our family, who remained in Klobuck. A few weeks later my elder sister, Chaya-Sarah, was taken to a camp.

My brother, Yehudah-Arye, and my sister, Leah, stayed in the Zagorz camp close to Klobuck. My father and my youngest brother, Pinchas-Menachem, along with other Klobucker Jews, were sent away by the Germans and never came back.

[Page 220]

Moniek Merin, the Organizer
of the *Judenrat* [Jewish council] in Klobuck

by Yaacov Szmulewicz

Translated from the Yiddish by his nephew Asher Szmulewicz

From the very first day of the outbreak of the war, Klobuck, located close to the German-Polish border, witnessed and was subjected to German cruelty. On Friday morning, September 1st (1939), the German airplanes brought unexpected death and devastation to our shtetl. The first Jewish victims fell: Gitel Brat, Yossef Meir Langer, Zisser Berkowicz, Yechiel Rosen and other Jewish women, men and children whose names cannot be remembered.

First the German "black reign" started (their destruction) by torching 200 houses, mostly Jewish ones. The Jewish hope in God was gone with the smoke. The Jewish library was also burned, with (the loss of) almost three thousand books. Immediately thereafter, the well-known systematic German persecution and extermination of the Jews started.

Jews of Klobuck had to wear an armband with a "Magen David" (Star of David) and were not allowed to be present in various places (or after the curfew). The Polish population was allowed to be out in the streets until 23:00 (11pm); Jews only until 18:00 (6pm).

All of the Jews from the shtetl from age eleven to fifty five had to gather every morning at the market place, and were ordered to perform clean-up work for the Germans. Every day brought new and bitter decrees.

The Jews of Klobuck found themselves oppressed and in a difficult situation. All trade was brought to a halt. Jews did not have the right to travel on trains or to trade (with other towns). The German authority seized Jewish shops and gave them to their trusted people, so called "Treuehender".

In this terrible and awful situation the rumor circulated, from and among the beaten Jews, that Merin, the well-known leader of the Sosnowiec Judenrat, was to arrive in the shtetl, escorted with a person named Jasne[i], with instructions from the German authority to organize a Judenrat in Klobuck. Such a Judenrat with Jasne and known elders was established. The former president of the community (kehilah), Baruch Szperling, declined all participation with the Judenrat.

Merin did not occupy himself with the activity of the Klobuck Judenrat, but he alone began to implement the cruel orders of the Germans against the Jews. Suddenly, Merin summoned all the Jews from the shtetl to gather in the courtyard of the mill. All the Jews from the shtetl assembled there and Merin gave them the following speech:

"Brother Jews, not one hair from your head, God forbid, will fall. No one will be "wischedlet" (sent out for extermination), the only condition is that all the men should (must) go to work in Germany. The men will be able to send back (to Klobuck) their wages to their parents, wives and children."

The assembled people understood immediately what was intended and started to negotiate with Merin, the well-known elder of the Sosnowiec region, seeking to diminish the number of Jews that had to go to Germany to work. They argued that the decree would ruin the Jewish settlement of Klobuck. The assembled people agreed to deliver only a part of the required contingent. Merin demanded 500 healthy men, that is to say every family head, since Klobuck numbered about 500 families at that time, about 2000 persons.

Two weeks before Sukkoth, 1940, the harassed Jews from the shtetl shivered with anxiety from the news that Merin had arrived in Klobuck, escorted by members of the Gestapo and with a commission of German doctors. The commission was to qualify the "free-willing" Jews who wanted to work in Germany. Few people turned themselves over to the commission. Among the men taken to work in Germany were blind, lame and sick people.

When the commission finished its work, Merin announced to the Jewish population that if the "contingent" is not delivered, the entire Jewish population would be expelled from Klobuck and put behind barbed wire.

Eight days after Sukkoth 1940, a group of 65 strong young men, including myself, "volunteered" to go to work in Germany. We assembled at the Skorupe[1] in the courtyard and immediately we were surrounded by the Gestapo. They took us to the synagogue. Straw had already been put on the floor in anticipation of staying overnight. Although we were under the Gestapo's watch, we were in a good mood. We did not lose our nerve, but our good mood did not last.

At midnight new victims were brought in. The Gestapo searched for Jews and took them out of their beds. In the morning we were brought outside in the courtyard. Gathered in front of the synagogue were the mothers, sisters and wives and close family members of the men who had volunteered, and the men who were dragged from their bed during the night. At the order of the Gestapo commander we lined up in three rows. The wives and the close family members had ten minutes to bring food and clothes to those who were about to be sent away. We marched to the waiting room of the train station. A train was standing ready to take us to an unknown camp.

At the train station, Nowy Herby, we met another transport from Krzepice, (with) Jews piled up in the same train. The contingent had not yet been fulfilled. The SS ordered the Klobuck community (kehilah) representatives to be brought before them: Benzion Swiertchewsky, Israel Lewkowicz, Yechiel Rosenthal and the president, Moshe Weissfelner. In the beginning of November, 1940 we left Klobuck.

Footnote

i.   The name Jasne, referred to in the text, has no relation whatsoever with the editor of our Yizkor book, A. Wolf-Jasny. A. Wolf-Jasny is only a pseudonym. The real first and last name of A. Wolf-Jasny is Abraham Wolf Tsiferman.

Translator's Footnote

1.   Polish word meaning crust (seems to be a name of a location in the shtetl)

[Page 223]

The Activities of the Judenrat
and the Battle for Existence
by Moshe Fajga

Translated from the Yiddish by Asher Szmulewicz

The head office of the Judenrat was in Sosnowiec, and a "branch" office was opened in Klobuck, with designated commissioners. The Sosnowiec members were: Berek Jasne; Winer and Shimon Merin[1]; and from Klobuck: Benzion Szwiertszewski; Yaacov Chade, who unfortunately tarnished his former superb Zionist activities with Judenrat work; Israel Lewkowicz; Moshe Weissfelner; Yechiel (Fogel) Rosenthal; Abraham Diamant; Yitzchak Buchweicz and Zisser Lapides.

*

Klobuck was annexed by the Third Reich. During the first year of the war, when people returned to their routines after the fire of the shtetl, the food supply was not too bad. Poles brought goods from Lodz and went back with food products, which sold well there. Jews traded with Poles. That is why in Klobuck it was still possible to make a living. The close town of Czestochowa was dependent on the "General Government"[2] and the Jews there, who had family in Klobuck, smuggled themselves into Klobuck, in order to obtain food to eat. It was these "foreign" Jews that the Judenrat gave special attention to.

One day, the Judenrat sent the Jewish policeman, S. Zacks, to look for the "foreign" Jews from Czestochowa, who were not registered in Klobuck. They were told that they were required to report to the Judenrat or they would be expelled from Klobuck. The Jews from Czestochowa reported to the Judenrat. There Berek Jasne, the commissioner from the Sosnowiec Judenrat headquarters, informed them that they must register in Klobuck and in order to register they were required to pay a significant amount of money. The "well to do" Jews sold some of their belongings and paid the Judenrat the required amount of money. The poor Jews, who couldn't pay, were expelled from the shtetl.

[Page 224]

Remembered here are three of the "foreign" Jews, who were turned over by the Judenrat to the Germans to be deported: my brother Chaim Fajga who was born in Klobuck. Due to personal reasons he settled in Czestochowa before the war. There he was active in the youth organization "Dror" (Liberty). Leib Szperling, also from Klobuck, who lived in Czestochowa and Kopel (butcher) Rosensweig. These three Jews worked as civil servants and they were sure that they did not need to register with the Judenrat and that they would not be expelled.

On a certain day the Jewish policeman, S. Zacks, told them that he had an order from the Judenrat to take them into custody and to turn them over to the German police. The order took place and the three were transferred to the German police Commander, Datczek, and then they were deported. In the year 1941, the wives of the three men received a letter from the SS-Commander, stating that their husbands had died in the camp.

The Smuggling Trade

Despite the difficult and pressing situation in which the Jews of Klobuck lived, they made strenuous efforts to sustain themselves and to find a source of living. They were forced to smuggle. They smuggled goods from Lodz and transferred them to Czestochowa, which belonged to the "General Government". The Jews also sewed clothes for Christians with the smuggled goods. If a Jew was caught smuggling by the Germans he was handed over to the German Gendarmerie. At that time there were two "Machers" (Fixers), Bertsze Green and Yitzik Berkowicz. They bribed the German Gendarmerie with big sums of money to free the Jews.

The "Fixers" also had relations with the "Landrat" (Regional council), which was located in Czlachow. With the "Landrat" the "Fixers" arranged for "Passport" for Jews who wanted to travel between Klobuck and Czestochowa. Later, when the "Judenrat" started its activities, there was no need for "Fixers" anymore since the "Judenrat" alone dealt with arranging all the matters with the German power.

[Page 225]

Meanwhile the German power grew. The Commander Datczek, who was nicknamed by Jews "Ober-Eichel" (Big Acorn), took over the management of the village. Datczek had his own police. The life for Jews became more difficult and more painful.

The smuggling of goods was operated by Aaron-Meir Goldberg, Avraham Gelbard, Yaacov Friedman, Avraham Anzel, Berl and Leibish Unglick, Yonah Pankower, Fiszel Fajga, Szaya Anzel, Wowe, Elie and Leibish Reich and the writer of these lines. Once we were traveling towards the border during a military exercise. The German soldiers surrounded us and took the goods. Those who were citizens of the General Government were freed, Elie Reich from Krzepice and Moshe Fajga (the writer) were brought back to Klobuck. We were sentenced to ten days of jail. We spent the ten days in Lublin.

After our liberation we went back to the border with back-packs on our shoulders full of goods to smuggle into Czestochowa. The border between the Third Reich and the "General-Government" was around Grabowka, close to the bridge where the small river was flowing. Later, smuggling became harder. The Germans chased the smugglers with dogs and shot at them. Yeszaya Anzel was confined to bed for a while after he was beaten by the Germans.

Once, during one of these "walking on the border" we met a group of Shiksim (non-Jews), who waited for us with knives. Our group included Moshe Hopek, Avraham Staszewski, my brother in-law, Wowe, his brothers, Leibush and Elie resisted with full energy. My brother in-law and his brothers Leibush and Elie Reich were stabbed. But the goods were not lost. Later it turned out that the leader of this group was a Czestochower Jew, Neiman.

Even afterwards when the Germans established a ghetto in Klobuck, and everyone who left the ghetto was punishable by death, the smuggling continued until the end of the year 1941, when people were sent away to work.

[Page 226]

The young people voluntarily reported for the work in the Klobuck's camp. There were a few men that were not accepted. Afterwards the deportation from ghetto started. The Judenrat assisted the Germans to make Klobuck free of Jews - "Judenrein". The majority of Jews were sent away to work camps in Germany, from where they did not return. Some Jews were forced to work on the " Reich's AltBahnStrasse"[3]. There they fell like fleas, as a result of the hunger and hard labor. The rest of Klobucker Jews were sent to death camps by the Germans to be gassed and burned.

*

In 1942 I found in Czestochowa the former Klobuck Judenrat members. They ran away when the Germans implemented the final liquidation of Klobuck. Then I told them: "murderers, you helped the Germans to exterminate the Jews of Klobuck and afterwards you ran away to save your lives. If I remain alive I will take revenge..."

During the liquidation of the Czestochowa ghetto they ran away, back to Klobuck. The Germans shot them and they died in the fields between Czestochowa and Klobuck. One of the former Klobuck Judenrat members survived.

Translator's Footnotes

1. "General Government" zone of Poland directly administered by a German General-Governor

2. Shimon Merin must be Moniek Merin of the previous chapter, Moniek being his Polish First Name and Shimon his Yiddish First Name

3. I think the writer meant Jews were sent to maintenance work on "the old German Railways"

[Page 226]

Pain and Self-Sacrifice of the Pious Jews
The Fight against the Judenrat
by Fishl Fajga
Translated from Yiddish to English Asher Szmulewicz

The Germans bombed the refugees, who fled from Klobuck and packed the roads. Near Kocin[1], a German bomb killed Gitel Brat, Zalman's wife. Many people were covered with soil and mud from the German's bombs. Several people succeeded, at the last minute, to pull Pesse Szperling and her child from the soil, which had covered them.

[Page 227]

Outside of Radomsk, Yechiel Rosen, a refugee from Klobuck, was shot. His body was taken to Radomsk, and he was buried there in the Jewish cemetery.

During our return to Klobuck, there was no place to flee from the Germans. We arrived in Lobodno (a small place 2 km NE of Klobuck with population of 9 people). A large scale slaughter occurred there. Many people were shot: Leib Zambek, Yehosha Leizer Gelbard, Gedalia Unglick, Mantshe's son, and his son in law, Simcha Yakubowicz. Mantshe's wife, Rode, had her hand injured. Many other Jews, whose names I don't remember, were also shot there.

Upon my return to Klobuck, I saw that half of the town had been destroyed by fire. I often went to Mantshe's house to pray. The miserable (grieving) father organized a Minyan (quorum - ten people for public prayer) to say Kaddish for his son and son in-law, who had been shot dead. A silence, full of sadness, filled and spread throughout the entire home. Everyone came to pray with their heads down as though they were all guilty for the death of the two men. Old Mantshe said Kaddish for his son, and little Moshele, in his childish voice, said Kaddish for his father. After the Minyan the people left the apartment with tears in their eyes.

In Klobuck the Germans shot Yossef Meir Lengner, who looked through the window of his apartment, Avraham Rosenthal and Zisser Berkowicz. Berkowicz was hiding in his cellar when the Germans searched the town and dragged people to work. They came into the apartment of the unfortunate Berkowicz, and found his wife. When they asked: "Where is your husband?", she became frightened and she called her husband. He came out of the cellar. The Germans took him out of the apartment and shot him.

In the village of Miedzno (5 km north of Klobuck), close to Klobuck, a few Jewish families lived. The local Poles reported to the Germans that the Jews were speculators, and impostors. The Germans arrested 14 Jews and deported them. Approximately eight days later, the Jewish community center of

Klobuck, received little boxes, full of ashes with the names of the arrested Jews.

[Page 228]

At that time, the community was still being led by the previous management, headed by Baruch Szperling. He took the boxes full of ashes and buried them in the Klobuck cemetery. Two of the fourteen deported Jews - Chaim Buchman and Berl Klug, remained alive.

Everyday Jews were required to assemble in the market place. The Germans persecution of the Jews was brutal. They enjoyed our suffering and pain. They ordered us to perform a drill: "bow yourself, lie down, stand up, sit down", and so on dozens of times. During this brutal exercise the Germans were helped by Poles and the hairdresser, Shuba, who was appointed Mayor by the Germans.

For Rosh Hashanah the Jews were afraid to pray in a Minyan (public prayer with a quorum of at least 10 men). The awe for God was stronger than the fear of the Germans, and many Jews took the risk, and gathered to pray in various other places. On Yom Kippur, the German murderers ran through the town like mad men, and dragged Jews to work.

My brother in law, Israel Blau, and I hid in an attic. From there we saw the horrible acts performed by the Germans on the Jews. We saw how Reb Avraham Shochat (slaughterer), was forced to sit in a truck full of pigs, and was ordered to hold a pig with both of his hands. A German then stabbed the pig, which tried to rip itself away from his hands, and screamed with frightening sounds. Reb Avraham had to hold the pig with both of his hands, and the German marched him and the pig to the slaughter house, where the pigs were ordered to be (ritually) slaughtered.

During Sukkot holiday the Germans found a group of Jews praying together. The Germans dragged the Jews with their Tallithim (prayer shawls) to the market place and forced the Jews to spread the Tallithim on the ground. The seventy year old Yonah Friedman did not let them take his Tallith. The persecutors violently tore the Tallith from the old man. The Jews were forced to set the Tallithim ablaze, and Reb Yonah, as a punishment for his defiance, had to dance bare footed on the burning Tallithim.

When we were sent to Zagorz to work, we already knew that many of us would not come back. We were hit with blows until we bled. The Germans persecuted us with brutal means that could not be compared to anything. The murderers forced Bunim Dudek, to bite the head of a half rotten pan-fried chicken. The only meat we received to eat was pork, with the order: "Jews you must eat this".

After eating, we were forced to say the after meal blessing. Our persecutors said forcefully: "Any one that does not pray will be beaten".

[Page 229]

Demonstration against the Judenrat

As previously described in another chapter, the Klobuck Judenrat was organized by three Jews from Sosnowiec, who were sent by the Central Judenrat located in Sosnowiec. In addition the following Klobuckers were chosen to help: Yaacov Chade, Benzion Szwiertszewski and Israel Lewkowicz. They were the governing body of the Klobuck Judenrat.

Once, while I was standing in front of the gate of my house, across from the post office, Yaacov Chade, whom I knew well, came by. He was walking with the Sosnowiec organizer. I called out to Yaacov Chade: "What is the purpose of a Judenrat for you? Are you giving him a tour of all the streets. If they want a Judenrat, they should make one by themselves. We Klobuckers should not help".

While I was standing and speaking to him, people gathered. Men, women and children were amongst them, including Yossef Szperling, Mordechai Szperling, Mrs Szilit and others. They started throwing stones at the Judenrat representatives. The above persons snatched the briefcase away from the Sosnowiecer, and tore up all of the documents. In front of the post office entrance stood a German policeman, who looked like a murderer, he was nicknamed "the smacker". The Sosnowiecer and Yaacov Chade appealed to the Germans, asking them to help them to control the Jewish crowd.

The German police did not know why the Jews were fighting, and they pushed the Judenrat members out of the post office. "Let the Jews fight with each other" said the Germans. The crowd became audacious and stoned the Sosnowiecer and Chade. They both fled away.

That afternoon, while I was again standing in front of the gate of my house, two German policemen approached me, and asked: "Does Fajga live here?" I did not lose my composure, and calmly answered that he lived further down the road, close to the marketplace.

They went away towards the marketplace, and I immediately fled and hid. In the evening, when it was dark, I left the shtetl and went on the Wilkowiecko road (Wilkowiecko is a small place 10 km WNW of Klobuck). I did not know where to go, it was late in the evening and I decided to sleep on a heap of straw.

After lying there on this "couch" for about two hours, suddenly I heard somebody coming nearby. I held my breath, and remained lying there for the whole night half dreaming. In the morning again I heard somebody moving in the straw. My curiosity was stronger than my fright. I raised my head and saw Yossef Szperling. I jumped down from the pile of hay, and we hugged one another. Our joy was great: there were now the two of us. Szperling told me that the police also were looking for him. We set out on the way to Wilkowiecko.

[Page 230]

A committee to fight the Judenrat

When we came close to the forest we went to sleep in the house of the peasant, Dachowski. During the night we heard Poles coming and going. Yossel told me: "Fishel I don't like this business". We made up our mind very quickly. We couldn't leave through the front door, so we jumped out of the window with our shoes in our hands. We spent the night in a barn, and at dawn we went to Wilkowiecko. There we found a third refugee, Mordechai Szperling, who was also sought by the German police.

Mordechai Szperling told us that he had a friend, a Christian, who lived in a small house in the fields. We went to his friend and stayed there. We sent our savior to Klobuck to tell our families where we were. Our host came back with the following news that my brother in law, Yaacov Aaron Blau, intervened with the Gendarmerie (country police). He bribed them with three gold rings and I was permitted to return back home.

I came back to Klobuck, but I didn't sleep at home.

During that same week two Germans came at night to our house, looking for me. They arrested Chaim Mass and Herszel Franck. The Germans still looked for me. Then, I slept in the attic in Yeshaya Enzel's home.

*

[Page 231]

The Judenrat learned that I came back home. They ordered me to report in their office. I knew they wanted to send me to a camp in Germany and so I didn't fulfilled their request.

We organized a committee, and named Herszel Szperling as the leader. Our mission was: Don't follow the Judenrat orders. Herszel Szperling made propaganda to the whole world. He told everyone not to pay the Judenrat taxes. "When you don't give, you cannot take" thus he said.

The Judenrat in addition to the "regular taxes", levied money from those who didn't go to work. Those that could not pay or did not work had to pay five marks per day. When people couldn't pay they confiscated all kind of objects from their homes. The implementation of the orders was done with the help of the German Police. They took a new sewing machine and bedding from Herszel Szperling's home. Herszel did not oppose the Judenrat, he just said: "Take the machine, if the world survives, there will be (other) machines".

The "Parisian", a so called Jew, who served as a courier for the Judenrat, came to my home. The "Parisian" came with a German and demanded that I should hand over my unique new sewing-machine, with which my wife made a modest living. I put some money into the Parisian's hand. Then he left without the new machine. The German who accompanied the Parisian, didn't care about the courier's mission, he came along just to accompany him. The Judenrat courier came several times to take goods and each time he left with nothing.

Finally, the Judenrat demanded that I show up in their office. I went there. In response to the question: "why aren't you paying the sums that we demanded from you", I answered that I did not have any money, and that they could take everything which was in my apartment. The Judenrat gave me a deadline of 14 days to bring the money.

In the meantime the following happened:

Once in the evening, I was outside late after the curfew hours set by the Police. A German and Korkasen, a Pole who liked to quarrel with Jews, walked in the street. The Pole pointed at me and shouted: "Jew, Jew". The German and the Pole chased me. I ran away, fell, got up and ran away again. I escaped and I arrived home. I had great pain in the hand. Dr Waitszik gave me a short document with a request that I be released from work. Thus I didn't have to pay any money to the Judenrat for not going to work.

[Page 232]

In a Work Camp

On March 20th 1941 the Judenrat together with the police posted notices calling for all the Jews to report to the courtyard of the Skorupa[2]. Those who wouldn't appear, would have their wives and children deported. The Jews ran around worried. "What should we do?", "Should we report to the police?" Everyone asked each other, but nobody knew what is the answer.

The day came when we had to report to the place. Only few minutes were left. Everyone looked at everyone else and finally all the men came to the courtyard of the Skorupa, as the Judenrat ordered. We were afraid that our wives and children would be deported.

I also reported. In the courtyard hundreds of Jews had already gathered, including Jews from Dzialoszyn and from all of the surrounding areas, who had "escaped" to Klobuck. The members of the Judenrat counted the "heads". We stood in a single line. They counted and counted again. Suddenly the German murderers, with helmets on their heads, came. They surrounded us. I saw, that it was the end and I pushed myself close to the meadow, planning to escape. A Klobucker, with whom I attended the Cheder, ran after me. My friend didn't let me escape. He shouted: "stand still". Being afraid that the Germans would shoot me, I came back to the line.

[Page 233]

Despite the heavy guard of the Germans, a few Jews managed to escape. I was among those who remained in the courtyard. We were marched to the Beit

HaMidrash, and from there to the Firefighter station, where we stayed for two to three days. Afterwards we were sent away to a work camp.

Translator's Footnotes

1. Pronounced Kotshin seems to be the actual Stary Kocin about 15 km NE of Klobuck

2. Polish word meaning shell or crust (seems to be a name of a location or a building in the shtetl)

[Page 234]

Forced Labor and Beastly Deeds

by Pesa Chorzewski Zlatnik

Translated from the Yiddish to English by Asher Szmulewicz

I fled Klobuck on Friday at dawn, September 1st, (1939), together with all of the other Jews, while the town was under attack by the Germans. Day and night we dragged ourselves through the fields and forests until we came to Jarek (⎺arki). The Germans were already there. There were ongoing skirmishes in all of the surrounding areas. I wanted to go back home to Klobuck, but the roads were full of dead people.

After two weeks of wandering, I returned to Klobuck, my birth place. In Klobuck there was a frightening silence. The streets were empty. Armed Germans patrolled the streets, and Jews started to come back to their destroyed and looted homes. (At first) we thought that we returned to the town of Klobuck, as it used to be. But soon the Germans started persecuting the Jews and forced them to work, and endure terrible sufferings.

One day I was taken to work. I was part of a group of fifty Jews, including Yehoshua and Baruch Unglick. We worked close to the bridge on the Krzepice road. The Germans forced us, all fifty Jews, to crawl into a water pipe, which connected the bridge to the canal. The Germans stood on both sides of the pipe with shovels in their hands, and any Jew who tried to lift his head to breathe fresh air received murderous blows.

Near the pipe there was a lot of debris that prevented the water from flowing. The Germans spared no effort to resume the water flow that entered the pipe to its full strength, and where the fifty Jews were suffocating. After working another hour, the sadistic Germans permitted us come out (of the pipe). We came out soaking wet, and still had to work in the water. A cold wind was blowing, and we had to continue working in such conditions until the evening.

[Page 235]

We worked the whole week, and on Friday the Germans subjected us to a special persecution day. We worked until noon. Then we were brought to the square in front of the Shul (Synagogue), and we had to clean up the square. Suddenly the Germans searched the men to check if they wore "Tzitzit" (Tassels or fringes on Tallith Katan). The sadistic Germans gave murderous blows to those wearing Tzitzit and burned all of the "Tallith Katan".

After cleaning the square, our persecutors ordered us to lie on the ground with our faces pointed upward, and the sadists trampled us with their boots. They also trampled on those with big stomachs, claiming to make them flat, while they laughed with wild giggles. They cut our hair with big scissors, and by doing so they also cut the skin on our heads.

After this bestial behavior, the Germans rounded up another group of Jews, led by Zisser Lapides[1]. They were forced and dragged into a cellar, and there they were beaten with murderous blows. The cries of the beaten Jews were heard throughout the streets. Women and children came out and wept and lamented. We all were sure that the persecuted Jews would not come out of the cellar alive. In the evening the persecutors (finally) let them go.

For several weeks I was dragged to forced labor, and then I decided to stop going to work. I went to see (the small) Zisser Lapides. He had the authority to send people to various other work projects. While I was in Lapides' apartment, German soldiers came in and forced me to go with them to the half destroyed Shul. There already were many other Jews there that the Germans held as hostages, which accounted for the town's quiet condition.

Among the arrested people were the Rav and Reb Wolff Weiss. We stayed in the synagogue for the entire Shabbat. The Rav asked the Jews to say Tehilim (Psalms). No one slept that night. We said Tehilim. At 4:00AM we heard gun shots. With a broken voice the Rav requested of everybody: "Jews pray to God, a calamity has occurred." With frantic fright we waited for dawn. Around 10:00AM we learned that a man had been shot, and we, the hostages, were being held responsible for that. In the evening I was freed. After a few weeks everybody else was freed.

*

[Page 236]

The Klobuck Judenrat was in charge of the Jews in Klobuck. Pursuant to its orders Jews were assigned to work, or were sent away to the camps, at the cost of blood and loss of life for those assigned to work or sent to the camps.

The Judenrat ordered that one man from every household was required to go to a work camp. Convoy after convoy were sent away. People were dragged from their beds during the night. We stayed in hidden places throughout days and nights. Suddenly it was announced that houses on the Third of May street (Trzeciego Maja), where I lived and where I was in hiding, were going to be demolished. The Judenrat sent an advanced notice to leave the apartments, because the buildings were going to be demolished. I had to move into Yeshaya Enzel's house.

We left our houses, and then we received another order, directing that all the Jews were required to work and demolish all of the buildings on the street. Jews had to register to demolish their own houses, and armed German soldiers forced everyone to assemble in the hall inside the Firefighter station. Aaron Szmulewicz, Chaskel Rosen and I tried to escape through a backdoor. When we opened the door, a soldier shouted that he was going to shoot. I was the first one out, and I escaped outside, by standing in the shadows, so as not to get noticed. I stood behind a half demolished wall, and heard the tumult in the Firefighter station caused by my escape. Hershel Weichman and a few Germans came out to look for me. One of the Germans said that they intended to kill my parents if they couldn't catch me. I entered the apartment of Elie Friedman, who was an invalid; he was therefore exempt from the order which required going to work. I sat at the table. Shortly thereafter a German came in and asked for identification documents. Since I had nothing to give him, he took me back to the Firefighter station, and turned me over to the Germans in charge of the guard, in order to be shot. The highest ranking military man said that it was a pity to waste a bullet on the "Juden" (Jews), and instead he administered murderous blows on me.

[Page 237]

I laid unconscious, covered with blood. I was taken away from there. The Germans who had been looking for me came back. Their leader saw me lying and bleeding. He "honored" me with a few more boot kicks, and declared that he would finish me in the camp.

I remained in my condition, worrying about my big troubles. Throughout the entire night, transports departed. At dawn trucks came again to take people away. My friends advised me to go, so that the German murderer would not know where I was. If he found me again, he would immediately shoot me. I followed my friends' advice, and I left with the transport.

I arrived in the camp, Klein-Mangelsdorf (Germany). Many Jews from Klobuck worked there. Many died from starvation and hard labor. While there, I also suffered through the difficult hard labor and pain. Many times I felt that my life had come to its end. Yet, I endured and survived until the liberation.

Just before the liberation, the German murderers dragged us from camp to camp. At the end they brought us to Hamburg, and intended to put us on a boat and drown us at sea. However, the Hamburg harbor was no longer reachable, because it was under attack by English fire. For three days we waited, while the bombing continued. Then the Germans marched us to Bergen-Belsen, which was captured eight days later by the English army. That is where we were liberated.

Translator's Footnote

1. Zisser Lapides was a member of the Judenrat. He was not in the cellar, he brought the Jews along with the Germans.

[Page 238]

The Last Jewish Kindergarten in Klobuck

by Adele Unglik, Australia

Translated from the Yiddish to English by Asher Szmulewicz

The Wandering Path between Death and Extermination

The kindergarten's teachers were: Natke Granek[1], the daughter of Mordechai Granek and Chanele from Pabienice. The two young girls founded the kindergarten in 1941 and it lasted until the final liquidation of the Klobuck Jews.

The children, like all children everywhere in the world, were happy and went cheerfully to their children "home" (the kindergarten), and spent day after day, week after week singing and dancing, without knowing what might happen to them tomorrow. Their little faces were gentle; their stare was guiltless and innocent. Yet they were snatched from their parents and executed by the German murderers.

In this last children home was Chavele, my sister's daughter. She was like my own child, I cannot refer to her otherwise. I saw her play with her friends; how she sang and danced. Then the ruthless devil extended its black wings above all of our heads.

Last Kindergarten in Klobuck
The teachers are standing on the right and on the left

[Page 239]

These children from the last kindergarten of Klobuck have no one to remember them, no one to drop a tear on their unfinished childhood. Their parents and families were exterminated by the Germans.

Therefore, my modest lines should be a Remembrance (Yizkor) for these innocent children of the last kindergarten of Klobuck, who were persecuted by the Germans.

Translator's Footnote

1. The name of the second teacher is missing.

[Page 240]

The Klobuck Ghetto:
"Selections," and the Torture Camps
by Tsile Witelzon-Zambek
Translated from the Yiddish to English by Asher Szmulewicz

The Wandering Path between Death and Extermination

On the third day after the outbreak of the war, we returned home to Klobuck, aware that there was nothing to be accomplished by running away. The Germans already were everywhere. Five kilometers before arriving at Klobuck, the Germans noticed the long beard of my observant father. They took him away. We did not stand by idly; for 14 days we looked for him, and we finally found his dead body not far from Klobuck.

We learned that the Germans forced him to dig his own grave, and then they shot him. He was one of the first Jewish victims of Klobuck.

My mother was widowed and left with seven children. My brothers were forced to work at various labor works, and they endured terrible persecutions (by the Germans). Often, I picked up their shovel and went to work instead of one of them, because I was afraid that they would be deported. The risk of deportation of women was much less than that for the men.

In the year 1940 we were notified that the "Arbeit Einsatz" (Labor Supply) was established, and that all of the men between the ages of 18 to 45 had to register (for work assignment). The Judenrat Elder, Moshe Merin[1], together with Gestapo personnel, arrived from Sosnowiec. Merin demanded that one young man from every family was required to go to the work camp. The Judenrat Elder promised a "golden good fortune": going to the camp assured that the worker would receive food, a salary and be able to survive the war.

The reality was different: the young people were sent away to suffer from the cold and hunger in the Eichenwald camp in Germany. The (young people) children wrote terrible letters, (begging) that we should have pity for them and send them kohlrabi and carrots, because no other products were allowed to be given to them. The work was very difficult: they cut wood in the forest. Only a small percentage of those who were sent to work in that camp survived the very difficult conditions. From our family, my brother Shlomo was sent to work. He never came back.

[Page 241]

Then there was another "Arbeit Einsatz" (Labor Supply) order. Nobody wanted to go. People were dragged from their beds, beaten, and murdered. Every night we ran to "sleep" (hide) in another attic; we didn't know what we could do. The world closed in on us. My second brother, Chaim, and my uncle, Niedziela, were sent (into forced labor), and they never came back.

My elder brother, Yitzhak-Wolf, remained at home, and we hid him from the third Labor Supply. My uncle, Pinchas Niedziela, procured a job for him in a German dairy. The Judenrat told my mother that she was "covered," and that the (remaining) children would not be sent away. But that good fortune did not last long.

On June 21, 1942 there was turmoil in the ghetto. News came from Sosnowiec that at night there would be "heimleich" (meaning a comfortable or cozy situation, like being at home).[ii] People knew there would be trouble and ran around frenzied, looking for any means to escape.

My mother and her children went to the home of a Pole in the village of Zagorz. From there they wanted to go to Pienczin, where another county administrator lived. Unfortunately it was too late. The deportation started during the night. I wanted to flee to Zagorz, where my sister was. On the way I met my uncle, Moshe Niedziela, and he advised me not to go back to the ghetto, because the road was full of lurking German gendarmes. They were arresting all of the Jews that they came across.

On the way back, my uncle, his wife and I did not return to the (Klobuck) ghetto, but went to the home of a Christian acquaintance of ours, in an attempt to hide ourselves in his barn. In the middle of the night we heard terrible crying and shouting. We understood that it was the end of the Jews in Klobuck. Soon thereafter, the County Commander, the Gestapo, with their trained dogs, and Jewish policemen came from Sosnowiec. We were dragged out and assembled at the gathering point in the Firefighter station hall. All the way, we were beaten and pushed around.

The Jewish policemen calmed us down, and asked us not to become hysterical. They said that no harm would happen to us, and that we would be sent to a work camp. I asked them to let my uncle, Moshe, and my aunt, Chana Rosa, go because they were elderly people, and that they could not survive the deportation. My request was ignored. We were all dragged away.

[Page 242]

At the gathering point in the Klobuck Firefighter hall, there were dreadful scenes, that should never again be seen by human beings. The Germans let their dogs free to attack and bite the elderly and the children. All of the sick and infirm people were shot. At the end, we were forced into transport trucks, which were heavily guarded, and the guards subjected us to unsparing blows. We were driven to Kiznitske. A young man from Krzepice, who tried to escape, was shot by the Germans. He fell wounded. The murderers trampled on his body, and then released the dogs on him.

When the martyrized man was lying unconscious, bitten all over by the dogs, the tormentors threw him in a river.

In Kiznitske we were dragged inside the Shul (Synagogue), where there were many Jews from Krzepice. There the "selection" was performed by the Sosnowiec Judenrat Elder, Moshe Merin. No one believed that we were chosen to die in the gas chambers and crematoriums. The Judenrat Elder convinced us that the elderly and the children would be sent to special camps. The food rations would be smaller for them, but they would be able to survive the war.

Twenty five young women, including myself, and one young man, Yaacov Diment, were chosen to go to a work camp. We were sent back to the Kiznitske shul. There I found my aunt, Neche Granek, and her children. Her eldest daughter was 14 years old, and she was not tall. I smuggled her out of the transport, and took her in our group of young girls. I placed a stone in her shoes so she would look taller. In that manner I was able to take the young girl from the (transport) and out of the camp. She came along with us to Sosnowiec, where there was a transit camp (durchgangs Lager "Dulag"). We were examined by doctors. My cousin was rejected because of her small height. She did not come along with us.

[Page 243]

After eight days in "Dulag", all of the 25 young girls were sent to the work camp, Grinberg. We worked hard there, and we did not receive enough food to eat. Day by day we became feebler, but we survived.

After a year of work, the camp was liquidated. We were then sent to Neusaltz. We met up with many Klobucker Jews there, from the first "labor supply," and among them was my sister, Bela. Other members of our group also found their sisters. Among them were: Feigel Blitz, Chana Unglick and Edga Granek. Mirel Unglick and Edga Granek died in the camp, following a long illness.

My sister, Bela, and I remained together until the liberation. We survived together throughout all of the stages of the German persecution and hell. We worked hard, and we became as thin as skeletons. However, we held on to a spark of hope that we would survive the war, and that hope sustained us and gave us the will to remain alive. Many of the young girls did not endure the terrible situation, and they collapsed.

In December, 1944 we were taken out of the Neusaltz camp, under a heavy guard of Gestapo personnel. The move was ordered to "protect" us from the Russian bombings. For six weeks the armed Germans dragged us from camp to camp. Every day we were forced to walk 30 kilometers, through deep snow, even though we had only wooden shoes, or were bare footed. Our feet were swollen. Many of the young girls, including young girls from Klobuck, fainted on the roads, and their short lives came to their end.

We walked through the Sudeten region, the Czech region, and the beautiful town of Marienbad. In the end the SS soldiers confined and locked us up in train carriages for three days, without food. That is how we arrived at the extermination camp of Bergen-Belsen. It was our good fortune that we spent only four weeks there, because we could not have survived more than that.

[Page 244]

Every day thousands of Jews were killed by the filth and the hunger. The dead corpses were piled up, and the living people wandered around like walking skeletons. We only received some soup once a day, without even a piece of bread. When the soup pot was brought,there was a scramble; and the "kapo," a woman, beat us on our heads until we bled. That is how we got some watered soup. Drinking water was under lock. During these four weeks we could not wash ourselves even once. Vermin were eating us alive.

By April 15, 1945 we were lying among the dead, when we were freed by the Englishmen. In the camp a typhus epidemic outbreak occurred. The Englishmen brought us to an hospital. We were washed, cleaned and healed. After two months my sister, Bela, and I left the hospital, and went to Sweden.

Translator's Footnote

1. In some chapters Moshe Merin is called Shimon Merin or Moniek Merin. From the all the chapters context it must be the same person. Moniek seems to be his Polish name and Moshe his Jewish name.

Reviewer's Footnote

i.   The writer is being sarcastic.

Page 244]

Final Liquidation of the Ghetto

by Karala Benszkowska

Translated from Yiddish to English by Asher Szmulewicz

My parents originated from Klobuck. When we were small children, my parents moved to Lodz.

My mother often travelled to Klobuck to visit her ancestors' graves. In my youth I did not realize the special significance and deep feelings that were closely connected to the journey to my mother's ancestors' graves. We, the children, rejoiced when we could join our my mother during her trips to Klobuck. I traveled to and visited this shtetl several times, and I have fond memories of it.

When World War II broke out, we traveled back to our parents' old home in Klobuck, and all of us met each other and came together there.

At the beginning of the occupation, men and women were taken to forced labor (nearby), and initially we liked it. We thought that it (the war) would not last long. This "happiness" did not last for long. The Germans started to send people away to work. Soon a new decree was issued: it was ordered that all of the young girls had to register, and then would be sent away to work. As was my fate, I was not spared or overlooked.

[Page 246]

In the middle of the night, I was ordered out of my bed. I shivered from fright, because it was the first time in my life that I was torn away from the thing I held closest and most dear – my home.

I did not know where I was being taken. However, I thought that my going away would spare the rest of my family from the worst. I was therefore ready to sacrifice myself for my family. I could not imagine that I had hugged and pressed my dear parents to my heart for the last time.

To this day I remember the image in front of my eyes of how the Germans brought us to the station. My mother ran after me, through the field, in her attempt to, at least, see me from afar. I saw my mother fall in the field, exhausted from running after me; yet she got up again as fast as she could, so that she could see me for the last time. She instinctively knew that it was the last time she would see me.

During 1942, when I was in the camp, I received a few letters. Shortly thereafter the "deportation" of Klobuck started. Everyone tried as best as they could to escape from the deportation. Everyone rushed to get into the work camp at Zagorz. My mother's only concern was for her children, and she did not think about herself; she agonized over how she could save them, and how to secure their lives. She brought my young sister, Marile, to the Zagorz work camp, and returned to her home alone. At home she was with my grand-mother and with my sister, Frimet, and her child, and waited for the coming fate of her sad life.

Indeed, on the very same night, the "deportation" of Klobuck occurred. My sister, Marile, knew that our mother, our grand-mother, our sister, Frimet, and her child were hidden behind the closet (in our apartment). Marile tried to find a means to travel to town, and find out what happened to our family.

[Page 246]

f Marile and Edge Epstein travelled to town with the ood caldron for the workers. They were detained by armed Germans, who checked their identification, and were told to sit in a truck. Three men were already sitting in the truck: Yechiel Mass, a father of 7 children; the 14 year old, Unglick; and the 13 year old, Dzialowski. They were all brought to the Jewish cemetery to be shot.

Marile and Edge stood facing the cemetery wall, while the men were digging a mass grave. When Marile tried to turn around, she received a blow to her head with a rubber stick. Her eyes were covered with blood. She wanted the pain to be over, because waiting for death was too much for her. But often redemption comes at the last moment before death. The town commissioner arrived and saved Marile and Edge (Chana) from death.

As soon as they walked a few steps away, they heard the shots. The Germans took the lives of three innocent victims – the Jews.

After two days, all of the people who remained in the Zagorz camp were brought to town (Klobuck) to clean up the houses of the Jews who were deported to the death camps. Marile and Chana were also in the "clean up committee," and by chance she happened to clean up our apartment, where our mother was still hiding, with our grand-mother and our sister, Frimet, with her child.

Marile asked the troop leader for permission to take them with her to the Zagorz camp. As a reward she promised to show him where our grand-mother hid her treasure. The troop leader accepted the "deal", but as they were about to leave, the Gendarmes came, with their sniffing dogs, and (the hidden Jews) were taken away.

A Polish neighbor, named, Dgizba, asked that he be allowed to take the child, Chanele, Frimet's daughter. He offered to bribe the Germans, but his efforts were useless. The Gendarmes took away the arrested persons.

*

[Page 247]

Not long afterwards, the last Klobucker Jews were deportedto work camps in Germany. Among the deported Jews were my father, and my two brothers, Yitzek and Alek. My father did not reflect on the difficult moral and psychic experiences of his life: he lost his wife, a daughter and a grandchild, yet he was determined to go on with life, and work for the German murderers, believing that he would survive Hitler's hell.

Yitzek and Alek did everything they could in the camp to facilitate our father's survival, by helping him with his difficult sufferings. Often, they gave him their food portion. He wanted to survive his bitter fate, but several months before the liberation there was a decree to remove all of the old people from the work camps, including my father.

One of my brothers volunteered to take my father's place, but it was impossible. The German murderers tore my father away from my brothers' arms, and sent him to the gas chambers.

Where are our dearest (and departed loved ones)? Where are their graves? How can we travel to our ancestors' graves, like my mother did for her parents' graves?

May their souls rest in eternal peace.

The Christian "Help" for the Klobucker Jews

by Pesa Chorzewski Zlatnik

Translated from Yiddish to English by Asher Szmulewicz

One day before the deportation of the Klobucker Jews from the ghetto, my mother and sister, with the help of a Christian, left their home and left the shtetl. They intended to smuggle themselves across the "border" and into Czestochowa, where my brother, Emanuel, already was living. During the journey, the Christian had regrets, (changed his mind), and no longer was willing to help my mother and sister.

They were left alone, approximately half way from their destination. They decided to go back to Klobuck. On their way back, Germans shot at them. Peasants warned the two women not to go back to Klobuck, because the Germans were shooting Jews.

[Page 248]

My mother and sister went to another village. There a Christian took pity on them, and for a large amount of money, arranged with a peasant to smuggle both of them into Czestochowa.

My father's painful wanderings were very different.

My father did not want to leave his home. At the beginning, when the German murderers behaved bestially in the ghetto streets, my father successfully escaped to the home of a Christian acquaintance, called Pierchowski. The good Christian hid the Jew (my father) in his attic from the evening until 11:00 PM. At that time Pierchowski went to my father and asked him to immediately leave his house, because he was afraid that the Germans would shoot his whole family. That was how the Germans were punishing Poles who were hiding Jews.

My father had to wander again. He went to the home of another Christian acquaintance, called Zmielnick, from village of Zakrzew[1] (Zakshew). Once he arrived there he received the same answer. This was the almost universal response that was given to the hunted and desperate Jews from his Christian acquaintances. My father wandered through the fields and woods, and broke into peasant barns or attics during the night to find a place to sleep. In the end he came back to Klobuck, because a Christian acquaintance told him that there was a "Jewish Committee" in Klobuck.

My father went to the "Committee," and met the Judenrat leaders Wiener and Jasne. The Judenrat elders became afraid when they suddenly saw a Klobucker Jew in the shtetl (after the deportation). They gave him a piece of bread, and advised him to hide in an attic. They told him that they would take him to the camp the next morning. My father did not hide in an attic, but again he left the shtetl, because he was afraid that the Judenrat elders intended to hand him over to the Germans.

[Page 249]

On his long journey, my father encountered drunk German railway workers, who held him prisoner. After many arguments and the payment of 10 marks, the murderers let my father go. My father was left in a field; he was physically and emotionally exhausted. A Christian passed by, and my father asked him to take him to Czestochowa. The Christian saw that my father had a gold pocket watch, and he asked that my father give him his watch as a reward.

My father gave him his pocket watch, and the Christian took him to the border, but then told him to go the rest of the way alone. My father had no choice, and he dragged his tired and swollen feet until he arrived at Czestochowa. But then, there was another problem: how to get into the ghetto?

The Jew (my father) went into a Christian shop, where he bought a glass of soda water. After drinking the soda, he asked the shopkeeper to ask someone to bring him inside the ghetto. For two Zlotys a Christian boy brought him to the Kadafsker Bridge, and on the other side there was the large ghetto (In Czestochowa were 2 ghettos: a large one and a small one).

Jews on the other side, (in the ghetto), saw my father. Risking their lives, they rushed to bring my father into the ghetto, so that the murderers would not notice him. After all of his long wanderings, my father finally arrived at his son's house, and we remained together until Sukkot eve.

On Sukkot's eve there was a second "Action"[2] in Czestochowa. My parents left their (son's) home, and went to a bunker, where they stayed for six weeks. Afterwards, when things calmed down for Jews, my parents came back to the ghetto. But the situation had changed and things were much more difficult. People were afraid to permit old people, or people who were unable to work, to remain.

After long and strenuous efforts, my sister, Ite, found a cellar room for my parents. They lived there for three months, suffering with their fright, and from hunger and the cold. Then there was another "Action". With the help of Jewish policemen, the Germans searched for and arrested my parents, and they were sent from the Czestochowa ghetto to Treblinka. This happened in January, 1943.

Translator's Footnotes

1. Zakrzew was a village to the south of Klobuck. Today the village is included within the town.

2. "Aktse", or Action in English, means a roundup of Jews for the purpose of sending them to an extermination camp. This particular Action was very long during the month of October, 1942. Six transports were organized by the Germans, resulting in the deportation to Treblinka of 36,000 Jews from the large ghetto of Czestochowa.

[Page 250]

Klobucker Jews in Extermination Camps

The Zagórz Concentration Camp

By Dora Wajs

Translated from Yiddish to English by Asher Szmulewicz

The village of Zagórz was located close to Klobuck. There, the Germans established a "free willing" work camp (as explained below) to serve the German economy and the surrounding areas. The work entailed breaking stones, taking apart houses or building new buildings.

The Zagórz camp was established before the "Yamim Noraim" (Days of Awe) in 1941. Its first "inhabitants" were a group of Jews from Zabrze in the Bielsk region, Sosnowiec County. Later Jews came from Klobuck and its surroundings, as "free willing." "Free Willing" meant that the people asked to be accepted to work in the camp. This was a result of the fact that the Jewish council (Judenrat) accepted the German rules. These rules compelled large numbers of Jews to "volunteer" to travel and work in the German camps. In the Klobuck Ghetto people were frightened. The rebellious ones, who did not want to leave Klobuck, were in constant fear of death. That is why the Zagórz camp was seen as a lifeboat for the desperate Jews, who were drowning in blood.

Klobuck Jewish people in the Zagórz Concentration Camp, at work

[Page 251]

The liquidation of the Klobuck Ghetto occurred on June 21st 1942. "Useful Jews" were permitted to stay, and among them were: Leizer Franck and his wife, a dentist; Petchia Tsintsinatus; Yaacov Aaron Blau; Itzik Elie Besser, with his family; Chaim Mendelewicz; Shalom Unglick; and Yankel Libski. All of them remained in Klobuck and received apartments.

After Klobuck became "Judenrein" (without Jews), the Germans established in the former ghetto a "Service Unit" of workshops for tailors and shoemakers, which was close to a supply room and a kitchen. There the "useful Jews" who remained were employed.

A significant number of Jews fled from the murderous deportation and were hidden in the forest and by peasants. The Klobuck region "Service Units" formed a network of "free" camps to attract the escaped and the hidden Jews, with the intent that those Jews would voluntarily register to work, and then be exterminated by the Germans at a later and determined time.

This diabolic plan succeeded. The most successful camp of the Klobuck "service units" was Zagórz. Not only did the escaped and hidden Jews come there, but also Jews from nearby Czestochowa, who depended of the "General Government".[1] The Jews from Czestochowa smuggled themselves through the "border" with dedication so that they could reach the "happy" Zagórz camp. In the Zagórz camp were 500 Jews before the liquidation. A few similar type camps like the Klobuck "Service Units" were located in Biala, Werenczice, Wilkowiek, Krzepice etc. The work was hard there, but compared to anywhere else it was "a good place".

The supposedly "good" time in the camp did not last long.

[Page 252]

During July, 1943 the Zagórz camp was surrounded by SS troops. They ordered everyone to get dressed fast and everybody was dragged to the police station. Jews from the other camps that made up the Klobuck region "Service Units" were also brought there. The police station was surrounded by a special unit of SS troops. Everyone instinctively knew that the liquidation had started, but there was nothing that could be done.

In this hopeless situation, a few audacious Jews tried to save their lives. When the bread was brought for those sentenced to death, Avraham Weiss, Nechama Kitner and Avraham Liberman escaped. Avraham Weiss was caught. A few Jews, Petchia Tsintsinatus with his wife, and Chaim Silberberg ripped off the gate and tried to escape. The Germans chased them. One of them was shot, the others were brought back. They received murderous blows. The murderous SS put all of them against a wall and prepared to execute them. At that moment, an SS officer arrived and said to his "comrades" that they were not worth the cartridges: "They will rot to death (like animals) anyway". The execution was cancelled.

The next morning, two females and one male jumped over the fence. They were caught. The guard had been fortified with SS people and a trained dog. At the end, all of the persecuted Jews were brought to the train and were sent in freight cars to the Blechhammer camp. A "selection" occurred, during which a few persons and the children were sent to the gas chambers, and those people able to work were sent to work camps. Only a few of those came back.

Translator's Footnote

1. The General Government of Poland was the part of Poland under German control and administered by a German General Governor. Klobuck was so close of the 1939 German border that it was annexed to Germany. That is why Jews from Czestochowa had to cross the "border".

[Page 253]

Out of Hiding and Away to the Zagórz Concentration Camp

By Avraham Enzel

Translated from Yiddish to English by Asher Szmulewicz

Three days before the deportation from Klobuck, I was aware of what was going to happen. I informed all my acquaintances about the reports of the impending danger. Within two hours, the frightening news spread throughout the Ghetto, and everybody looked for ways to escape. Young men, women and girls ran to the Zagórz camp. Older people stayed, letting fate decide. A portion of the community ran away and crossed the "border" to the "General Government"[1].

My wife, Karola, and I together with the Unglick family decided to hide in a prepared double attic inside a building next to our house.

On the last evening, when we were ready to enter our hideout, I met Yachet Ripstein. She asked me: "Where should I go and what should I do"? I invited her to join us in our hideout. She told me that she knew a Christian acquaintance and that she intended go to him, and ask him to hide her. We emotionally parted, and I never saw her again...

During a calm and dark night, as the people of the Klobuck Ghetto were being rounded up and the town was empty, we entered our hideout and locked the door from the inside with a bar. In the morning we suddenly heard frightening knocks on the building gate, and the wellknown beastly voices of Germans: "Jews open up". We also heard gun shots and people screaming and crying as they were being dragged out. From our hideout, we saw Esther Skorupa, standing with her child close to the building gate, crying.

The Germans broke into the building where we were hiding. They searched every room, but they did not find our hideout. The Germans left. We stayed in our hideout for three days without food or water.

During the fourth night we decided to go one by one to the Zagórz camp, because we heard news that in the camp it was possible to manage and survive. We left our bunker and went to the camp.

Translator's Footnote

1. The General Government of Poland was the part of Poland under German control and administered by a German General Governor. Klobuck was so close to the 1939 German border that it was annexed to Germany. The nearby city of Czestochowa on the other hand was inside the General Government of Poland

[Page 254]

The Struggle for Life and Existence

By Moshe Fajga

Translated from Yiddish to English by Asher Szmulewicz

I successfully escaped the Hasag camp in Czestochowa in the year 1943. Czestochowa was then part of the (Polish) "General Government," and I had to flee across the "border" to reach Klobuck, which was annexed by the (German) "Third Reich". I left the camp with the other workers to go to work. While going to work in a line, I walked away from the line and onto a side street to a Christian, who was known to be a "smuggler". With this Pole were several Jews, among them: Aaron Franck from Krzepice, Moshe Tsintsinatus from Klobuck and a few others. Our "savior" hid us in a cellar in the second room. During the night we came out of the cellar, ate something and prepared to go.

At midnight, we started to walk towards Klobuck. We crossed the "border" close to Jabienitz(□abieniec) without problem, and we arrived at the Zagórz camp at approximately three o'clock (in the morning). The "smuggler" brought us to the pig sty, which was the home of the Jews working in Zagórz. In the pig sty former Klobuck landlords and respectable Jews were sleeping on bare wood plank cots.

Our arrival woke them up. They welcomed us warmly, and started asking about their families, who were living in Czestochowa. One of the Jews from the camp, Mordechai Ross-Gelbard, instructed us to lie down, because the "Uncle" would soon come in. "Uncle" was the nickname of the "Kapo," Reuven Shnieber.

It did not take long and the "Kapo" came in and said to me: "Moshe, you came back again. You want to tease with the commander of the camp. Go away from here". At the same time, Aaron Frenck[1] received blows from the "Kapo".

I asked him: "Where can I go at night? I will be caught.

[Page 255]

Tomorrow morning when everyone goes to work, I will go with them, and then I will disappear".

It happened as I predicted. In the morning we went out to work (with the others). Aaron Frenck, Moshe Tsintsinatus and I left, and each of us went to another place. Aaron Frenck's brother was a "Reklamirter Jew", which meant that he was a dentist and worked for the Germans and lived in Klobuck. Aaron Frenck went to his brother. Moshe Tsintsinatus and I went to Tsintsinatus' brother, Petchia, also a "Reklamirter Jew", who worked as a painter for the Germans. We hid there for eight days.

Our hope was that we would be accepted in the tailor camp. There young women worked, and amongst them were my nieces, Libe and Dina. I had already informed them about my coming, and Dina had already visited me in my hideout. She told me that her father and his two sons, Chaskel and Levi, were in the Zagórz camp. Her mother (my sister) was in the Sosnowiec hospital and she (Dina) and her sister Libe were working in the tailor camp, which was part of the "Service Unit". For the time being it was not possible to apply for a job in the tailor camp, because the young women were accused of stealing laundry. No one was caught, but the camp commander punished everyone by ordering confinement in the cellar for ten days. Since the work had to continue, the workers were confined in the cellar on a rotation basis. Thus, those in hiding had to wait until the punishment was over.

We remained hidden under a closet in Tsintsinatus' brother, Petchia's, apartment. My niece was liberated from the cellar punishment, and she asked the camp commander to accept to the camp two Jews who came out from their hideout. She said they will be "Useful Jews". The camp commander agreed.

Dina came to see me, and announced the good news that I could work under the supervision of Reuven Feiner, who was involved in tearing down Shlomo Alars' house (see my note at the end). I went to see Feiner to inform him that the camp commander enrolled me. Reuven Feiner demanded that I give him money for the right to work with him.

[Page 256]

Since I had no money, he punished me by having me carry several heavy metal bars over a long distance.

For four weeks, my work was to break stones, until one day a few stones sheared off and hit my foot. I was taken away with a broken right foot in the car that transported the stones and was driven to the Zagórz camp.

The young women, who were busy in the kitchen, came out joyfully towards the car. They thought that a potato delivery was being made, but then saw me lying in the car with a broken foot. I was taken off the car to lie down on a dirty plank cot in the pig sty.

There was a Jewish doctor in the camp, but the Jews did not trust him. They brought a Polish doctor to me, who had previously treated many Jews in the camp. The doctor put a bandage on my foot. Later the Jewish doctor came. He was very upset that the Jews did not trust him, but did trust a "Goy" (non Jew). He re-did the bandage. The Polish doctor told the troop leader, Eldering, about what happened, and asked that I be transferred to the Sosnowiec hospital.

My brother in law, Yossef Mendelewicz, tried to intervene so that I would remain in the camp, but he could not help. The German said that he had instructions from the doctor, and that he had to comply with them. The Jews said their good-byes to me. A few calmed me down, and told me not to be afraid, and that I would come back healed. Mrs. Macha Weinman shed tears.

The next morning I was sent to the Sosnowiec hospital, escorted by two men. I was laid down on the ground floor. I was told that my sister, Tsvia, was there ill on the first floor. She did not know that I was in the same hospital. The nurse told me about Tsvia and how sick she was. I instructed the nurse not to tell Tsvia about my illness. Why should I give her more grief?

[Page 257]

The hospital was full of sick Jews, who were brought from the German camps. The Jews worked in coal mines in Silesia andwere brought with broken hands and legs, and other wounds on their body. I was visited by Mordechai Elia Mass, and he brought me news about my sister.

One day the doctor, Frisher, a surgeon who treated our limbs, disappeared. There was a rumor that the doctor trafficked in identification papers and that he had fled to Switzerland. Two Polish doctors came and they examined us. A few days later "SS" were seen in the hospital, and the people who were seriously ill were taken out of the hospital. I was left alone for the moment, likely because the cars were full. I wrote to my nieces in the Klobuck camp that they should save me.

My niece came to the hospital with the troop leader, Eldering, to take her mother, who was ill in the hospital, back home. On this occasion my niece asked the troop leader to bring back two more people from Klobuck, who had recovered and were able to work. The German agreed to bring us back.

We drove to the train station. With much difficulty, my niece put her mother in the wagon. It was even harder and more difficult with me. I could not walk. My friend Mordechai Mass and Libe carried me. When we arrived at the train platform, we learned that the train had already left. The SS troop leader spoke with the station master to let me go on the next train, which was due to leave in one hour.

I could not stand any longer hanging on with my hands on the shoulders of my friend. My foot was in gypsum. I was weak and nervous. I asked the troop leader to shoot me, because my life was no longer worthwhile. Our death was inevitable. The troop leader answered: "nonsense".

It was time to go. Mordechai Mass got a cart and brought the luggage to the platform. Libe and Mordechai put me on the cart and took me to the train. With great difficulty they put me on the train. In Kroleswka Hute I found my sister, Tsvia. The unexpected meeting gave us great joy.

[Page 258]

We arrived that night in the Klobuck camp. The Jewishinmates rejoiced with us. Each of the new arrivals, Mordechai Mass, my sister and myself, went to his own camp. Klobuck was the headquarters of the camps which were located in Krzepice, Wilkowiec, Werenszice etc...

The camps had a good reputation and were a refuge. The Jews, former Klobuck inhabitants, came from Czestochowa, looking for an escape in the camps from the Germans' wild conduct, in Czestochowa . They came to the camps during the night. Since it was known that the "Kapo", Reuven Shnieber-Feiner, beat the newcomers, the established inmates took the newcomers to the women camp, which was 200 meters away. There they were hidden in an attic.

It is worthwhile to detail the crooked activities of the "Kapo". He had three children in the camp, two daughters about 8-10 years old, and a 12 year old son, Beniek. The daughters helped their father with his "livelihood." They showed him where the newcomers were hidden. The "Kapo" then dragged the Jews from their hideout, took their belongings, and threw them out of the camp. In contrast, the son of the "Kapo", Beniek, had sympathy for the persecuted refugees from Czestochowa. With the well-known exclamation, "Six", he warned the hideaways that "the father comes," and that they had to hide.

The father, the "Kapo", did not like his son. Many times he was beaten and shouted at him that the little (girl) children had more wisdom than the older son.

The life in the camp and the role of the "Kapo"

Several young men and women worked in the kitchen, or in the laundry, and the rest of the people, the majority of men, worked tearing down houses, pulling weeds, or breaking stones. While several Jews were breaking stones in the streets, I remember once that a Jew was beaten by Reuven Shnieber, because he was yawning while working.

[Page 259]

The Jews of the camp were forced by the Germansto dismantle the Jewish cemetery. Berl Szmulewicz came back with a small piece of the tombstone of his father, as a souvenir. I thought: we will be buried, but the tombstones will remain.

The women did the same difficult work as the men. After a hard day of work, a train arrived with a delivery of bricks. Everyone, men, women, children and old people were ordered out of the camp. In the middle of the night we were marched to the train station and ordered to unload the bricks from the train. When we returned from the work, the "Kapo" was standing on a balcony and he threw out a few pieces of bread to a few Jews. In that way he gained the sympathy of the Jewish inmates. "Nevertheless he has a Jewish heart", argued a few.

I did not go to work because my foot was still in gypsum. When I saw the "Kapo", I started getting busy in the laundry Rivka Unglick and Yankel Ajzner's wife worked also in the laundry. When the "Kapo" came in the laundry he told me: "Moshe, if you speak about politics, I will send you directly to Auschwitz".

The "Kapo" had a mistress in the camp, a daughter of a shochet who came from Zdu□ska Wola. She always said: "I live with him in order to hold him back, so that he will not make trouble for you". She died in the BlechHammer camp because of her lover.

Reuven Shnieber, the "Kapo", was from B☐dzin "underworld". There was a rumor that before the war he bet for 5 pounds that he could eat a frog. He indeed "swallowed" a frog, and it was said that was the reason why he spoke in a hoarse voice. In the Klobuck camp he usually was drunk, and had a good livelihood, by looting from the dead people as well as from the living.

Our camp was an open camp, supervised by a troop leader, and not enclosed by fences like other camps. We were not allowed to leave. We had to be careful, not to be caught outside of the camp. During work time there was a foreman. We were not watched by Germans. We were always afraid that the "Kapo" Reuven, the "Uncle", would come by and stop by our work.

In Czestochowa's ghetto the situation worsened. Jews fled to our camp as the only place for rescue.

[Page 260]

The "Kapo" chased and hunted them. They turned to the troop leader, and he registered them into the camp.

We received news that in the Klobuck region, there were partisans. Therefore we called a meeting. The following people participated in the meeting: Berl Szmulewicz, Moshe Feige, Avraham Weiss, Avraham Enzel and Yidl Szperling. We decided that by all possible means we should get money and weapons.

A few days later, on Sunday, we sent Heniek Szilit to Truskolas. In the evening a Pole ran into the camp with a letter from Heniek: "Friends, pity on myself, save me, I am under arrest at the Truskolas police station in a cellar". The Jews went to the troop leader and asked him to save Heniek. They promised him a reward. His wife did not want him to go, but he wanted to. The question was where could we get a horse and a cart? At that point Reuven Unglick came to the rescue.

Reuven Unglick worked for a Romanian Christian, whose name was Kobiak. Reuven asked him to harness his horse, and the Gentile agreed. Together with the troop leader they went to Truskolas. Once there they learned that the arrested man was transferred to Fashistanie.

The troop leader went to Fashistanie and identified himself to the police. He declared that Heniek Szilit was detained there, and that he had escaped from the camp under his command. He said that he wanted to take him back to the camp, where he would hang him in front of all the Jews. After this punishment and by seeing such a hanging, no other Jews will try to escape the camp anymore.

This trick worked and everybody came back home safe.

[Page 261]

The Romanians prepared themselves for a pogrom against the Jews in camp

I told you about a Romanian called Kobiak, who lived in Klobuck's neighborhood . He was not the only Romanian Christian in this region. For an unknown reason the Germans settled Romanians in this region.

I have already mentioned the Kubiak.Reuven Unglick, who worked as the Kobiak's foreman, was sent from the camp to work with his landlord, the Kubiak. They went to Biale, but they did not come back. Kobiak's wife went to Biale to find out what happened to her husband and was told that her husband travelled back home the same night he arrived. Also no one at the police station knew what happened of him.

The next morning the Christian's wife came into the camp and demanded that Reuven Unglick's parents tell her who had killed her husband. Chava, Reuven's mother, weeped, tore the hair from her head and swore that she did not know anything. The Christian's wife left the Zagórz camp and went to the Romanians. They told her, vehemently, that they would make a pogrom against the Jews in retaliation of her husband killing. So she told them that a Jew from the camp went with her husband to Biale to deliver goods; that the Jew got drunk; killed her husband; and fled with the horse to the partisans. The Christians believed her and therefore they prepared themselves for a pogrom on the third day. In the camp everyone was frightened to death. The Unglick family cried about their missing son, and here at the same time a pogrom was being prepared against the Jews in the camp.

The troop leader was away, and the camp commander in Klobuck was informed about what the Romanian Christians were preparing against us. He sent another camp commander to the camp to "protect" us...

On the third day, just when they were ready to attack, the Christian (Kobiak) returned. He told the people that they got drunk and fell asleep in the cart. The horse, instead of returning to Klobuck, went to Bejenice, and they were held on the border. The Christian was released on the third day. Reuven, his foreman, remained there. Reuven's mother and father cried, and tore the hair from their head.

[Page 262]

They contacted a "Volk Deutsch"[2], and paid him a lot of money in order to go and save their son. The "Volks Deutsch" came back with the news that Reuven was sent to Wielun. The mother again gave money to the "Volks Deutsch" and sent him to Wielun. He came back with the answer that from there he was sent to Auschwitz. The parents understood that they could do nothing about it. They wept about their son who lost his life in Auschwitz.

During the month of August, the woman' Baltshe ó tobrode[3] (Joltobrode) fell sick. I asked Reuven Shnieber, the "Kapo": since I cannot work, because I cannot walk on my foot, can I be the night watcher and can I also escort the young women to the Krzepice hospital." He agreed. At the Krzepice hospital I found my brother in law, Yossel. While I was speaking with him, the "Kapo", Mendele Bank, came into the hospital and made a list of all the sick Jews. I understood what was the purpose for the list.

The liquidation of the Zagórz ghetto

I immediately travelled back to Klobuck and warned the camp that we should be prepared for news. During the night I was at my post as a watchman. I told my friends in the camp that when the Germans arrive I will give them a sign. Berl Szmulewicz and other people prepared metal rods. Mordechai Klapack came to me several times during the night to ask if all is quiet. He could not longer sleep.

Night. The dogs barked. I opened the small gate, I looked around, it was very dark and I saw no one. I woke up my friend Moshe Mordechai Klapack. He told me: "when one dog barks, all the dogs bark. It is nothing". I stood outside on the road and listened. It was calm. I didn't hear anybody coming and the dogs barked again. I was nervous, and I couldn't calm down. I walked in circle in the street, in the courtyard.

[Page 263]

Suddenly Germans jumped over the fence, pointing their rifles towards me. "Hands up". I told them that I was the night watchman. One of them was ready to shoot at me, and the second told him: leave him alone. He asked me: "where does the camp commander live"? I pointed to the direction with my hand and he told me to keep my hands up and to turn around my face to the wall. I counted the minutes, I thought that he was going to shoot me. After a short time, the troop leader came out, he told me to come back inside the camp.

In the camp there was turmoil. People knew that it was the end and everybody prepared himself for death. People threw away all their belongings; money, gold what people prepared for the last minutes in order to save their lives. The Germans ordered everybody to get dressed. They put us in a row outside and prepared to send us away.

Nachele Szilit (née Zigelbaum) said to the Germans: "where are you going to murder me and my child, kill us now". The Germen laughed. We are leading you away to Klobuck in the Skorupa house[4]. A few Jews were able to jump over the fence outside and started running away. Among the Christians, immediately somebody denounced them. The Jews were caught, and they were lined up with their faces against the wall. We thought that they were going to be shot. At that moment Ludwig, the "Major", came out and gave an order not to shoot.

During the time we spent on the Skorupa courtyard, surrounded by police, another group of policemen gathered Jews from other camps and brought them to the same courtyard. In the Werenszice camp, the Jews saw in advance that the Germans were coming and that it was the end of the camp. They ran unfortunately to the forest. We envied them.

Around midday, two Jews came in from the forest and notified the Germans that the Jews from the forest wanted to come back and they asked to be taken back. The Germans drove with the two Jews to the forest. All the Jews that escaped brought back. The Jews understood that they would not be able to survive in the forest for a long time in the forest.

During the night we stayed on the ground. Next morning we were driven to the train station. We were packed inside wagons and the train left for an unknown location.

Translator's Footnotes

1. Must be the same person as Aaron Franck (typo)

2. German people

3. This family name comes from Polish word □ó□tobrody which means yellow beard

4. Skorupa means crust, shell in Polish

General note of the translator

There a few inconsistencies in this long chapter. The writer speaks of an open camp and then he was night watchman and there were fences. I think that the writer was first at an open camp in Klobuck and then went to Zagórz camp which was just on the outskirts of Klobuck and was a camp surrounded by fences. The open camp in Klobuck was the head quarters for all the camps surrounding Klobuck. In the last part of the chapter, all the Jews from all the surrounding camps were gathered to the Skorupa courtyard before their deportation.

Other inconsistency: how could the writer escort a young woman to the hospital while he could not walk because of his broken leg?

[Page 264]

Hunger and Hard Labor

By Berl Yakubowicz

Translated from Yiddish to English by Asher Szmulewicz

We travelled to Germany. In a train station in the Alps, the Germans attached a few additional cars with Jews to our train. The Jews were from Miszkaw and Krzepice.

We arrived at a small train station and the Germans started shouting: "everybody out". We got out of the train cars and saw that we arrived in a small train station named "Eichenthal". In front of the train station trucks were waiting; we were crammed inside the trucks and driven to an unknown location.

After about five kilometers, the trucks stopped. On one side we saw a forest and on the other side wooden barracks, enclosed with barbed wire three meters high. It was getting dark. We didn't know where we were. The gate opened and we walked inside in rows of three. Twenty six men were counted out and were directed to go inside the barracks, row by row. Inside the barracks there were thirteen beds, (two persons per bed), a table and a few stools. We were ordered to fill up our straw bags with straw and go to sleep.

The next morning, we were awakened by the Germans, who shouted: "Everybody up" and arrange the beds like in a military camp. We were young men, who had not been in military service, and we did not know what to do.

Everyone was pushed outside into the square, and we were counted, to check that no one had escaped. In each of the four corners of the camp, there was a watch towermanned by German soldiers with machine guns. Close to the gate soldiers stood with rifles around their shoulders.

[Page 265]

In the morning we got black coffee, half bread, about 400 grams, and about 20 grams of margarine. We were notified that that was all the food we would receive for the rest of the day, and now we should go outside to work, and that when we returned in the evening we would get a meal.

We marched outside in rows of three. The German soldiers watched us from both sides. They commanded us to march in foot steps like soldiers. We marched about four kilometers. From a wooden booth each of us received tools to work with: a shovel, a spade and a crowbar. We were then divided into groups. One group was ordered to shovel soil into little steel carts on thin rails, which allowed the carts to move on. Another group was ordered to do various other tasks.

We started working, shoveling the black soil into the carts. A German civilian stood in front of us and shouted: "faster pace!" threatening us with the handle of a shovel, "anyone who does not fill up the cart will be beaten with this stick".

After the carts were full, a small locomotive arrived, and was connected to the carts and dragged them away. Immediately thereafter we had to fill empty boxes until the carts came back, so that we were unable to rest even for a minute. We worked this way all day long.

At 4 PM we received an order: "all the tools must be cleaned; they had to be returned as clean as they were received". We were then immediately ordered again to form rows of three and to march back to the camp. Everybody was hungry and exhausted. In the camp they counted us again to check that no one escaped. We were warned that if somebody escaped, we will be put in a row and one out of ten would be shot. Every time we returned from work we heard the same kind of threats and demands.

We were ordered to stand in a single line, and were marched to the dining room for a meal. Everyone received a plate of food, which was a mixture of water with kohlrabi and very few potatoes. Everyone who still had another receptacle he brought from home ran in order to get some more of the food. But unfortunately it did not last very long.

[Page 266]

Food package from home and migration to a new camp

We wrote letters home. Every letter went through censorship. Any letter that did not please them (the Germans) was burned. We were allowed to write only in Latin letters. It was forbidden to write in Yiddish and that was what we yearned for. We wrote: "we are healthy and we send regards to the baker". Our parents understood what we meant. After a few days we received from home, bread, meat and various other food like sugar. We understood that our parents deprived themselves and sacrificed for us. They sent us (food) as frequently as they could, but we did not receive everything. The Germans checked for secret things in every parcel. They (the Germans) also mixed sugar with kasha or pasta with tea etc, to anger us, and so that we couldn't use the food we received from home.

Receiving parcels from home was a treat for us. We felt the gentle hand of our mother or father, who thought about us while packing these food parcels: "with this my child will stay alive and, God forbid, he will not starve". I am sure that a lot of tears flowed while these parcels were sent to the camp.

We worked approximately ten weeks. After a hard day of work in the field, during which the rain and wind chilled us to our bones, we returned to the camp, and we were notified that all the steel workers, locksmiths, ironworkers, tinsmiths, blacksmiths, as well as drivers and carpenters were ordered to go to work in a factory, because there was a shortage of those craftsman. We had no choice but to surrender to the bitter fate. We also had to separate from our friends from Klobuck.

Shortly afterward a military truck came and took about twenty healthy and vigorous people.

[Page 267]

With our luggage in one hand we climbed into the truck. Before leaving, everyone received a half kilogram of bread with 20 deca margarine. We said goodbye to our friends, and the truck got started, while we were guarded by two armed Germans, who travelled with us.

The journey lasted about two hours, and we again arrived at a fenced location. The barracks there were like the ones in Eichenthal. We got off the truck with our luggage, and we were lined up in one row. A German soldier examined us with an electric torch (flash light) in his hand, one by one in particular, and then we were marched into the camp.

We were confronted with new problems. We were given empty straw bags and we were ordered to fill them with straw, which served as our mattresses to sleep on. Everyone was in the same room. This occurred in January 1941.

On the next day in the morning, instead of working in a factory, we were sent to the field to dig trenches. During the work we were watched by German soldiers, foremen and engineers, who supervised the work.

All of the locksmiths and the blacksmiths carried thin rails. Carpenters carried wooden blocks and the others dug deep trenches. We made friends with the civil Germans, who worked there as professionals. They told us that a bridge for the Reich Highway would be built there. They pointed out the river over which the bridge was going to cross. It was the historical river Neisse[1].

Thus we worked every day from morning to nightfall on the highway bridge from January 1941 to March 1942.

We dug pits 6 meters deep. We stood in water above our knees, and removed the clay and sandy soil. When we came back to the camp after a arduous day of work, we had to clean the camp and throw away the garbage. We hitched up a truck and brought the garbage to a field far away. We washed ourselves and we had to mend our clothes by ourselves. There were about 500 Jews in the camp from shtetls throughout Poland. The majority were from Silesia, Bedzin, Sosnowiec, Klobuck, Krzepice, Miszkaw, etc ...

[Page 268]

We lived among ourselves like friends, because everybody was in the same boat. We received letters from our parents and also some food from home.

One summer day, one of us escaped. The Germans who guarded us were very upset. Before the escape they used to guard us only during the night and then disappeared; after the escape they started also to guard us during the day from the towers. They searched for the escapee. After a few hours the person who escaped was found. He said that he was hungry and went to find some food. We, all,were lucky that he was caught, because we were threatened that if he was not found we will be lined up in a row, and one out of ten of us would be shot.

From that escape on, the Germans conducted a "night service" for us. We worked very hard during the day and during the night one of us had to stay awake for two hours in order to prevent escapes.

It is becoming worse, the last letter from Klobuck.

In March 1942, an order was issued to send us to another camp. We were sent to Tarnowskie Góry, which was called Tarnowitz during the German occupation.

In Tarnowskie Góry new problems arose. We were packed together with a hundred men in one barracks, which comprised thirty five beds on three levels. One person slept above the other. We were ordered outside to work on the railroad. The work was to carry heavy rails to enlarge the train station. We worked with shovels and filled carts with heavy soil, some of which was wet and clay. We were not strong enough for this work. The Germans, who watched us, beat us with the wooden handles of the shovels.

In the camp we received less food to eat. Three men were given a kilogram of bread a day, with 2 deca margarin. The food parcels from home became rare and scarce, because the situation also became worse in Klobuck. The Germans were persecuting us more and more.

That was how very hard and bitter we were worked in Tarnowskie Góry, where approximately ten people from Klobuck were from. We rarely received letters from home.

[Page 269]

And when we received a letter from home, we were told that all of the Jews from Klobuck now lived in the ghetto and that they were being deported to Oswiecim (Auschwitz). We already understood what that meant.

During the month of Tammuz (July), 1942 I received a last letter from Klobuck, from my mother, and she wrote:

"My dear son, I write you a letter today, possibly the last letter, because everybody from Klobuck has already been deported. There was an attack (action) during the night on the shtetl, and all of the Jews were dragged to the train. Your father was among them (taken away). Your brother was also taken away to a camp, I think. I can not write anything more precise, because I don't know. Stay well, and hopefully we will meet as soon as possible at home..."

No return address, no signature. I only recognized my mother's delicate handwriting, with which she wrote this last letter.

The camp inmates from Klobuck who learned that I received a letter, came to me, and I read them the letter. Everybody wept silently. We did not know what to do. Each of us felt that everything was lost. Until now, we had parents, some of us were married with children, had family, a home to which we all hoped to be able to go back to once the war ended... And now it was the end of everything.

I took the letter again and read it from all its sides. I saw from the postage stamp that it was posted in Dzia☐oszyn[2] (Jaloshin). I couldn't calm down; Why was my mother was in Dzia☐oszyn? I kept the letter as a treasure. Unfortunately I could not keep this letter for a long time.

The encounter with my brother in a camp.

In October we received the order to move to another camp. We didn't know where we were being sent. The following morning we did not go to work. We were ordered to pack up and we were marched to the train. Again, we travelled in an unknown direction. Around 2 pm we arrived at a small train station. We saw a sign board with black printed letters: Markstatt. From the train station we were marched into the camp.

[Page 270]

As we arrived in the new camp, I met a friend from Klobuck, with whom I was in the first camp, Eichenthal. I learned from him that my brother was here. I could not leave my place, and I asked my friend to go and call my brother. He left and brought back my brother. We were standing 5 meters apart. We were separated in different barracks. When it came my turn, I asked that I be assigned to the same barracks with my brother. I don't know what effect it had on the block Elders, but they put me with my brother in the same room.

After the full inspection, that lasted two hours, I reunited with my brother. We hugged and kissed and we could not separate from each other, having been separated for two years. I was eager to know what happened with my parents.

We received one bed, my brother slept on the upper level, I slept in the lower level. It was a two level bed. My brother told me everything, and how the deportation occurred. All of the Jews from the shtetl were gathered together, including the children and the old people. The people who could work were taken to a camp, the other ones were taken to the train. We were almost sure that they were deported to Oswiecim (Auschwitz). We stayed awake all night and he told me everything.

He told me how once my mother went to the committee (Judenrat) and broke all the windows, because the committee had promised that people would come back from the camp after two months. Almost two years had gone by and no one had come back. Rejoiced to be with my brother, we went every day to the hard work. We did not receive any more letters from anybody. Also there were no more parcels from anyone. The food in camp became worse and worse. Thus, we worked from October 1942 until March 1943.

[Page 271]

The mutual brotherhood help from the persecuted Jews.

One day in March I became very feeble. Although I couldn't work, I had to go out to work because I didn't have fever -- but I couldn't move and I could not feel my limbs. I was indifferent to everything, my life was not worth anything anymore. I had lost all hope. The German supervisor beat me severely, accusing me of being a "saboteur", because I didn't want to work for the "Deutschen Sieg" (German victory). I remained lying all day in a closet, with a few other Jews who couldn't work.

At the end of the day when everybody returned to the camp from work, the other Jews carried us four people on their shoulders and brought us back to the camp.

My brother waited for me every day at the camp gate, because he returned half an hour earlier than I, since his workplace was closer to the camp. He saw that I was being dragged, almost as if I was dead, and he did not know what he could do for me. All of the people who were brought back as sick were immediately brought to the "sick rooms". There were special blocks for the sick people, and from there every week sick people were sent to Oswiecim (Auschwitz). They called it being sent to "recovery". Not one of them saw the world again.

In the block for sick people, we all received a meal with a portion of bread. My brother also brought me his own bread portion to eat, so I could regain my strength. After a few pieces of bread, I immediately felt vigorous and normal. My brother advised me to go back to my barracks, because it was dangerous to stay in the rooms with the sick people; very often sick people were "sent away" from there. I couldn't yet walk on my feet.

There were approximately 150 sick people. Every day new sick people were brought to the infirmary, -- those who could not work anymore; had swollen feet, or with injuries that did not heal because of the bad food and difficult work. (In a short time) we

[Page 272]

were 300 men, comprising of Jews from various villages, young and old. We were sent to Brand during the month of March in the year 1943.

We all wept during the journey. We were saying goodbye to the world of the living. Almost all of us were young men between 15 and 40 years old. After a few hours of travel, we arrived in the camp named Brand. There we were "welcomed" with sticks and blows from murderous hands. Those of us who couldn't walk by ourselves were immediately thrown into special barracks where their fate was sealed. Those who could walk by themselves were divided in group of 39 men per barrack room, with three level beds and more. We received food and bread, clothes to change into, and a small piece of soap on which was written "RJF" (Reine Juden Fett)[3].

After ten days in the camp, our strength returned to us. Every day there was a roll call of the healthy ones. At 8 o'clock in the morning we showed up in rows of three. We had to be clean, shaved with a short hair cut, our clothes not torn and shined shoes. Under our nails had to be clean, and our pockets empty, except for a handkerchief, and no cigarettes (were permitted) whatsoever. The handkerchief had to be clean; it could be a piece of rag (schmate), but a clean one. The roll call lasted two to three hours. It did not matter if it rained or snowed, or even if it was in the greatest cold.

*

Since I was sick I was lying in one of the sick person rooms. I felt "happy", because I didn't have to stay outdoors for so many hours. The healthy people didn't have the right to enter the sick person block. The healthy persons (those who recovered) worked only inside the camp which was a rally camp (for the sick people) from all the camps. The sick people from this camp were sent to Oswiecim (Auschwitz).

We also had a Jewish Elder, like the other camps. The Jewish Elder had somewhat better relations with the people since he dealt only with sick people. The Jewish Elder was allowed to visit the sick people. He came every day. One day, he came in our room, where 39 people were lying. He spoke to each of us separately and asked us: "Who of you wanted to stand up and join the healthy people?"

[Page 273]

It was understandable that we believed it was better to rest, having suffered two and half years of hard labor, rather than again subject our bodies to the German blows, and return to forced labor. But the Jewish Elder told us that in several days the SS would come, and will send all of the sick people to Oswiecim (Auschwitz). Every person who remained in bed, would be registered and sent away.

We didn't consider the issue for a long time, and we reported to the Jewish Elder that tomorrow morning we would appear at the roll call and we would remain among the healthy persons. The Jewish Elder immediately sent us clothes, trousers, jackets, shoes and socks and other various things. While we were sick, we only had the clothes we wore, and not even a pair of shoes.

The next morning, we all stood straight at the roll call. We stood in rows of three, and we attentively were observed by the Germans. We stood this way every day. In the afternoon, all of the healthy prisoners had to work in the camp. I was unable to do the difficult work, so I got beaten by a German soldier. He beat me on the head with the handle of a shovel, and as I protected my face with my hand I received a severe blow on my left hand; the bone was immediately broken.

I could not move my fingers and I went in the ambulance to the doctor, who treated the sick people. I told him the whole story about my hand. He examined me and diagnosed that my hand was broken. They had to put my hand in gypsum. The doctor, about 45 years old, was a French Jew, and he like us, the Polish Jews, was locked up in the camp.

With no choice, I let my hand be set with gypsum, and a sling around my shoulders held my hand. I was immediately registered as sick, and every day I could be sent away to Oswiecim (Auschwitz). I had no other choice.

[Page 274]

The next morning I did not go to the roll call.

One day in April 1943, we were notified that on the following day the "Sturmbannführer" (major) from the German SS would come, and that he ordered a roll call. All the prisoners found lying in the "sick rooms" would be sent away to Oswiecim (Auschwitz). Of course it was better to have as many healthy persons as possible, and as few sick persons as possible. Not knowing what to do, I ran to the doctor and asked him for his advice, because I didn't want to be sent to Auschwitz.

The doctor, a person of feeling and compassion, because he was imprisoned like all of us, told me that tomorrow, when the SS came, I should go out with the healthy persons, with my hand without the sling around my shoulder, stand straight with my hands along my body and nobody would pay attention. I thanked the doctor and left his room.

The next day in the morning everybody was pushed out of the rooms. We were told that everything had to be clean, because a controller was coming. We already knew who was going to come; we nicknamed him "the angel of death". About 400 men stood in rows. Everybody was shaved and clean, as if it was a great holiday for us. I stood in the middle of everybody, with my broken hand. My heart was beating like a heavy hammer. Thoughts knocked around my head: either I stay among the living, or among those who would be sent away to die.

We stood from 8 o'clock until 11. I watched the SS man; he was a man around 50 years old, and limped slightly from one foot. Slowly by slowly he came in front of me, escorted by a German, the Jewish Elder and the Jewish doctor. All the ones who didn't look good, and all the ones who displeased the SS where taken out of the row. He looked at me and asked the doctor, "what happened to him?" The doctor said "in about 10 days, I can go back to work." "If you lie ,doctor, you will go to Auschwitz" the SS man grumbled. The doctor snapped his heels, like a soldier in front of a general, and shouted with a frightened voice "Jawohl"! (Yes Sir).

The Jews' murderer made a list of about 200 sick people and ordered the Germans: "All of the sick people I chose put in one barrack". During the night we heard cars coming by. We saw through the window long carts with horses parked in front the barrack of the sick people. At about 2 o'clock in the morning, the door of the barrack was opened and all of the sick people were ordered to climb into the carts. Those who could not climb in were thrown inside like a potato bag, one on top of the other.

[Page 275]

The cries and the shouting filled the entire camp. The Germans shouted: "any one who is not silent, will get shot". It did not help, not the shouting, nor the blows. The people knew that they were being sent to Auschwitz. The carts with the heavy horses moved slowly out of the camp, one after the other.

A camp: a "paradise"

The night ended. Again we heard shouting: "Everyone out of the beds, stand up, straighten the beds, polish your shoes, in one hour outside to the roll call!"

We came out into the big square. Looking at the sick people block, we didn't see any of the sick people, everything was empty. Everybody knew what had happened, but everyone was afraid to ask anything about the sick people. During the roll call a German civilian showed up, he was the camp commander. He asked who among you want to go outside to work. My hand felt better, I made a step forward and I registered to work outside. About twenty men also took a step forward. The German shouted that he needed thirty people. Another ten people stepped forward. We were now thirty men standing one step ahead, three in a row.

At the gate a civilian truck was waiting for us. We passed through the gate, escorted by two Germans, and we drove in the direction of the train station. On a side track there was a wagon full of coal, needed to be unload. The Germans told us that when we finished unloading the coal we would return to the camp.

Across from us, about twenty meters away, a closed carriage stood by, on which was written Oswiecim (Auschwitz). From inside of the carriage we heard weeping, we understood immediately where these people came from – from the sick block.

[Page 276]

We couldn't believe that they could pack two hundred men in one carriage. The carriage stood in the Brand train station, closed and locked up. How these young men souls exhaled and how they suffocated together. This happened in March 1943.

One morning, during the roll call, we were asked who wanted to be sent away to work. I stepped out as the first one. A few others did the same. The number of candidates to go away increased, we were thirty five Jews, all young men between twenty and thirty years old. We were soon registered. We receive bread, double ration, also clothes, shoes, trousers. We got everything in double, towel, shaver.

In the afternoon, the thirty five persons who registered were called to depart. In front of the camp, at the gate, waited a truck with two soldiers serving as escorts. We drove in an unknown direction. We drove through Breslau (Wroclaw). A few kilometers after Breslau, we came to a warehouse of the "Deutscher Luftwaffe" (German Air Force), and inside the warehouse was a smaller camp, enclosed like all other camps. It was a Jewish camp with a Jewish Elder. The place was called Gintebrick.

The two German soldiers ordered us: "fast, step down from the truck!"

We arranged ourselves in three rows. A German civilian, about 40 years old, with a big belly, showed up. He called the Jewish Elder. Everyone was inspected by the German. The two German soldiers turned us over to the civilian and said that the Jews had been in the sick person camp at Brand. All of them were sick, but now they are again healthy and able to work. The two soldiers saluted the civilian with a "Heil Hitler" and went away.

We were received by the Jewish Elder. The whole camp consisted of one barrack with four rooms. The total number of Jewish inmates was around eighty. We were well received, and with great compassion from the other Jews because we were sick. The majority of the Jews in the camp were young men from Poland: Upper Silesia, B dzin, Sosnowiec, Dombrowe and from the surrounding towns. We, the thirty five new comers, were also from various villages around Poland. I was the only one from Klobuck.

[Page 277]

We were divided among four rooms and received a double food ration. The next morning, we went out to work. The work was not far from the camp. Everyone was courteous. There was no shouting at the Jews, nobody was beaten, everybody was obedient. There was more or less enough food, at least more than in the other camps. We received clean clothes every Saturday. We almost weren't watched. Only one German soldier sat at the gate, without a rifle, but he always kept the gate locked. The whole camp was inside a bigger area that belonged to the "Deutscher Luftwaffe" (German Air Force). Our work was to load and unload trucks with various military goods. The work was not too difficult.

We woke up at 6:00AM. We got breakfast and we walked a few steps to go to work. We worked from 7:00AM until 12:00. The hour from 12:00 to 01:00PM was lunch time . We went back to the camp to have the lunch. We received a fresh soup. I must say that the food was cooked cleanly. Afterwards we worked from 01:00PM until 04:00PM. From 04:00PM we had free time, and we could lie and rest.

During June, 1943 it was announced that the camp would be closed and the first thirty five men who came in would have to go away. The Jewish Elder finalized a list of the thirty people to be sent away. I was on the list. We had to pack, and I together with the 30 other people, did not go to work. We received clothes, trousers and a shaver. In the afternoon we went out to the big square with our packages. A military truck stood In front of the gate.

Again we travelled to an unknown location, nobody knew where. Our fate was in the German hands. After a two hour journey we arrived in Gerlitz and stopped in a big square. In the place there was a car factory. Not far away from there, were three long barracks with Jews.

We were received by an old German man. He arranged us in rows. Soon the German guard showed up with the Jewish Elder of the camp. He told us that this was a new camp, and that if we were good workers and behaved ourselves, he would be good to us.

We marched inside the camp. The Jewish Elder registered us, and we received food. In the entire camp there were only fifty Jews. During the following days new additional groups of Jews came, with the total number was three hundred Jews, all of them young people.

The construction work and the plumbing were shared every day by seventy, fifty and thirty people per group and other smaller groups. The work was conducted inside the camp, where there was a factory. We were enclosed twice, once by the camp and once by the factory. In the camp there were also Russian, French, Polish workers and workers, from other nationalities. All of them were prisoners of wars. Thus we worked hard and had bitter life from June 1943 to March 1944.

Again there was an order that tomorrow we weren't going out to work. We all go away to another camp. We stayed in the Reich AutoBahn (German Highways) camp until March, 1944, a forced labor camp. In March 1944 onward we were in the K. Z. camps, (Konzentrationslager Katzet[4]) concentration camps.

The penultimate stage of the events taken place before the effective liquidation of the camps.

March 1944

Again we were sent to an unknown location. We drove for about 3 hours until we came to a forest, to a gate to an area enclosed with barbed wire. Every four meters a sign was posted: "high voltage!" There were two rows of barbed wire, and between them armed German soldiers were on patrol.

We arranged ourselves in rows of three, with our "baggage" in hand. The Jewish Elder came out with a stick in his hand. He wore a "prisoner suit", of blue and white stripes with a triangle sewn on his breast; the triangle was red and had a serial number on it. We were counted and anyone who did not stand straight or moved his head immediately received a blow from the stick on his head.

Amidst blows and shouting from the Jewish Elder, and rushing out of fear, we were pushed inside the camp. The blocks were empty. We marched inside one block, and the Jewish Elder gave an order: undress and put your clothes aside.

[Page 279]

We received prisoner clothes: underwear, a shirt, trousers, a jacket, a round hat, a pair of shoes and a pair of socks.

Hairdressers showed up. Everyone had their head shaved except for a strip (in the middle) of two fingers wide. We were ordered to stand in a row, and everyone received a serial number. My serial number was 19266. The belongings we brought from the former camp were taken away from us. Everyone received the same clothes, without any exception. We were divided into groups of 90 men per block, with three stories beds. The floor was concrete. Everyone received a straw bag with two blankets. We all looked alike, like we were disguised.

The next morning we marched to the roll call square. We stood five in a row. We were counted, there were about 1230 men. We were divided into groups, received bread and black coffee and escorted by armed guards, we were marched to work. After about an hour we arrived at the work place.

We were inside a forest where entire blocks were being constructed. In the forest there was an armament camp. Thus we worked every day in the camp. Our work was hard and bitter.

Here in this camp we felt our insignificance. Whoever died was not buried, like in the other camps. There the dead were buried in a wooden coffin, not far from the camp. In the K. Z. camp, where we were, all the dead bodies were sent to Gross-Rosen to be incinerated. Our camp was a part of Gross-Rosen, where people were incinerated in several furnaces.

From March, 1944, when we entered the K. Z. camp, we were not called Jews anymore, but "prisoners", or "detainees". When one of us had fever, he did not have to go outside to work. Every day there were a few hundred sick people, who became candidates for the Gross-Rosen furnaces. In May, 1944 a transport from Oswiecim (Auschwitz) arrived, about 800 men, and they told us about the atrocities that occurred there. We could not believe their stories. We suffered through many troubles, but compared to what they told us, we remained congealed like fish in water.

[Page 280]

The attitude of the civilian workers on the construction site changed. We became aware that the war was not going as well for the Germans as it had when the war started. We learned about the great setback of the German on the west front from the civilian workers who worked with us. Every day complaints were heard that the war could end anytime. The belief that any day we could be free gave us courage to survive. Construction materials started to be in short supply. Also due to various reasons, the work was interrupted.

Thus we lived throughout the summer, 1944, with the joyful hope that the war was going to end. Often there were alarms. The sirens started to sound. The lights were turned off, sometimes for an hour or even more. We stayed inside the barracks during the alarms. We also heard the noise of the airplanes, full squadrons. We knew that they were the airplanes of our liberators, who flew to bomb Berlin.

The summer went by. The winter came. We did not have any winter clothes. Almost every day the sirens were blowing. The German towns were being bombed more and more. During the alarms, for security reasons, we remained in the camp, without going out to work for many days. Thus we lived in hardship and cold weather until February 9th, 1945.

February 9th, 1945 at 7:00 AM, during the morning call, the healthy people were put on one side, and the sick ones on another side. The healthy ones received the order to pack because they had to leave the camp. The Russian Army was 20 kilometers away from the camp. The sick ones were ordered to stay.

Nobody really wanted to move, thinking it was better to stay in place for a few hours until the Red Army arrived. About 200 sick and feeble people stayed.

Simultaneously we realized that the Germans were burying something in the ground at the four corners of the camp. We understood that at the last minute they were going to blow up the camp together with all of the sick people. We struggled with our thoughts and dilemma - leave the camp or stay with the prospect of being freed and helped. But in the end we had to follow the order.

[Page 281]

The bestial means the Germans used to kill the last inmates in the camp

After we received a half loaf of bread and some margarine, about 1000 people marched away from the camp, escorted by armed Germans on all sides. Our hope, to set ourselves free after four and one-half years of being enslaved, was beyond description. During all the time that we were imprisoned, we never had been so close to freedom. It was like hanging on to life, until the last moment, because we already knew that the Red Army was only 20 kilometers away and behind us.

We marched farther and farther and received very little to eat. Days passed; we were lead away hungry, without rest for even a moment because the Red Army was behind us. The Germans dragged us this way for days after days. The people who stopped and could not march anymore were taken aside to a field and shot.

Together with us, German civilians ran away because they feared the Russians. The Germans ran away with horses and carts, and with their young children. At night we slept sometimes in the fields, sometimes in a shed. We did not wash for weeks. We wandered from February 9th until April 4th when we arrived in Buchenwald.

We arrived at 2:00 PM in the camp. We were sent to the wash room where we waited until 7:00 PM. We were told that we were going to have a shower. We had a look at the camp barracks, which were spread over a very large area. At that time there were about 70,000 men in the camp: Jews, Russians, Gypsies, Englishmen, Finnish, Belgians, Dutchmen, Norwegians, Italians, and Spaniards etc...

[Page 282]

We did not have a shower. We saw that in a barrack naked people stood, enwrapped in a blanket. Everything was taken away from them, and they did not get clothes. Three thousand Jews were standing barefoot on the concrete. During the same time, Jews from all of the other barracks were pushed outside. There were already five thousand Jews gathered outside. Nobody knew what our fate would be now.

The prisoners from the other nations were let back into the barracks. Only the Jews were gathered under the open sky. Most of the Jews that were pushed outside were those who were in the barracks with the Poles.

We were in Buchenwald under the open sky, staying that way from April 4th until April 9th, five days without receiving any food to eat. Every night many airplane squadrons flew above our heads. We prayed that they would drop a bomb on us. We would rather die than suffer so much from cold and hunger, or die from a German bullet. Unfortunately our prayer was not fulfilled.

The number of dead people was growing. There was a mountain of dead bodies close to the crematorium that were not incinerated during the last few days. The living took the clothes from the dead to wear for themselves in order to get some warmth. People became insane from hunger. They cut the ears of the dead people to satisfy their hunger. Some people hid between the dead during the night to get some warmth. Some hid between the dead not to be dragged again. There were rumors that we would have to walk again during the coming months. There were tragic scenes when the persecuted people recognized a family member among the dead. The vast majority of dead people were Jews.

Shabbat morning, 9 April 1945, we again were arranged five in a row, and guarded on both sides by Ukrainians, with big German shepherd dogs. Those who didn't stand straight were attacked by the unleashed, wild dogs, that jumped on them, and brought them down by their trousers and biting. We were counted. I heard that we were about 4,500 Jews. We were divided into three transports: 1,500, 1,650 and the third one about 1,350. I was in the second transport with 1,650 Jews.

[Page 283]

We marched out of Buchenwald, without receiving any food or water whatsoever. We were almost barefoot, with no shoes. For months we didn't wash our clothes. We walked out of the camp. Dead bodies were lying on both sides of the road. These were people who were on the first transport, the one that preceded our transport. They were shot. In our transport, the shooting continued.

Those who didn't march straight or those who looked inside the woods, thinking to escape, were immediately shot. Every day 40 to 50 Jews were shot. Our transport dwindled every day. Around 100 Ukrainian SS men and 10 big German shepherd dogs were guarding us. The dogs kept biting and the "dogs" with two feet kept shooting. While we walked, the weapons were firing. During the night we were lying in the fields guarded by a dog.

We marched about two weeks. On April 22nd 1945 we arrived in the Flossenburg camp. Out of the 1,650 Jews at the start of the march, only 800 Jews remained alive. We thought that we would stay in this camp. But after a few hours we left the Flossenburg camp. We were again gathered, and counted. We were only 750. Some were kept in the camp.

We marched away from the camp. We were shot like animals in the forest. Every day we were fewer and fewer. Also the Ukrainian guards became fewer. They fled from us every day. At last, we received a piece of bread and some water.

It was April 25th only 500 Jews were left. Every minute seemed like a year' we couldn't see the end. Thus the days went by. On April 29th only 200 men were left. The murderers shot 70-80 Jews every day. The weapons worked all day long. On April 30th only 150 Jews were left... May 1st, May 2nd the number of people who remained alive diminished. We were less than 110 and still not freed... We witnessed how the Germans shot 1,500 Jews during 4 weeks. Those thoughts didn't let us rest...

We marched again and carried the German murders' bags, in each of which there were civilian clothes, which they intended to use to escape.

[Page 284]

Thus we walked between fields and forests, between two Ukrainian bandits who were watching us. There was a rumor: "tomorrow May 3rd there was nowhere else to go. During the night we will stay in a village, and the next morning each SS man will take 3 or 4 Jews in the woods and kill them. Then the transport would be over. Every soldier will change from military to civilian clothes and will no longer be a soldier". One of us over heard this rumor from two SS men. He stood still, without showing any interest to what they said.

We went into a peasant's house and we were locked up with 5 bandits, who guarded us with weapons. Our friend, who heard the conversation between the two Ukrainian mass murderers, told us what was going to happen tomorrow... We decided that we had to escape, no matter what happened. We didn't sleep the entire night, thinking only how we would escape.

It was dawn. We heard one SS man asking the other SS man what time is was. We heard the answer: "4:30 AM, we will stay here for another half hour". We saw the daylight coming through the cracks, and decided to break open the door, and that anyone who wanted to should flee. We decided not to run out together in case they will fire their weapons at us, and to shoot all of us to prevent us from fleeing. We spread out as wide as we could on the sides.

Without thinking, with a friend I opened the door, and with the speed of lightning we ran out, not knowing where. My friend took a blanket and he threw it over the SS man standing in front of the door, and pushed him to the ground. I even didn't pay attention what was on the floor, I stepped on him ran away. Thus we 11 Jews escaped. The remaining ones were all shot in the morning. One of us was slightly wounded, but without paying attention to his wound, he continued running. The two Jews running in front of me thought that I was chasing them and I thought that the two Jews that were running behind me were chasing me. Five of us arrived at the edge of the woods and felt free...

Translator's Footnotes

1. The river Neisse is part of the post 1945 border between Germany and Poland known as The Oder-Neisse border

2. Dzia□oszyn is about 20 kilometers north of Klobuck

3. Pure Jewish Fat

4. Katzet abbreviation for Konzentrationslager

[Page 285]

Attempts at Resistance in the Camps

The Work of the Tailors Workshop

by Moshe Fajga

Translated by Gloria Berkenstat Freund

We entered the Blechhammer camp at night. A group was selected to be sent to Annaberg. I joined the group that consisted of 30 people. I was in Annaberg for about two months together with Lev Mendelowicz, my nephew. We often spoke about our situation and came to the conclusion that we had nothing to lose. If a transport was selected, we would be included. Perhaps we would meet someone in our family. A transport actually was selected almost immediately and we went with it. We were sent to Kletendorf; we met Jews there from the Klobuck camp.

The Klobuckers were considered dangerous people. They were denounced as wanting to escape. Berish, the *judenelterster* [Jew chosen by the Germans as the camp inmate leader], placed all of them in one barrack and at night they were locked in. The Jew who denounced them regretted his denunciation, but he could not change things.

When I entered the camp, I immediately was warned that I should say that I am from Lodz and not from Klobuck; I answered that I actually was from Lodz. I had lived a considerable number of years in Lodz.

A roll call took place every morning. Several men were called to work in the iron camp. It was difficult for me to carry iron bars. I turned to the *judenelterster* and said that I could not carry any iron with my broken foot. He told this to the *kapo* [trustee]; he ordered me to stand in the wagon and pass the iron, but I also could not do this. In addition, I walked several kilometers

[Page 286]

to work. Working with me were Pinkhas Niedziela and Lewkowicz. By chance, my situation improved. Mordekhai Frenk once came to me and asked that I make a pair of pants for him. I answered that if the *meister* [mastercraftsman] in the workshop would permit me to do so I would sew the pants. The meister permitted me to do so. When he saw that I could work, he told me to put aside the pants and ordered me to sew for the work leader. This is how I began to work in the tailors workshop. In the morning I went to work with all of the camp inmates. At night I went to work in the workshop. For my work I received enough to eat. I divided it with Lev Mendelowicz, my nephew. In the end, I was taken on permanently to work in the workshop.

*

I received a bit of news from Blechhammer that all of the boys were murdered there. I did not want to tell that to Lev, that his brother, Chaskel, was no longer alive.

Another transport was sent from our camp. I was not successful in keeping Lev with me. He said to me: "Uncle Moshe, do not worry, fate is taking me. Perhaps I will find someone in the camp, my mother, father or my sisters." After the last transport only 130 remained of 700 people in our camp.

It was not bad for me in Kletendorf. I worked for the quartermaster; we organized a secret group and established contact with two Breslauer quartermasters; the second one was called *Zeydele* [little grandfather] - an old Social Democrat. They told us that if a malicious edict were issued against us, they would come to our aid; they would set a barrack on fire. That would be a sign that we needed to escape.

Not far from us was a camp, Markshtadt. The camp was liquidated and the people and their *kapos* - Leibele Bosak and Hershl Muk, both Bedzin louts - were sent to us. The group of artisans, shoemakers, tailors, laundrymen who were employed in the workshops informed the *judenelterster* that they would take revenge

[Page 287]

against the unfamiliar *kapos* who beat our brothers. He answered us: "Do it, I know of nothing." We beat the *kapos*. They ran and complained to the *wache* [guard] and then met the Germans with whom we had a connection. The *kapos* received blows from them and they were sent away with a transport a few days later.

In the Torture Camp (*Katzet* [Nazi Concentration Camp])

The S.S. men surrounded the camp during the month of October. We were sent to the Waldenburg camp. There, everyone had to undress completely and instead of our own clothes, we received paper bags. They took everything I had with me. The blows I received did not matter to me; neither did the clothes that were taken from me, only that they took the photographs of my wife and child. Because of this I was completely dejected. There was not a great deal of time to think in the *katzet*. We went to work.

Those who were last were beaten with rifle butts by the guards. We worked very hard. When Shramer [possibly Schramel], the camp leader, came to the construction job, he would take a brick and hit someone in the head. When blood flowed, he asked him, who did this to you, when the victim answered that he did not know, the murderer laughed and went away satisfied.

When we arrived in the camp, Schramel, the camp leader, told us to fall. We fell with our faces in the snow. He ordered us to stand up and again fall and we lay like this for a long time and he pressed our heads into the snow with his heavy-booted feet. Then he ordered us to stand up and to fall on our backs. Thus the torturing was constantly repeated. There was no day and night. We had to toil without food and without sleep.

[Page 288]

He brought in "prizes" that were the greatest misfortune for a person. The prize consisted of a watery lunch and five cigarettes. There were passionate smokers. They gave away their piece of bread for the entire day for one cigarette. The people became swollen from not eating. The miracle was that it already was close to the liberation.

A friend came to me and said: he did not know what to do; he had succeeded in "arranging" a little chopped straw with bran that he had taken out of the horse sacks while they were eating. He took a can of water and set this to cook and now he had to leave it and return to the camp. He could not find a solution; they were having the roll call and they would see that one was missing. If they caught him, things would be miserable. I advised my friend that he forget about the food and go to the camp.

We were afraid that we would be sent away with a transport because we had heard that they were murdering those on the transports along the way. It was said that the Russians were nearby. We would survive the hardships and live to see the liberation.

On the 4th of May the camp leader came to the electrified entrance. He threw the keys into us and said that the *judeneltester* would soon tell us everything and the Germans escaped along with the "guard" who watched over us at the electrified wire.

This was on the 5th of May. At a quarter after four, the chief *kapo* gathered 30 of us men. I broke into the middle. He told us that the *oberscharfurher* [senior squad leader] had been good to the Jews and that we would take him into the camp and hide him. He lived in a wagon room not far from the camp.

I turned to the tortured men: Comrades, the camp leader and the "guard" are not here; do not be afraid of the chief *kapo*, Berek from Jaworzno.

I tore off my black shirt that once had been white. I made a white flag out of it that I placed on a stick. I went in front. The camp prisoners followed behind me. The kapo trembled for his skin. The Russians came with tanks. A tank stopped. A member of the Red Army asked what kind of people were we? There was among us one who knew English, Spanish and Russian. He informed them that we were

[Page 289]

"concentration camp inmates." They threw us bread with chicken fat and traveled on. Men immediately ran into the streets. The Germans, the great "heroes" had run away before the Russians [arrived] and had left everything unguarded.

The liberated prisoners entered the stores, quenched their thirst and returned to the camp. The food to which they were unaccustomed immediately was bad for their health. Many became ill, many died. I escaped right away. I took a bicycle from the Germans and rode to Breslau.

In Breslau I met a friend of mine and he told me that he had a room and that I should live with him because it was impossible to travel to Czenstochow. I accepted his invitation. In the morning I went out into the street and saw a sign with the inscription, "Committee of P.P.R."[1] I went into the committee and offered my cooperation. I received a rifle and, later, a revolver. Two Germans, Weiss and Frentsel, who declared themselves as communists showed me where the Nazis were hiding. I pulled them out of their hiding place and stilled my thirst for revenge.

We received food in the Soviet *stolowke* (canteen). I had no money. People began to conduct business. All of this did not matter to me. I protected the premises of the P.P.R. and searched for Nazi-Germans.

I met an acquaintance from Czenstochow; he delivered a greeting to me from my brother Fishl and sister. I wrote a letter to them. My brother came to me. I gave him the rifle. He took my place at the P.P.R. and I traveled to Czenstochow to see my sister, Leah, a cousin and a sister-in-law.

In Czenstochow I met a woman who with great difficulty took her five-year old child from the Poles. She became my wife.

[Page 290]

All of us - my sister, my wife, the cousin and sister-in-law - came back to Wroclaw [Polish name for Breslau] and we settled into an apartment together in the same house in which my brother Fishl lived. To him came Bluma Razin, Mendl Razin and Yakov Ahron Blau. Thus a homey environment was created.

A year after the war we learned that our brother Yankl was alive in Germany. We decided to travel to him. I occupied myself with Zionist activity in Germany and in 1948 I came to Eretz-Yisroel.

Translator's Footnote

1. *Polska Partia Robotnicza* - Polish Workers Party (Communists)

[Page 290]

In a German Camp with Members
of the Klobuck *Judenrat* [Jewish council]

by Fishl Fajga

Translated from Yiddish to English by Asher Szmulewicz

Before we were sent from Klobuck to Germany, two members of the Judenrat: Yaacov Chade and Benzion Szwiertszewski, were brought to us at the gathering place, in the courtyard of the Skorupa[1]. In the ghetto there were a few Jews who were jealous of the success (special treatment) of the Judenrat members, and they bypassed the Judenrat, and had direct contact with the Gendarmerie (country police). With presents of boots, suits and money, these Jews "bought" the Gendarmes (county policemen). The Judenrat members wanted to prevent "private people" from having (direct) relations with the Germans. The Gendarmes resented the Judenrat members, who meddled in their business; therefore, they arrested Yaacov Chade and Benzion Szwiertszewski, and sent them away together with the other Jews.

The Gendarmes did not forget the Jews who gave them presents. They were taken out of the rows as "useful Jews". The majority of them were craftsman, tailors, shoemakers, tinsmiths, watchmakers and others. They were immediately set free.

From Klobuck we were sent to Germany, separated in two groups: the bigger group, in which I belonged, was sent to Sakra (Germany). The Klobuckers, including myself, were installed in three rooms. Among us also were the two Judenrat members: Yaacov Chade and Benzion Szwiertszewski. Shlomo Unglick, Hershl Szperling's son in law, wanted to take revenge against the Judenrat members, because of the persecution they inflicted on his father in law.

[Page 291]

One day Shlomo Unglick brought the mail for the camp's Jewish inmates. There was a letter addressed to the two Judenrat members. Shlomo took the letter and later read it in front of all of the Klobucker camp inmates. In this letter, the secretary of the remaining Judenrat in Klobuck, wrote: "do not worry, I will soon bring you home. Jasne will be in Sosnowiec this week, and everything will be arranged. It is a pity that you were not in Klobuck when Hershl Szperling was expelled from his apartment, and put in a cellar with water up to his knees". The letter was signed by Davtshe Diament, the secretary of the Judenrat.

After reading the letter, Shlomo Unglick shouted again that he would take his revenge; whatever he was able to do, he would do. A few days later a taxi came with Gestapo people, and they called for Chade and Szwiertszewski. They were accused of being communists. The former Judenrat members answered that they were loyal people, and with their identification papers, they showed that they were Judenrat members. The Gestapo people wondered: "How did you get here?" They answered that they were brought with the other Jews into the camp, and then they were detained. It did not take long, and the two Judenrat members were sent back to Klobuck.

Among us was the Klobucker, Kapel Zaks. One day he was sent away from the camp. Before his departure he said: "friends, I was torn away from Klobuck, and I am being sent to another camp. I beg of you one thing: Those of you who will survive the war, if one of the Judenrat members is still alive, take revenge, for my uncle, Israel Lewkowicz, take revenge for him. With the words: "take care", he bitterly wept.

From Sakra we were sent to Birkenheim and from Birkenheim to Sarne.

[Page 292]

In the transport there were a few people from Klobuck: Baruch Azjner, Pinchas Unglick, Shlomo Unglick and others; we were about 500 men. In Gross Sarne was the well-known murderer, Salek Maler, and the German watchmaster, Pietshak, who also was not a small murderer. Salek Maler choose eight Jews, including me, to be room elders. I was assigned to the room number 4. In my room were people from Klobuck, Krzepice, Miedzno and Dzialozyn.

Once, late in the evening the watchmaster, Pietshak, and the Juden Elder, Maler, came into our room. Baruch Azjner shouted: "Beware". Everybody stood up. Baruch reported: "Room number 4 includes 50 men. I was resting in bed, being allowed to stay in bed as a room elder. The watchmaster counted the men, and one man was missing. There were only 49 men. As a punishment, the men were put in 2 rows, face to face, and they had to hit one another in the face until they bled. It turned out that two brothers, Pinchas and Shlomo Unglick, stood face to face from each other, and they had to hit each other until they bled, and they could not stop before then. That night remained very clear in my memory.

After that we walked 15 kilometers to go to work. We started when it was still dark outside. The watchmaster came with his dog and chased us. We ran kilometers with wooden shoes in deep snow, one after the other. Yehoshua Rosenczweig ran and fell, and could not stand up again. We brought him back to the camp dead. People fainted and fell: one from Klobuck, Zilberberg and one from Dzialozyn. We dragged them with us, but on the way Pietshak shot them.

The tragic encounter of a father and a son

A few days later we were sent out of Gross-Maselewicz. In the train carriages we met Jews from other camps. But it was forbidden to sit together with the other Jews. Suddenly we heard a cry: "Daddy!" Pinchas Unglick's son jumped with a cry to his father. They had not seen each other for three years.

The watchmaster allowed them to sit together. The discipline was not as strict as it was in the camp. But the separation of the son and father was so tragic.

[Page 293]

We were dropped off the train in Breslau, and the others Jews from the other camps remained on the train, and continued their journey. Pinchas Unglick met his son once more in the Direnfort camp. During the evacuation, Pinchas Unglick could not walk anymore, every Jew that stopped walking was immediately shot by the murderers. Since Pinchas' son saw that his father couldn't walk anymore, he did not leave his father alone, and then the Germans shot the father with his son.

A young man saved the life of dozens of Jews from Klobuck

I was sent again to Koliz to a "Katzet"[2] (concentration camp). There I found other people from Klobuck. In Koliz died: Shlomo Kurtzbard, Yehonatan's son, and my brother in law, Moshe Zelten.

Avraham Mass' son was also there. He worked in the kitchen, when he left Klobuck he was 15 or 16 years old. He kept dozens of Jews from Klobuck alive. He gave food to the feeble ones. Every night Jews stood by the window and shouted in the kitchen: "Leib Baruch give me a piece of food", and whatever he could, he gave them food. Out of the 20 men working in the kitchen, he was he only one to give extra food (to the Jews); the other ones gave blows. He sustained and kept many people alive.

Here comes the liberation

On February 21st 1945 the first Russian soldiers arrived, and they found only sick people in beds and lying on the floor. I remained sick for two months. I longed for my Jewish Klobuck, and I went back to Klobuck, even though I was still exhausted. I walked and also travelled a little bit in cars, when non-Jews took me along. I also went by train. The war was not completely over. After two months of wandering I arrived in Klobuck. I found only one Jew, Mrs. Rachel Leah Lapides. I spent one night in her house. The next morning I went into the streets, penniless and with a shameful face. A Pole took pity on me, and a second one asked me: "Czy jestece ¯yjesz?" (You are still alive?)

[Page 294]

I soon left Klobuck, and went immediately to Czestochowa, and from there back to Germany in a D. P. camp (Displaced Person camp)

There I learned that in the town of Bayreuth there were a few people from Klobuck. I moved to Bayreuth, and really found a few Klobucker Jews. There we organized the first Hazkarah (Remembrance ceremony) for the Jews from Klobuck in 1946.

Translator Footnotes

1. Polish word meaning crust (seems to be a name of a location in the shtetl)

2. Katzet abbreviation for Konzentrationslager

With Klobuckers in the Torture Camps

by Yitzhak Szperling

Translated by Gloria Berkenstat Freund

My brother and I worked in the Niederkirche camp building highways. It was a camp of 250 people from Klobuck, Krzepice and the area. We worked there for three months until the camp was abandoned and we were brought to Camp Markshtadt (Lower Silesia). There were 3,000 Jews located there.

We also worked hard there at various hard labor, building munitions factories.

In January 1943 we were sent to the *Funf Teichen* [Five Rivers] concentration camp, not far from Markshtadt, where the true suffering began: at four o'clock in the morning, winter in the greatest cold, we were chased into the street. We stood for hours until we left for work. We worked 12 hours a day; we endured various pain at the same work as at Markshtadt. During the same year, 1943, my brother, Ahron Meir, died in the camp. I did not even know what happened to his remains. I remained alone, lonely, not knowing about my family. I was in the camp with other Klobucker Jews.

[Page 295]

In 1944 I was sent with other Klobuckers to the Wieselburg camp. I worked there with the Klobockers: Lipa Birnbaum, Shlomo Birnbaum, Dovid Mass, Mordekhai Wajsman, Nehemia Wajsman.

We worked there breaking stones. The Germans, who guarded us, received their lunch from the military kitchen that was located three kilometers from the workplace. They ordered us to carry the empty casks back to the kitchen. I left to take the casks back to the kitchen. There was a warehouse of potatoes in the same barracks as the kitchen. I went into it and took a few potatoes in a small sack in order to quiet the long-lasting hunger for just a moment. Suddenly the cook, an *S.S.*-man, entered the warehouse and ordered me to pour out the potatoes. He locked the door and quickly returned with a bayonet. He stabbed me until the blood ran from me... Then he unlocked the door and told me to go out. In the street, he again beat me on the head with an iron bar. I ran a few meters and fell on the ground in a faint. The blood flowed from me.

I lay on the ground for a long time. When I gained a little consciousness, I stood up and began to drag myself to the workplace.

My comrades saw that I had not returned after such a long time; one comrade came to look for me. He met me on the way in such a state, when all of my things were covered in blood. He led me to the work place. My comrades gave me clothes to change into and after work took me into the camp. There was a commission in the camp that chose the weakest people and sent them to Oswiecim [Auschwitz]. "The selection" took place in the following manner: everyone stood in a row; each person had to run past the Germans. In this way they removed the weak, those who could not run. I was not in good condition as I ran, but through some miracle from God I went past their eyes and I entered the camp.

My comrade Lipa Birnbaum led me to the camp doctor. He gave me an injection and said that he had no

[Page 296]

place for me in the sick barracks and told to go the barracks in which I lived. I should return early in the morning.

The night was a nightmare for me. I could not find a place, not sitting and not standing, not lying down and not sleeping because of the wounds I had received from the murderer. I was going crazy until I finally saw the day. When the day began I went to the doctor. He sent me to the sick barracks.

I lay for two months and could not move from the spot. I did not receive any remedies to heal my wounds. Yet, I recovered a little. When I could stand on my feet, they sent us further.

We walked from the Wieselburg camp from early morning to late at night, across fields and woods. Late at night we arrived in a German village. We remained there overnight. In the morning we had to go further. We were taken to a second village. We remained there in an empty field in two large empty barns.

We all lay pressed together like herring. We were there for six days. Many died from hunger and cold.

After six days, we again wandered. We were taken to a train station, 15 kilometers [about nine miles] from the village. The Germans told us that whoever could not go further or felt weak could remain in the village.

I was not in a condition to go further, but I knew that they would finish [kill] those who remained in the village. I went further with my last strength until we arrived at the train station. There they packed us in a freight train in open cars up to 70 men in a car. We traveled like this in the frost and cold for several days and nights. Many died from hunger and cold on the way. The Germans threw the dead out at the station when the train stopped.

[Page 297]

We traveled through Czechoslovakia. The Czechs threw bread into the cars. The German murderers did not permit them to come close to us and whoever caught a piece of bread was lucky. One threw himself on another to catch a piece of bread.

After several days and nights of traveling we arrived in a concentration camp near Austria where our hell began. We arrived in the morning. The torturers stood us out in the snow and in the frost under the open sky until the middle of the next day. Many of us died of hunger and cold. They remained lying right on the spot. One of the tortured asked for a little water. The *kapo* [prisoner functionary – prisoner who performed administrative tasks] answered: You are about to die, so why do you still need water? The *kapos* with the rubber whips in their hands beat the unlucky ones who lay in the snow to see who was alive and who was dead. I did not believe that I would leave this *gehenim* [hell] and remain alive.

In the morning we were taken to the wash barracks where we bathed ourselves with cold water. Then they led us into the barracks where we were for two weeks, exposed to terrible pain, chased out half naked into the street every day. We stood in the snow and the greatest cold for hours.

After the two weeks we went out to work where we labored at building a tunnel in the mountain. We worked there for 12 hours a day and also at night. Returning to the camp, they chased us from one spot to another. We received 100 grams of dark bread to eat and a little water boiled with potato peels. These were the provisions for an entire 24 hours. There was no way to avoid the blows. There were dozens of dead every day; the people fell like flies. The crematoria in the camp burned day and night. This was a camp of 40,000 people of various nationalities. We were cut off from the open world. Several Klobucker Jews died there. Although I grew weaker from day to day, I held out until the liberation.

[Page 298]

This was on the 6th of May 1945, when the American military freed us. We did not want to believe our own eyes. I did not know what to do with my great joy. I was a living skeleton and could not stand on my feet. We all became ill when the Americans gave us food because we could no longer digest the food. Many died immediately after eating their fill. I slowly recovered and little by little began to return to being a person.

Savage Exploitation and Final Liquidation

by Yaacov Szmulewicz, Paris

Translated from Yiddish to English by his nephew Asher Szmulewicz

On November 11, 1940 we arrived in a camp named Eichental in the Alps region. The camp was located in a forest and was comprised of wooden barracks. It is worthwhile to give an accurate description of what it looked like, since it was one of the first German labor camps, that became a tomb for tens of thousands of Jews and non-Jews alike.

At the entrance of the camp the "watch-house" was situated, and further on the left was the kitchen and in the courtyard there was a bath, as well and other facilities. At first sight it was difficult to imagine that people would come into (the camp), but would not leave alive.

The barracks were not finished (and were barren). There were no amenities (beds or toilet facilities), and the bath did not operate. We slept on the bare floor and we washed ourselves (in the open air), subjected to the severest cold (and weather conditions) in the courtyard close to the well. There were thirty people in each barrack.

On arrival at the camp, everybody was given a small bowl, a spoon and a cup. Each person had to look after these utensils "like his own eyes", because if your utensils broke or disappeared, there were no replacements, and (lost utensils) also meant that food for the day was forfeited, and instead of food, 15 lashes on the lower back side were given. Everybody had to watch after his own kitchenware so that another camp mate could not steal it from him.

In the beginning we received food parcels from home. The mood among the camp prisoners was not that bad. Despite the harsh (circumstances and) regime we were joyful and even optimistic. During our free time we organized entertainments. However, the camp prisoners who left a wife or children at home were sad and in a depressed state of mind.

Our work was to build a highway. The year 1940 went by without any eventful shocks. The year 1941 started with special and cruel tortures for the prisoners. One day in January, all the prisoners were gathered on the "roll call square". In cold, windy and snowy weather we were forced to stand outside for 5 hours. A whistle was blown by Moshe Weissfelner from Klobuck, who was named as the representative of the Jews, in order to warn his comrades. The German "Truppenführer" (Commander) appeared and made the following announcement:

The sending of food parcels by Jews to Jewish detainees was dirtying the German trains. Therefore receiving (food) parcels was prohibited from then on.

That was the beginning of conditions getting worse and worse.

During the year 1942 the Germans liquidated all of the small camps in the Alps including Eichental. All the prisoners were concentrated (and sent) to a larger camp, named "Markstel – concentration camp Fünf Teichen" (five ponds). We referred to the concentration camp as "the hell", because in addition to the hard work we had, we were burned, roasted and tortured (and subjected to) all kind of mistreatment.. Two thousand Jews arrived at the "Fünf Teichen concentration camp", and after only one month we were reduced to only 1400 persons. Six hundred (of us) were murdered or died. Among the deceased were Jews from Klobuck like Berl Unglick and others.

The number of prisoners (sent to the camp) increased to the level of six thousand persons. People from various countries were sent. The number of prisoners (at the camp) was to remain constant. (As prisoners died), in place of the executed and tortured prisoners, the German brought in fresh victims. Not all the people died quickly. Weak people who could not work anymore but stayed alive were deported for a "healing" – on the orders of the SS – to Oswiecim (Auschwitz). In the transports to Auschwitz were Jews from Klobuck. I remember the following names: Shlomo Kurtzpartsis, Reuven Rosensweig, Pinchas and Reuven Klopak and Shmulik Szmulewicz.

In spite of all the problems, pain and destruction we always thought about our close relatives, who were left in Klobuck. Then the "Yov Bessoreh"[1] (terrible news) arrived in the camp, although I don't remember how:

On June 22, 1942 the Klobuck ghetto was liquidated.

We took the news very hard. During the liquidation of the ghetto, the Germans shot and killed with cruelty a great number of the Jews from Klobuck. They dragged them out from the shtetl. Sniffer dogs and local Germans[2] looked for people that went into hiding. A lot of people were bitten by the dogs. Other unfortunate Jews were forced to dig their own graves and then were shot dead. The small number of Jews from Klobuck who were still alive in the camp already knew that their home was destroyed, eradicated and wiped out.

Translator Footnotes

1. From Hebrew expression "Bessorat Yov" meaning very bad news, used to announce that somebody passed away.

2. Klobuck was located 17 kilometers from the German-Polish border in 1939, so German locals were not far away.

[Page 300]

Liquidation of the concentration camps and the Germanintention to exterminate the Jews who remained alive

by Yaacov Szmulewicz, Paris

Translated from Yiddish to English by his nephew Asher Szmulewicz

In the beginning of January 1945, when the Russian Armies entered Germany, the Germans took steps to evacuate the concentration camps. The unfortunate prisoners were dragged (from camp to camp) in a cruel manner. The feeble ones, who could not walk, were left in the camp to die from hunger.

In deep snow and frost the "healthy ones" were dragged toward (concentration camp) Gross-Rosen. The weak ones who (could not march and) stayed behind were shot by the SS guards. Chilke Weissfelner was among the killed ones from Klobuck. He was always comforting us by saying we will survive this tragedy and his body remained in the impure (tameh) soil of Germany.

Thousands of prisoners were gathered in one block of the Gross-Rosen camp by the Germans. We slept on the bare ground, (and forced) to sit with our legs stretched out, and intermeshed with another prisoner sitting in the same position in the opposite direction because there was not enough space for everybody. After (spending) such a painful night, we had to stand at the roll call in the morning. In the snow and the frost, dressed in our light concentration camp clothing, we were forced to stand for a few hours until they sent us back to the cold barracks.

In this abyss of pain and hardship I suddenly had a great surprise. Among the thousand prisoners, I recognized my elder brother, Berl. He told me that his transport came from a camp named Blech-Hammer. He told me that he wanted to end his life several times, but he did not have the (emotional) strength to commit suicide. During our long journey we became separated, and my brother Berl Szmulewicz[1] was shot by the Germans in Buchenwald together with six thousand (other) Jews.

We were also sent to Buchenwald. There was a roll call before departing with the transport, and during this roll call the Polish "Kapos" selected from the rows (of prisoners) three victims: a Pole, a Russian and a Jew. Those miserable (ones) were crushed to death in front of everybody. I will never forget this image of bestial murder. The martyred Jew was Itzik Zaks from Klobuck.

After these bestial murders, the painful journey started. We travelled in opened trucks, (suffering) from hunger and the cold. We arrived in Buchenwald after four days. However, because of overcrowding we were sent further to Dachau.

In the meantime the Allied armies advanced. The German SS criminals disappeared and ran away. As they (the Germans) realized that it was close to their end, they started liquidating the camp and its inmates. We were dragged from place to place. We learned later that there was a German SS plan to blow up the camp with all the prisoners inside. The fast advance of the Allied armies prevented this bestial German plan of (additional) mass murder to be implemented.

April 28, 1945, Dachau, with all its detainees, was liberated. The healthy ones (immediately) started to look for the SS criminals in order to have them account for their crimes. During the first two days the situation turned into anarchy. Afterwards the American soldiers became our caretakers. They restored order and we were again confined in the barracks. Those who tried to escape through the fence were shot, and a few people were wounded. This situation lasted only a few months. Thereafter we asked for the intervention of the American military rabbinate, and we received documents that allowed us to move freely.

After the liberation, everybody started to look for their relatives. I looked for my younger brother Yossel. He was liberated from the camp named Staltack nach Feldafing. We met in the former SS barracks in Schlossheim close to Munich, and a few other Jews from Klobuck were also there. My brother travelled back to Poland to visit Klobuck to see if any of our relatives remained alive (in our town). I was unable to travel because I was ill at that time. My brother wrote to me and said that he did not find any of our close family or relatives. The Germans had desecrated the Jewish cemetery. The "matzevot" (gravestones) were ripped out and used to pave the roads. The tombs were plowed under.

Only a few Jews from Klobuck survived. They scattered around the world, including Israel. There are no Jews living today in Klobuck[2] . As a remembrance of the days when Jews lived in Klobuck, the Shule (synagogue) was left, but standing "orphaned" without doors and windows.

Translator Footnotes

1. Berl Szmulewicz was shot on February 17 1945 in Buchenwald.

2. This book was published in 1960 and it is still true in 2013.

[Page 303]

We Wanted to Fight Against the Murderers, But We Did Not Have Any Weapons

by Avraham Wajs, Tel Aviv

Translated from Yiddish to English by Asher Szmulewicz

I was not born and did not originate from Klobuck, but my father, Elchanan Wajs, was born in Klobuck. But as fate decided, at some point during my difficult wartime experience, I was in my father's birthplace, the shtetl of Klobuck. There I married Dora Szperling, the daughter of the Klobucker politician, Baruch Szperling.

I came to Klobuck during year 1942, when I escaped from death during the liquidation of Jews in my birthplace, Pienczne. My escape was linked to the terrible death of 12 Pienczner Jews, who were arrested by the Gestapo from Wielun, sent to the Lodz ghetto, and hanged there.;[1] I was among the arrested Jews, but I successfully escaped before (they were transported and hanged).

I left the Pienczne ghetto and smuggled myself through the so called "border" established by the Germans between "Warthegau[2] and the "General-Government". Anyone caught crossing the border could be shot by the Germans without any charges or trial. When I arrived in Radomsk, which was located in the (Polish) "General-Government", I learned that the Pienczne ghetto had been liquidated. In Radomsk, people spoke about the liquidation of the Radomsk ghetto, and many believed that people were sent away to work somewhere in Germany or in a camp.

[Page 304]

In Radomsk I met young men, who like me, did not believe that the Germans sent people away to work. We already knew that the bestial Germans were sending the Jews to death. We organized ourselves as a group, and together we discussed how to escape from the German extermination. Our group was comprised of refugees from various shtels, which already had been liquidated, and everyone had in their minds the horrible pictures of the death of their close family members.

We contacted Poles who provided us with false identification papers, but there was nothing we could do with them. No Poles wanted to give us shelter in their apartments. They were afraid for themselves and for the welfare of their households. Our Polish friends advised us to go to Klobuck, where there was a Judenrat, which was established after the liquidation of the Klobuck ghetto. Jews were working there, and nobody did harm to them there.

Suddenly we learned from a Polish policeman that on the following day the Radomsk ghetto would be liquidated. There wasn't any more time to think. We had to escape immediately. We split ourselves into small groups, and we left the ghetto unharmed. My group constituted four men and three women.

We wandered through the forests. We hid during the day, and looked for good peasants during the night, who would take pity on us and take us in. In the Wewiedka Wola village we found such a good peasant called Baranek. He was like an Angel for us. He hid us in his barn for four weeks. He provided us with food, and only took money from us for his expenses. Even now his kindness to us was a mystery. We no longer could stay in Baranek's barn, because he told us that bad people started to murmur about him that he hid "Jidkes" (Jews).

[Page 305]

We decided to go to Klobuck, where the "happy" camp for Jews was to be found. "Jews were working there unharmed". We had to walk 80 kilometers to reach the "happy place". We walked for an entire day and for one night, through a region of great danger, because it was supposed to be "Judenrein" (without any Jews). At the end we reached our goal. We "happily" went into the Klobuck camp. The Jews in the camp already knew the fate of the Jews sent to Treblinka, and they waited, being afraid for their own fate.

In the camp, together with the Klobuckers, we established an organized group. We again strove to contact Polish partisans, even though we knew that the only ones active in this region were the A. K. "Armie Krajowa" (The Polish secret under-ground forces), whose members included some of the greatest enemy of the Jews. We had little confidence in them. Our only aspiration was to obtain armaments, which we intended to use to resist when the impending liquidation was to proceed.

In our resistance group were the following Klobuckers: Moshe Feige, Avraham Enzel, Berl Szmulewicz, Ptichia Tsinsenatus, Shalom Unglick, Hela Mantel and my wife Dora Szperling. From Pienczne: Yidel Szperling, Avraham Liberman, Chemia Kutner, David and Yossef Szwierczewski, Avraham Wajs (the author of this article), and a group called "Bunkerowtses," because the people associated with this group were formerly hidden in by a Pole in a "bunker". I brought them to Klobuck and into the camp.

This group finally linked up with Polish partisans, but before we succeeded in doing anything, the end came. During the night in July, 1943, when everyone was asleep, the camp was surrounded by S.S people, and at dawn everyone was brought to the courtyard of the Polish police[3]. There the Germans gathered the Jews from all of the neighboring camps. We stayed there for days and nights, and waited until the Germans finished up with all of their Jewish victims.

[Page 306]

Our group knew that we had to prepare for the last journey towards Auschwitz. We discussed what we could do, and how we could obtain armament. How could we save the women and the children? We came to the conclusion that we were powerless, and decided that each one of us should escape as best we could.

One morning the Germans requisitioned 10 men to bring bread to all of the arrested people. Ten people from our group volunteered for this task. The intention was to take the opportunity to escape. Accompanied with one S.S guard, we were brought back to the camp. Three out of the ten persons: Avraham Liberman, Nechemia Kutner and myself, jumped over the fence. The remaining ones were afraid and did not move. The S.S chased us and shot at us. My two friends successfully escaped. I was caught by the German and he inflicted on me murderous blows.

I was lying shriveled and waited for death to come. Meanwhile two Jews came by, and they implored the German to take them in because they had nowhere else to go. The German "invited" the two Jews into the camp, and then gave the three of us murderous blows. The two exhausted and persecuted Jews asked to be shot, but the German got more pleasure persecuting us rather than killing us.

An S.S Officer came. He watched how his comrade beat us with cruelty, and said to the German that killing the Jews was not worth a bullet. "They will die anyway in the camp". We were sent back to Klobuck to the courtyard of the Klobuck police station. The next day at dawn we were taken to the train under a strong guard of S.S people with dogs. We were packed into the rail carriages and sent away.

We thought that the destination was Auschwitz, but we came to the Blechhammer camp in Germany. There the Germans made a strict selection. Old people, sick people and children were separated to be killed. Healthy people were sent to various camps. Only a few of my fellow-sufferers survived.

[Page 307]

The majority died from hunger, sickness and hard labor. Many were shot. I am among the few, who after hard persecutions, waited for the liberation.

Translator Footnotes

1. There is no archive or document or testimony of the Lodz ghetto where the awful event of hanging 12 Jews is related during the year 1942.

2. Warthegau (Wartheland) is the German name of the region of northern and western part of Poland that was annexed to the Reich in 1939. Klobuck was inside this region very close to its border. Czestochowa and Radomsk were outside of Wartheland, in the General-Government.

3. The Polish police building is the Skorupa, as described in other chapters)

[Page 307]

The Heroic Death of the Old Man Hershl Fajga

by Moshe Fajga

Translated from Yiddish to English by Asher Szmulewicz

At the beginning of the war my father was already 85 years old. During his old age one misfortune followed another. In 1940 two of his daughters died, Rachel and Aidel Nache. Then his wife, Mirel, passed away. Overwhelmed by the grief, he decided to leave Klobuck and go (by attempting to smuggle through the border) to Czestochowa in the Polish "General-Government". The attempt to re-locate did not succeed. The old man had to go back to Klobuck, where he lived with his son-in-law, Arye Besser, He received financial assistance from his son, Moshe Arye.

The old man did not know tranquility. He was informed that his son Henech, who was sent to forced labor, became sick there. Henech was sent to the Sosnowiec hospital. He was in danger of passing away in the hospital. Reb Hershl decided to secretly take his son from the hospital. For this purpose he hired a Pole he knew, who went to Sosnowiec, and took Henech out from the hospital. The Pole brought Henech to Klobuck. When he arrived there he (Henech) was informed that his wife and her brother, Leizer Green, were brutally killed.

Despite all of these difficult and painful experiences, the old man did not (emotionally) break down. On Rosh Hashanah, 1940, all of our living family members gathered to wish my old uncle a happy new year. Reb Hershl comforted us: "The downfall of Hitler will come". He said to me:

[Page 308]

"I am already an old man. Being 85 years old I cannot do anything. You will be able to take revenge on the Germans".

I remember the last tragic moments of the old man's life. It was Yom Kippur, in 1942. I was compelled to work at the "Vulcan", a factory that once belonged to Shmuel Gelersztein. On my way (to work) I remembered that it was Yom Kippur, and I went to greet my uncle, the old man, Hershl Fajga. I found him praying at the Warszewer shtibel. My uncle asked me if I was going to work (on Yom Kippur). Not wanting to cause him distress, I denied the fact that I was going to the factory. The old man told me then: "There is no point of working for the Germans, because they will kill us anyway. The (train) carriages are ready to send us away". At the end (of our visit), the old man suggested that I accompany him to a bunker (and hide ourselves). I thanked him and walked away to go to work.

Indeed, at the end of Yom Kippur the first deportation started. The Germans shot (people) in the streets. Jews fled to bunkers. I was allowed to enter the factory that formerly belonged to Goldsztein, where I had worked. In the factory, there was a gathering place for the "useful craftsmen". The majority of the Jews from Klobuck were sent to Treblinka, to death.

I was among the "useful craftsmen", who were sent to Czestochowa to the "Hasag" factory. After three months of hard labor I escaped from the "Hasag-camp", and hid myself in the small ghetto in Czestochowa. There I was with my brother-in-law, Wone Reich . He told me about the heroic death of my 85 year old uncle, Hershl Fajga.

Wone Reich, together with other Jews, remained in Klobuck after the deportation, and he worked in the "Command-Room", which was responsible for moving the furniture and the other Jewish belongings that was left after the deportation of the Jews. Wone, together with other Jews from the "Command-Room", did the work under a heavy German guard.

[Page 309]

Once they went to Berek Joselewicz street and saw a group of Germans taking Jews out of a bunker. There was the old man, Hershl Fajga, and his son, Henech, his daughter, Chaye Sarah, his sister Ita Szmulewicz and others.

The old man spoke to Wone: "Now you will be able to see what the Germans will do to us".

The Germans forced the Jews to walk to the marketplace, from where they were going to be sent to work. The old man, Hershl Fajga, answered: "You can shoot us here, I am not moving from here". The Germans immediately shot my uncle, and the 85 year old Hershl Fajga, fell dead. All of the others who were with him let themselves be led by the Germans, and they were all shot. This mass murder of the Jews of Klobuck was conducted by the Germans a few days after Yom Kippur in 1942.

*

Baruch Szimkowicz gave us the following portrait of Reb Hershl Fajga:

He always worked for the community in Klobuck, and was always a faithful, devoted, Gerer Chasid. During the last Rabbi election, Reb Hershl Fajga, with his heart and soul, defended the candidate of the Gerer Court, who was a grandson of the first Gerer Rebbe: the "Baal Chidoushei Harim"[1]. During the winter, Reb Hershl Fajga took great pleasure by staying among the common people, close to the tile-oven in the Beit Midrash, where he told of the deeds of the Gerer Court.

Translator's footnote:

1. Rabbi Yitzhak Meir Rottenberg Alter was the founder of Chassidut Gur, called Baal Chidoushei Harim (Harim from Rabbi Yitzhak Meir).

[Page 310]

Liberation and Still Between Life and Death

by Berl Yakubowicz

Translated from Yiddish to English by Asher Szmulewicz

This happened on May 3rd 1945, at 6 o'clock in the morning. After five years of being threatened by a gun, I stood at the edge of the forest, listening for any movement. I was hungry, like a wolf in the woods. Close to the woods there was a field with potatoes. We grabbed the half rotten potatoes and ate them. Afterwards, we decided that we had to get rid of our prison clothes, with their stripes. Thus we dug a hole and buried our clothes, so that people would not know that we were Jews from a "Katzet" (concentration camp). I was left only with my shirt.

We decided to separate into two groups, of three and two (persons). Thus, if we were caught, we would not be a large group, and be mistaken as spies or paratroopers. Two of us left, and I stayed with the other two people.

Later my two friends went away, and I remained alone in the woods. I thought about what I should do. I was afraid to approach a German. I decided to go to the first house (I saw), and I would go in. Being afraid of meeting Germans, I entered in a stable. In the stable there was a cart and various plows.

I noticed that in a corner there was a small attic. There was no need of a ladder to get up there. With two strides I jumped into the attic, which was under the roof.

I decided to stay in the attic until the Americans (arrived), and I would be set free. If this took a few more days, I decided to go into the woods during the day, and sleep in the attic during the night. In case I was caught, I no longer would (identify myself) as a Jew anymore. I decided to say that I was a Pole, who worked for a German farmer in Silesia, and when the Russians got close, we all fled so as not to be caught by the Russians.

[Page 311]

Looking through a crack, I saw a farmer, about 40 years old, prepare his car, into which he put a sack of clothes and various other things, and I heard him say to his wife that he was not going to surrender to the "cursed Americans". His wife and their two children decided to stay. The farmer looked at his wife and children and disappeared. Listening to this conversation I decided that when it became dark I would go to the house of the farmer's wife, and ask for something to eat and for some clothes.

Suddenly there was a loud explosion, and the whole building, where I was hiding, was jolted from the blast. At the same time I heard squadrons of small aircraft shooting their machine guns. I thought then that the liberation must be coming. My heart was pounding like a hammer. After 5 years in camp, I will finally be free.

Looking from the cracks, I saw on the road a row of heavy tanks. Close to the road people were standing waving white handkerchiefs. Soon white flags were hung. I understood that the Americans had arrived here. After 10 minutes I decided to go out to be free.

I went to a German house, and asked for food and clothes. They did not ask who I was. They served me bread, milk and gave me a bag to take away. I was very hungry, and without patience, I opened the bag and started to eat.

The American tanks drove in one direction. I went to the other side of the road. An officer in a jeep paid attention to me. He stopped and called to me and started to speak English. I shrugged (not understanding him). He stopped a tank, and the tank left the row, so that the other ones could continue. A soldier came out and spoke with me in German. I answered him. A second soldier came out and spoke with me in Polish. The officer left and disappeared with the jeep.

I stood for about 15 minutes, close to the tank, and told them everything. Soon there was a soldier and another one who spoke English, German, Polish, Russian, French and other various languages. The soldiers told

me that I was free. It was evening, and my joy was indescribable. After 5 years I was again free.

[Page 312]

Among Germans after the Liberation

I went to the village. The village was called Abing. I went inside the first house of the village, and asked for something to eat. They gave me something to eat and to drink. It was already night. The American armored vehicles were driving by, without interruption.

In the house where I was, I asked the Germans to give me clothes to wear. I asked for trousers, and shoes – and I received everything (I asked for).

The old German couple prepared a bed for me to sleep in. I turned down the offer to sleep in the bed, because I did not trust sleeping with the old Germans in the same room. I asked them to prepare a cot bed in the attic. They prepared a cot bed for me in the attic, although I could not fall asleep. The tanks passed by the whole night. The house was shaking from the tanks, and my heart was jumping from joy. I was free. Also the food I ate, being satiated after being hungry for so long, did not let me sleep. It was liking cutting my stomach with knives. The uncleanliness also weakened my body. I did not sleep for the whole night.

When the day came, I left the attic fast. The old people asked me who I was and where I came from. I told them something, and asked for warm water to wash myself. They had a wooden bathtub, similar to the one that was in the Klobuck mikveh (ritual bath house). They warmed up several pots of water, and the wooden bath tub was put in the stable because it was warm there. I washed extensively, because it had been several months since I had any water to wash my body. I shaved, I ate and went out in the village to look for my friends, but I did not find them.

I lived like this for a few days in the old couple, farmers' house. After a week I found my friends; they had acquired food from the best sources.

[Page 313]

We were satiated: meat, alcohol and other good things. Immediately I felt weak and had stomach pain and fever. I was bedridden for several days in my friends' apartment. They brought a nurse, who measured my fever, and told me that I had to go to the hospital.

My friends and the nurse brought me to the hospital, which was a small house with four rooms. There was no expert doctor, only the village doctor. I was put in a room by myself because I had stomach typhus. The nurse and the doctor took great care of me. When I arrived in the hospital I was afraid to say that I was a Jew, being afraid that they may poison me. I said that I was a Christian, and that my name was Boleslav Yakubowski.

The head nurse was Italian. I received various injections, but the fever did not go down. The compress did not help either. Every day a priest came to visit the sick people, and since I said I was a Christian, he came to visit me also.

The fever was higher every day, until it went up to 41.8 degrees centigrade. The nurse called the doctor. He came and gave me injections. Suddenly I noticed the priest in the room, with his cassock; a large, white, silvered sewn stripe around his neck (stole); and an octagon shaped hat on his head. On his chest hung a big cross, and in his hand was a prayer book.

The head nurse, with two candlesticks, also entered the room with him. She laid the candlesticks on the table, and set two candles in them. She left the room. I remained alone with the priest. With a soft voice he told me: since we are all Christians believing in Jesus, we believe that when somebody is sick, the priest must pray to God for his recovery. He asked me to answer everything he was to ask me. I was still and calm, hearing his questions, but did not have the strength to answer him. He told me to nod with my head to give him a sign for yes or no.

[Page 314]

He asked me if I knew the Ten Commandments, and if I followed them. He turned a few pages, he said a few words, took a piece of cotton and dipped it in a glass with wine and made the sign of the cross above my head and said a few words from the prayer book.

At the end he wished that God will help me, and that I would be healthy and again be an observant Catholic, and he left the room. After he left the room I started to whisper Vidui (Prayer to be said before passing away), and I fell asleep.

When I woke up, the nurse told me that I had slept 16-17 hours straight. She measured the fever: 35.3 degrees centigrade. She immediately called the doctor. He came at once and she gave him a report of the night. They measured the temperature again, and I had 35.4. I received injections to fortify myself. The doctor went away. The head nurse told me that the crisis was over and that I would recover.

After a few days an American military ambulance came with three soldiers, who had red crosses on their arms. They told me that I must go with them because I had typhus, and that I needed a special treatment from a bigger hospital, that specialized in typhus.

I did not want to go, but the doctor who cared for me came and told me that I must go with them, because it will be better for me there. I allowed myself to be convinced. They took me on a stretcher and put me in the ambulance. A nurse accompanied me and we arrived in the hospital. I received clothes. I was in a wooden barrack. Soon several Jews came in and greeted me with "Amcho" (from our people). In the barrack there were about twenty Jews.

I was in the hospital several weeks, which was located in Trassberg (Bavaria). When I recovered, I was again

a free man, but alone and solitary, without parents and family, a lonely person in the world.

[Page 315]

In 1948 I made my Aliyah to Israel. The small Greek boat, "Panama", struggled with the waves of the Mediterranean sea and made its way to the Israel coast. On Shabbat, the day after the proclamation of Independence, May 15th 1948, I arrived in Tel-Aviv.

Page 316]

Episodes from the Time of Extermination

In German Captivity

by Mordechai Weissfelner

Translated from Yiddish to English by Asher Szmulewicz

I will recall here a few episodes from the horrible period of Hitler.

When the war started I was enrolled in the Polish army. After three weeks, while retreating from the front, I was captured with my unit by the Germans. I escaped and I hid in the forest. The next morning I came to the village, known as Szidlowcze, which is close to Kielce. The Germans were already there with their tanks, aircraft and horses. They tore open the Jewish shops and threw all of the goods to the Poles. I spent two days in the village and on the third day I left, and returned to my parents. We walked as full units of Polish soldiers, still in our uniforms. The German military came and an officer ordered us to stop. I did not say that I was a Jew.

We were dragged back to the same village where we had come from. We were put in a cellar, where we were almost sitting on one another. After two days we were transported by trucks to Kielce, to the barracks previously used by the Polish army. There were thousands of people there. Then the real hell started for the Jews.

The Germans separated the Jews from the Poles. We were a group of 500 Jews. They immediately started to persecute us. We had to kneel and keep our hands up. With our eyes directed at the sun, they kept us like this for the entire day.

[Page 317]

The sun burned us terribly. Representatives of the Polish Red Cross came and gave us bread and water. The Germans did not allow them to give us the bread, but only one cup of water per person.

That is how 5000 Jews were gathered, and left outside for three weeks. We slept on the ground. For three days we did not receive any food. On the fourth day we received one meal consisting of watered soup with peas. Many died from starvation and exhaustion.

After three weeks I managed to leave the Jewish group, and I joined the Polish group that was being liberated. I registered as a Pole, and escaped from the persecutions. In Kielce a train with carriages was waiting. Another Jew and I wanted to travel to Czestochowa. The Germans who were standing around the train started to shoot at us, but we successfully escaped. We walked for two days and arrived in Czestochowa.

My family's joy was overwhelming, but it did not last for long. My persecuted life began, both in the German camp near Klobuck, and then in the camps in Germany. I was in about ten camps, and I saw a lot of persecution, and I was persecuted myself.

Today it is impossible to understand how people and I survived such starvation. The best was when we found a "good garbage can" where there were enough peels from rotten potatoes and rotten cabbages. The one who caught such a "bargain" was the happiest man in the world.

[Page 318]

"The Mikvenik" (mikveh attendant)

I will never forget the German persecutor, by the name "mikvenik", who was very well known in the camps. I knew him well from his original way of beating us. He always had (whip) with a knot (at the end), a "bukowiece", which he used to hit people in the face; anyone who received a blow, remembered it for a long time. The nickname "mikvenik" was given to him because he took special pleasure to beat his victims while they were in the barrack's shower, where people stood nude.

A second German tormentor was nicknamed "timtam"; he received his nickname because of his appearance: a smooth chin without any sign of a beard. He walked the entire day with a stick, beating and roaring: "Jewish swine". He received his "reward" for all his bestial actions. When the Russians invaded Germany, he was caught and shot.

The Master of Burning Dead People

This was one of my most terrible experiences. After traveling eight days in open train carriages, without food and water, with about 200 persons per carriage, we arrived in the camp on the ninth day. We were divided into groups for different work. I was assigned to carry dead people. The "master", that is how we called the German, who was responsible of the work, asked us if we knew what a pyre was. Then he opened a large barrack in front of us where thousands of dead people laid, lying like herrings in a line. We had to take them out to the field, and lay them in layers and then prepare a pyre, in the following manner.

We spread kindling wood on the ground, and on top of the wood we put 70 dead bodies. On top of the bodies we put more wood, and on top of the wood, again 70 dead bodies, until there were a total of approximately 500 (dead) people, layer after layer; and then we lit the fire. We worked like this for four weeks, until we (burned) all of the dead bodies. Every day we made a pyre, in which we burned people from the camp, who died from various diseases, hunger and suffering.

The work of burning the dead people was performed in a very "professional" manner. The German "master", who conducted the work, was very exacting and precise in this "trade". In addition to the dead bodies from the barracks, we had to dig out corpses who were buried in very shallow graves in the ground. We used a pickaxes for this work.

[Page 319]

The German master told us that we will be the "next ones" on the pyre.

I have seen several films about war, but none of them displayed the reality of the cruelty of the German extermination. The Germans professionally filmed their extermination work, and then destroyed the films when the liberators entered Germany.

The Last Jews in the Klobuck Ghetto and German Extermination in Czenstochow

by Yehuda Szperling

Translated by Gloria Berkenstat Freund

When they began to say in the Klobuck ghetto that the Germans would send out all of the Jews and liquidate the ghetto, I sent those closest to me – my wife, daughter and mother-in-law – to Czenstochow. The lived in the ghetto with my brother, Yitzhak Leib. My father and my youngest brother, Pinkhas Menakhem, were hiding with a Christian in a village. Two brothers and a sister were in Germany in labor camps.

After the liquidation of the Klobuck ghetto, which took place in June 1942, I remained in the former ghetto as a "useful Jew," a tailor. I was employed cleaning the emptied Jewish houses.

I learned one day that the last Jews were also being sent out of Klobuck. The *shtetl* [town] would be "*Judenrein*" [free of Jews]. I did not wait until they sent me out and I went to a Polish acquaintance. He took me over the border[1] to Czenstochow for an appropriate reward. I met my wife and daughter and received employment in the ammunition factory, "HASAG" [Hugo Schneider AG – German arms manufacturer]. The deportations of the Czenstochow Jews took place four months later after *Yom-Kippur*. Our entire family, 30 people, went out at six in the morning and appeared at the gathering point. There we were counted. I remained alone. Everyone was sent to Treblinka. Before sending away the people at the gathering point, the director of the "HASAG" factory where I worked arrived and he chose "his Jews" amounting to 500 people. He wanted to take us to work, but the Gestapo office, which was in charge of the "deportation," answered him that he could not take anyone for work during the deportation – this was the highest wish of the "Fuehrer."

The director did not yield. He telephoned the highest authority in Radom and asked that "his Jews," who he had to have to work in the factory, be freed. The highest authority yielded to his plea and we were removed from the deportation. We were placed in barracks in the factory. We ate there, we slept there on the hard floor and we worked.

A small ghetto of approximately 4,000 Jews remained in Czenstochow. When a deportation again took place, a comrade from *Hashomer Hatzair* [The Youth Guard – a socialist-Zionist organization] wanted to shoot the leader of the Gestapo. But the revolver jammed. The Gestapo then chose 28 men and two girls, the healthiest and the best looking, and shot them in the presence of all the Jews who stood in the square.

There were still small children in the ghetto. The Gestapo leader, [Paul] Degenhardt, ordered the Jewish leaders to arrange a kindergarten where the children could spend time. Degenhardt made sure that the children received milk. This lasted for several weeks. Suddenly, when all of the children were in the educational home, Degenhardt and the Gestapo surrounded the house and they began to lead the children out. The crying and shouting reached toward the heavens. Armed Gestapo members led the children away to their deaths.

[Page 321]

Later the Jewish leaders received an order to register the Jews who had relatives in *Eretz-Yisroel*. It was mainly doctors and their families who registered and almost the entire *Judenrat* and the chairman. One day the Germans ordered all of the candidates for travel to *Eretz-Yisroel* to appear at the gathering spot with baggage up to 10 kilos and they would be sent to *Eretz-Yisroel* to their relatives.

Cars were waiting for them at the gathering point. The group was seated in them and they began to go. In the middle of the trip, the Jews noticed that they were being driven to the cemetery. There was turmoil. The Jewish leaders took poison. Two people were successful in escaping. The remainder, approximately 200 Jews, men, women and children were taken to the cemetery. Graves had already been prepared there. The Germans shot the children first, then the women and finally the men.

In the Czenstochow ghetto, Degenhardt chose the leader of the Jewish police as the leader of the community. All of this happened in the winter of 1943. The shooting of the candidates for travel to *Eretz-Yisroel* took place on the Fast of Ester of that year [18 February 1943].

After the shooting, I received a letter from my sister who was in the Zagórze labor camp, near Klobuck. She wrote to me that I should come to the camp. Although such a trip was full of deadly danger because I would have to go through the "border" between the General Government and "Wartenau," we – my cousin, four other people and I – decided to turn to a Pole to take us across the border. We bribed the German who took us to work, as well as the Pole. The "border smuggler" was well paid and we arrived in the Zagórze camp peacefully.

My sister hid us in the attic. We lay there for three days until my sister persuaded the camp leader to register me. Things again were good and I worked there until July 1943.

The Zagórze camp was surrounded on a Friday night and we were led out to German camps.

We were forced by the Germans from camp to camp between death and extermination. I saw how old people and children were sent to Oświęcim [Auschwitz]. The Jewish *kapos* [prisoner functionaries who supervised the forced labor and performed administrative work] tortured us more than the Germans. One *kapo* named Akiva Rozencwajg hanged himself after the liberation.

[Page 322]

The last camp in which I was until the liberation was called "*Sportschule*" [sport school] near Faulbrueck [Lower Silesia]. The women's camp where my sister was located was not far from there.

I was liberated on the 8th of May 1945. A roll call still occurred in the morning of the thousand camp arrestees. The members of the Gestapo told us to sing *Hatikvah* [*The Hope* – now the national anthem of Israel], which we sang with tears in our eyes. The German guards disappeared around noon. A white flag appeared and later a red flag.

I left the camp and ran to the women's camp. There I met my sister and a cousin. We cried for the entire time. Later the Russians came and permitted us to go to wherever we wished. I, my sister, my cousin and other acquaintances from Klobuck left for Reichenbach.

In 1946 I went to Klobuck. I mourned those closest to me who were tortured to death by the Germans, and began a new life. I married Chana Benszkowski. We left for Germany and from there, in 1948 to Israel.

Translator's footnote:

1. During the Second World War, Klobuck was part of the German Province of Oberschlesien – Upper Silesia – and Czenstochow was under the General Government in Poland.

In the Cleanup Command in Germany

by Mordechai Weissfelner

Translated from Yiddish to English by Asher Szmulewicz

As soon as the Germans entered Klobuck they started to persecute the Jews in a bestial manner. The sadists cut beards, forced men to eat their hair from their beards, and rounded up people and sent them to forced labor. Bitter news came from the people sent to forced labor in Germany: It is unbearable, the work is very hard and there is no food to eat. Thus everyone thought about how to hide.

[Page 323]

I also was caught for forced labor, with other Jews. We were confined in the "stra¿ak szope" (firefighters' shed). My mother came to visit me, and she brought peasant clothes for me. When nobody paid attention, I put on the clothes, and I escaped from there. I was hidden for a long time by Christians.

When the ghetto was established in Klobuck in 1941, I was caught and put in the ghetto. From there I was sent, together with a group of others, to Gliwice (Germany). Our work was to empty the Jewish houses. We were called the "Cleanup Command". We saw with our own eyes what was done with the Jewish belongings, and to the people who were sent away.

I managed to get an authorization to go back home for a few days, and I was able to stay in Klobuck for three days, on the condition that my friends were accountable for my return (to the camp). They guaranteed that I would come back, and I went back home.

I told everyone about the conditions, what was done with the Jewish belongings and with the Jews. My parents tried to convince me not to go back. I did not want to stay. I knew that my friends were responsible for my return, and I therefore returned to Germany. Later, I learned that during the "relocation" (deportation) of Klobuck, my parents fled to Czestochowa.

Our group was sent back to Zagorz, and to the camp there. In the Zagorz camp I was told that my little sister, Reisele, was in Klobuck, and was being hidden by Christians; and that my elder sister, Devorah, was in Germany in the Neuesaltz camp; and that my parents, together with their remaining children, were sent away to Treblinka.

[Page 324]

The twelve year old boy who escaped from Treblinka

While in Zagorz, I was informed that my youngest, 12 year old, brother, Yitzikl, survived the death camp in Treblinka. He later recounted what he saw in the terrible German extermination camp: large transports of Jews were brought in carriages, locked with iron bars. Chlorine was poured onto the carriage floor. In Treblinka, in a large area, several

gas chambers, and a large oven were located. First, people were sent to be gassed, and then to be burned. Everyone was taken inside a room, and were ordered to undress, so as to take a shower, and then to receive new clothes.

My little brother immediately understood that everybody was being sent to their death, and he hid in the heap of clothes and other belongings. When everything was calm and still (after the group of Jews were dead), several hours later, a group of young men came in to remove the clothes and belongings: separating the men's wear and the women's wear. In that group of men was my uncle, Moshe Weissfelner, and when the group of young men found the boy they wanted to notify the Germans, not willing to pay for the secret with their own lives. But my uncle, Moshe Weissfelner, identified the boy and did not let them notify the Germans.

Within the group a few people wanted to escape. My uncle did not want to escape. He said that he did not care about his own life, he already had lost his entire family. He just requested of his fellow-sufferers that they take the boy with them.

At 5 AM, at the wake up time, when people went to get a piece of bread and coffee, the Jews who prepared to escape, went out through the barbed wire, and they took my little brother with them. After wandering and many difficulties, they arrived in Warsaw. They had a lot of money and gold that they had gathered from the pockets of the murdered Jews. With this money, they saved their lives.

In Warsaw they obtained false Polish identification papers, but I don't know how, and they continued their traveling. They arrived in Czestochowa, where there was a camp with Jewish craftsmen.

I learned that my brother was in Czestochowa, and I obtained the service of a "black" Christian (meaning from the underworld). For a large sum of money, he was hired to bring my brother to the Zagorz camp. With many difficulties he successfully brought back my brother. My brother did not want to eat or drink, and he did not want to live. He was so shaken by what he lived through. I

[Page 325]

told him that now we were the parents of our remaining little sister, who was hidden by Christians, and that "you must regain your strength". In 1943 during the liquidation of the Zagorz camp, when people were sent to various work camps, we were separated, I was sent to Fashemacher camp, and my brother with my little sister were sent to Blechammer.

Later I was told that in Blechammer there was a selection, and all the youngest were sent to death, but my brother was able to arrive in the Keltendorf camp. Avraham Weiss was with him. He told me about his experiences. My little brother worked like an adult, and was kept well. Later a typhus epidemic broke out, and many people from Klobuck died; the healthy people were sent to the Falbrick camp. My brother was also sent there. In Falbrick, Wolf Unglick, from Klobuck, worked in the kitchen. He took my brother to work in the kitchen, where it was not that bad for him. He also gave food to other people.

Once a commission of doctors came, and my brother was categorized as "unfit". He was sent in a transport to his death, and he was finally murdered by the Germans.

That is how he ended his struggle with death.

[Page 326]

How I Caught the German Jew-murderer – Halschuld

by Moshe Fajga

Translated from Yiddish to English by Asher Szmulewicz

The German, Halschuld, "the horse dealer", as the persecuted Jews secretly called him, was the main inspector for the "Zonder Kommando"(special commando) work. During the deportation of the ghetto, he separated people with his stick: "left and right", which meant who went to (continue to live) a temporary life, or who went to their death.

I was "introduced" to him in Klobuck, and in the work camps in which I was persecuted. Holschuld came to the camp workplace, and the exhausted, starving slave workers, who did not please him, were sent to Auschwitz, to the gas chamber. In the camps, Jews called him "the horse dealer" or the "lame", because he had a limp.

On the seventh month of year 1947, which was after the liberation, I was walking on Mathias street in Breslau (today's Wroclaw), which was already under Polish rule. A limping German passed in front of me; he was well and smoothly groomed, had a cheek beard, and I seemed to know him from somewhere.

Being a member of the local militia, I stopped the German, and asked him: "who are you and what is your name?"

The German took out Russian documents and showed them to me. I could not read Russian, and I asked him what the documents were? He answered that his documents confirmed that he was a freedom fighter (during the war). While he spoke I recognized him, as the murderer of Jews, Halschuld. I took out my revolver, and shouted at him: "hands up".

The German, livid and afraid, followed my order. I took his documents and dragged him to the Polish headquarters. On my way to the headquarters I found an old, muddy, top hat, and I put it on the German's head, the murderer of Jews, and laughed at him, the way they (the Germans) laughed at Jews.

In the headquarters, another militiaman joined me, and together we brought the criminal to the Russian headquarters. There I was ordered to present two people who were in the camps with me, to testify that he was the same German that persecuted Jews. I immediately went to R. Grochowine (who today lives in Israel), and to Motel Berliner from Dombrowe, and told them about the captive, Jew murderer, the lame German.

[Page 327]

The next day we went to the Russian headquarters. We were introduced before a large room, full of Germans, and we were asked to wait until the German, the one we recognized as the Jew murderer, came in.

We waited for four hours. Germans were brought in and out of the room. At some point we saw the lame, "horse dealer", as we called him in the camps. I immediately gave him a slap. Motel Berliner came close and raised his hand to hit him, but his hand became stiff, and he couldn't bring it back down. The interrogation soon started. The Russian officer asked me how I knew this German. I answered: the first time I saw him he was in Klobuck, and then in Zagorz. When the camp was surrounded, and the Jews were taken out, the German hit the blind, Yeshaya, and he wanted to send me to Auschwitz. In the Dyhernfurth camp, he ordered that Jews be brought to the "bathroom", where he put a water pipe in each one's mouth, opened the faucet, and let the Jews suffocate from the water flow. R. Grochowine and Motel Berliner confirmed this.

The German understandably denied everything. He declared that he was only an inspector in the work command-room in the camps, and did not do any harm. He asked to verify (his account) with the Jewish Elder, Berish Welner, and said that if he was brought to the investigation, he would speak differently, about the alleged the lame German, the Jew murderer.

Later I left Germany and went to Israel. My friend Goldhammer, who I met in Israel, told me that in Wroclaw the lame German was convicted and he died in jail.

[Page 328]

Committee to Aid the Hungry in Zagorz Camp

by Avraham Enzel

Translated from Yiddish to English by Asher Szmulewicz

The nightmare of murder and extermination, implemented by the Germans, was unable to successfully suppress the humanity in the Jew, or the Jew from humanity. The example for me was Yossef Meir Kurland.

I was with him in the Zagorz camp. There Reb Yossef Meir, as we called him, established a kind of committee to help the hungry. When the Germans liquidated the camp and sent us to Auschwitz, I was with Kurland in the same (train) carriage. While on the way to his death, he demonstrated his courage and humanity.

Several young people cut a hole in the carriage, and prepared to jump out. Several Jews became angry at us, because they said that everyone would suffer (by reason of our escape). Reb Yossef Meir Kurland to the contrary, encouraged us and gave us his support and said: "Children save yourselves, if you still have living blood in yourselves." He just asked us to wait until we passed the railroad's crossroad. From there, one track went to Auschwitz, and the other one went to Gliwice. He said if the train goes to Auschwitz, then we should jump.

"Jump with Mazal (good fate), and God should watch over you, and take revenge for our sufferings", said Reb Yossef Meir.

His cheering strengthen us. We jumped from the train, which was heading to Auschwitz, and I saved myself.

[Page 329]

Esperiences of Klobuckers in France During the German Exterminations

Among the French Partisans

by Moshe Wajnman

Translated from Yiddish to English by Asher Szmulewicz

In memory of my dear parents, who passed away before the war, and of my persecuted sisters, brothers and family.

This happened in June, 1940. I was already on the front line for about a month. As a French citizen, I was called up in the French army. Our units retreated in terrible disorder, and on June 15th we fell into German captivity. We were sent to a camp in Germany as POWs. Three months later, in September, I escaped from the camp. My well known political views immediately led me to enlist in the ranks of the fighters against Hitler's oppression. We received the first news about the German cruelty and murderous activities against the Polish Jews.

Although in the beginning the anti-Hitler activities were not very strong in France, especially in the "Free Zone", the repression against Jews was extraordinarily strong. We always were in danger of death.

The first task of the resistance fighters against the enemy was to win the French population through anti-Hitler appeals and personal contacts. Among those in the Jewish underground movement, the primary question was how to save the thousands of Jewish

[Page 330]

children who were taken in by good non-Jewish French people. They hid Jewish lives, sometimes risking their own lives.

*

When the Soviet Army's counter attack against Hitler became noticeable and sustained, we changed our combat tactics. I was entrusted with (supervising) an important defense sector; I had a great responsibility for achieving good results in our struggle, and for the lives of my fellow fighters.

**Moshe Wajnman as a partisan in France
He lives in Israel.**

During the long hours, while preparing plans of attack, while awake in the long nights, I saw in full tragic light the great tragedy of the Polish Jewry, including the devastated Jewish homes of the Polish shtetls, and my birth place shtetl, Klobuck.

It was already 15 years since I had left my home place, but during those tragic days, during the night in the quarters of the French underground fighters, waiting for the enemy, like in a dream, I wandered again through the streets and the alleys of Klobuck, looking inside the Jewish apartments, and in our apartment, recalling the happy times when there was a Jewish life, with all of its joy and sorrow.

[Page 331]

My memories recalled a house from the old city. I looked inside my home, saw each corner, long ago when I still was a Cheder boy, learning from Dudel Shuster, Henchel, Yijke Yasse, the Melamed (Cheder Teacher), with the handsome large beard. Later I was in the Beit Midrash. My beloved father, although being a ribbon maker (I was called Moshe the ribbon maker), who weaved with his weaving loom the various colored ribbons, had a lot of free time, not only to read Tehilim (Psalms), but also to deepen his knowledge of sacred books and gemara, tossafot and other laws and edification books.

You were an honest, observant Jew, an honest and humble loving man. An Alexander Chasid, traveling to see the Rebbe and learning Torah. I see my father enwrapped in his talit (prayer shawl), in his kittel (white gown used on Yom Kippur) standing close to the pulpit on Yom Kippur, like a Shaliach Tzibur (prayer leader) during the Musaf prayer.

While all of these images passed in front of my eyes, I was staying in a small village on the edge of the Garonne river. In an isolated house 16 kilometers from the beautiful and so pleasant French town of Toulouse, in the south of France. Outside, two armed partisans were watching to protect us against an eventual Gestapo attack. All through the night it was dark, and during each minute I could lose my life, yet I thought again about Klobuck.

In front of my eyes passed the figures of my brothers, Levi and Leizer. They studied for a long time in the Beit Midrash. Your wish, my dear father, was partly fulfilled, your son, Levi, survived the Holocaust, but his wife died together with their seven children in Poland. He is now Rabbi and Shochet (ritual slaughterer) in Santa Fe in faraway Argentina. The German murderers did not spare my second brother and my sister. Where did your remains disappeared, which killer bullet cut your life short?

[Page 332]

Moshe Wajnman as a partisan with false identification documents. He lives in Israel.

Dear hometown Klobuck, from the French partisan quarters, my thoughts wandered in your direction. To all your Jews with perennial crafts and Jewish poverty.

My beloved mother, Hinde, like all of the Jewish mothers, worked hard, and was under pressure day and night, and during the winter days she suffered from cold and freezing weather in the market place, being the livelihood provider to allow her husband to study Torah.

My dear parents, who had the chance of dying of natural death, were not left in peace by the German vandals who destroyed and desecrated the cemetery. My parents wanted so much

[Page 333]

that my brother and I should be honest and observant Jews, and that we also become Rabbis.

For myself, the goal of my partisan activities is much clearer. A few days ago three of my dear comrades died trying to blow up a movie theater where the anti-Semitic film, " The Jew Suss", was screened. They were non-Jews that died for a wonderful human solidarity in the anti-Nazi struggle. A few days ago the Rabbi of Toulouse, Azanski, was arrested by the Gestapo; I had spoken to him a few days earlier at a meeting, where we worked out a plan to provide money for the needy families of Jewish refugees. Every day there are new victims. A few times already I manage to get out of very dangerous situations, but for how long?

I am here in the partisan camp. I, Moshe, the son of Hinde and Yaacov Yitzhak, the ribbon maker, feel on my shoulders the great responsibility this period placed on me, and the strong burning desire of retaliation for the innocent blood that was spilled.

My Experiences in France

by Noakh Rybsztajn

Translated from Yiddish to English by Asher Szmulewicz

I left my home and my birth place town, Klobuck, in 1934 and went to France. Two years later I was expelled from Paris and went to Eretz Israel to the "Maccabiah" (Maccabi Games). After staying illegally in Israel for two years I came back to France in 1937, and there I received my second residence permit with a bonus, one month in jail. The prisons were full of Jews and non-Jews expelled from France.

[Page 334]

The war brought more sufferings: the wandering on the roads from France, pursued by the German armies, heading toward Paris.

In 1941 I was interned in a camp for foreigners. When the French Hitler collaborators started to extradite the interned Jews, with their wives and children, to the Germans, to send them to the extermination camps, I escaped in February, when the trucks were already full with Jews.

I rambled for three weeks in the forest until I found a Swiss citizen who let me stay in his apartment. After a short time gendarmes (country police) came and arrested me. Again, I successfully escaped to the forest. The same day a French family let me in their apartment, where I stayed and ate for three weeks.

My wife and child were blackmailed by the Authorities. They demanded that they give them my hideout.

In 1942 I was taken to a camp. I escaped through the barbed wire. I was hunted by a trained dog. I was brought back to the camp bleeding. I was punished for my attempt to escape by limiting my time to see my child to only 10 minutes.

On Pesach, 1943 I again successfully got out of the camp. I went to a mountainous region, lived in an isolated house and linked myself with the resistance movement. I was given a mission to save the resistance fighters who escaped from the German surrounding areas, and to bring them, with their armaments through a water stream, to a safe place.

During my retreat from the barbed wire zone, my wife and my child travelled with me in a truck full of explosives, despite the formal order not to bring wives and children. After two days of wandering we waited for the arrival of the American army.

[Page 335]

We rejoiced that we survived. My joy soon vanished and transformed to sadness when I learned that during the extermination of the Jews by the Germans, my dear parents were killed, together with my beloved brother, Shlomo, and my entire family was brutally murdered.

**The Klobucker Leib Azjner fought in
the French army against the Germany**

[Page 336]

Extermination of the Jewish Communities of Miedzno and its Surroundings
Translated from Yiddish to English by Asher Szmulewicz

Miedzno is a village, not far from Klobuck, where a large number of Jews, about 30 families, lived. They had their own Shul (synagogue), with a Mikveh (ritual bath), and a Shochet (ritual slaughterer), who was financially supported by the Klobuck community. Jews made their living from village trades. There were also a few Jewish trades: a baker, a shoemaker and a tailor. Each Jew of the village had his own field.

When the Germans entered Klobuck and its surroundings, they sent fourteen Jews from Miedzno to Buchenwald. A few days later, the Germans sent back a small box with the ashes of the murdered Jews from Miedzno, which was later buried in the Klobuck cemetery.

The Shochet of Miedzno, Pinchas Rosental, was shot in the Zagorz forest by Polish thieves. His wife died soon afterwards from great sorrow. His two sons, Nete and Meir, were killed in Czestochowa. His third son, Heniek Itshe, lived in Pabienice, and was deported during the expulsion of Pabienice, together with his wife and children.

Of the fourteen deported Jews from Miedzno, only two survived: Chaim Buchman (who lives in Israel) and Klug (who lives in America).

In the Klobuck region there were also other small villages with Jewish populations that were linked with the Klobuck community. The villages were: Zagorz (where the Germans established a Camp for Jews during the occupation), Lobodno, Wr czyca, Ostrow, Kocin, Walenczow, and Z ochowice.

In the villages a few Jewish families lived, and they came to Klobuck to davenen (pray) during the high holidays. They were murdered by the Germans.

[Page 337]

German Exterminations

Photographs from Dachau Torture Camp

The following photographs of the German bestial murderous activities in the Dachau camp were contributed by Avraham Gelbard. He received these photographs from American officers who took these photographs immediately after they took over the camp.

**Avraham Gelbard in the camp attire.
He lives in Israel.**

[Page 338]

Entrance to the persecution camp – Dachau

The streets in camp – Dachau

[Page 339]

The barracks

The crematorium in Dachau

[Page 340]

The victims are sent to be creamated

Preparation to burn the dead people

[Page 341]

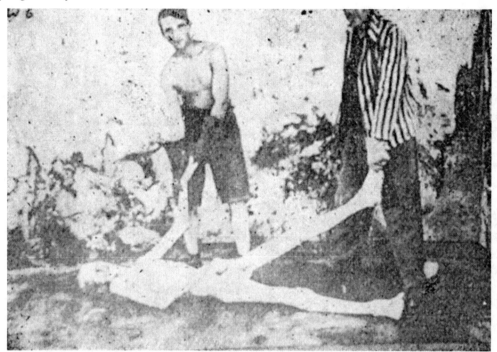

Preparation to burn the dead people

The victims are pushed inside the crematorium

[Page 342]

German extermination

German extermination

[Page 343]

German extermination

German extermination

[Page 344]

S.S. people caught a fleeing prisoner and hanged him

**American soldiers and officers describe
the terrible images of the German extermination**

[Page 345]

Jewish families Tortured by the Germans

The surviving Klobucker Jews perpetuate the remembrance of their families and close friends through the publishing of the photographs that were left and the description of their life and death.

The committee of the Yiskor Book strove to enter in the "Sefer Klobuck" the names, the photographs of all the Klobucker persecuted Jews. Unfortunately it was not possible to obtain a full list of names and to gather all of the materials from all of the deceased families.

[Page 346]

blank page

[Page 347]

El Malei Rachamim (God full of mercy)

God, full of mercy, Who dwells above, give rest on the wings of the Divine Presence , amongst the holy, pure and glorious who shine like the sky, to the holy souls of Klobucker Jews and surroundings, fathers, mothers, sons and daughters. Old and young people, infants and babies, children and women who were killed, burned, slaughtered, strangled, struck, murdered and were buried alive by the Germans descendants of Amalek.

Therefore, the Merciful One will protect their souls forever, and will merge their souls with eternal life. The Everlasting is their heritage, and they shall rest peacefully at their lying place, and let us say: Amen.

(translation partly from Wikipedia)

[Page 348]

blank page

[Page 349]

Photographs, Family Descriptions, Incomplete List by Name

Translated by Asher Szmulewicz

The Weichman Family

by Macha Weichman

I was born in Krzepice, but I was married in Klobuck to Zalman Weichman. We had six children. Three were already married (at the outbreak of the war). We were a family of twelve members until 1941. We lived with the hope that our family could hold on until the end of the war, but our bitter fate was different. When the Germans took all of the young people (Jews) from Klobuck and sent them to Germany, my son and my son-in-law were among them. Thereafter, my husband received an order to go to work every day. Afterwards, the Zagorz camp was established.

In July, 1942 during the Klobuck "Ausiedlung" (deportation), many people fled to Czestochowa, and I did also. We did not know where to go. Everybody fought against death. Those days and nights are profoundly kept in my memory. Whole families were torn apart.

Three months later, on Yom Kippur, (the deportation) started in Czestochowa. My daughter Rachel was deported. I returned and went back through the "border" to my husband and (remaining) children, who were in the Zagorz camp. Going through the border was really a death march; many were caught and were immediately shot.

I successfully got through the border without incident, and arrived in the Zagorz camp. We were 600 men and women working in Zagorz. We worked very hard. Then the Jewish cemetery was destroyed; the tombstones were removed and it was smoothed over with soil. I remember very well that day. My heart ached and I suffocated from tears, while the tombstones were removed and the earth was leveled, where our dear Klobucker Jews were resting "in peace."

[Page 350]

In July, 1943, when the camp was liquidated, we were put in closed and locked (train) carriages and sent away. My husband told our children that he said goodbye to Klobuck where he, his parents and grandparents were born.

In the locked carriages we were sent to the Blechammer work camp. A selection was made: young and healthy men were sent to work; children, ten to twelve's years old, also wanted to work, but their requests and tears did not help. The German murderer, the lame Ludwig[1], with his big evil dog, dragged all of the children and old ones, who did not pass the SS selection, to a cell and from there they were sent to Auschwitz forever. Although I was more than fifty years old, I looked younger, and I was allowed to go to work in an ammunition factory in Ludwigsdorf, not far away from Breslau (Wroclaw).

My husband, Zalman, worked in a concentration camp until 1944, when he died from hunger. My two sons and a son-in-law were killed a few hours before our liberation. I stayed alive because our camp was not liquidated, although we starved, but we survived until the Russian army came in on May 8th 1945 and set us free.

Today I am in Sweden with my children.

Translator's Footnote:

1. Seems to be Holschud that was caught after the liberation (see page 326)

The Unglick Family

by Yankel Moshe Unglick, Paris

On each occasion that our family members met, we discussed the origins of our family name, but we never discovered the source of this bizarre name, (Unglick means unhappy).

I will start the description of our family with our old grandmother, Aidel, and our old grandfather, Leibush.

[Page 351]

Reb Kopel Unglick and wife

They had six sons: Moshe, Kopel, Meshulam (Shilem), Shimshon, Itzik and David. Over time, the family grew. After the passing of our grandmother and grandfather, the names Aidel and Leibush were carried on in several (family) households. Thus, with time we could no longer refer to Leibush Unglick, because it became impossible to identify the specified person. We had to say Leibush Unglick from the Krzepice road, or give some other identifying details. And since many of our family members left Klobuck, and settled in all directions, there was no region in the vicinity without an Unglick family member originating from Klobuck.

I will remember here my close family member, my grandfather, Kopel Unglick, who lived until after WWI. He had his daughters marry men who were Torah learned. The eldest son-in-law, Yidel Dawidowicz, was born in Panstow, and later moved to London. The second son-in-law, Yossel Markowicz, was born in Dzialoszyn (about 25 kilometers north of Klobuck), was a good Torah student and an Alexander chassid. He was well known in Klobuck, being a Baal Tefilah (prayer leader), a Mohel (who performs ritual circumcision), and was always was involved in various institutions and societies that served the community.

Yossel Markowicz was a founder of the society "Bikur Cholim" (who comforted the families of the deceased or ill). During the Hitler-occupation he was persecuted by the Germans.

[Page 352]

Yehuda Dawidowicz and wife

Our grandmother Leah, before passing away, gathered her children and grandchildren and, before departing from them, her last words were: I am leaving from such a beautiful generation.

My parents, Meshulam and Frimet Sheindel, were shot by the Germans in Klobuck. They hid in an attic for a long period. Finally, when they were starving, they surrendered to the Germans and they were shot. Those who survived: Abraham (lives in Israel) and the writer of these remembrances.

[Page 353]

Meshulam Unglick and family

Survived: Abraham, second in the left in the upper row, and Yankel Moshe, third from the lower row on the left, who was then a child.

[Page 354]

The Guterman Family

by Arye Guterman

I am a grandson of Reb Yeshaya Hartzke and Freidel Guterman. They conducted a fine trade, and (maintained) a Chasidic house with tradition, Torah and mitzvot (commandments). They arranged honorable marriages for their children. For their daughters they looked for Chasidic sons–in–law, and for their sons they looked for good daughters–in–law. Both the grandfather and the grandmother passed away during the same week in Hechvan Tav Resh Peh Gimmel (Nov. 1923), and they were survived by nine children.

In Klobuck lived: Chana and her husband, Yehoshua Yissachar Rosencweig, with their four children. Yehoshua Yissachar was a Radomsker Chasid. They all perished together.

Tova and her husband, Shlomo, and their two children died together with the other Jews from Klobuck. Yaacov Feivel and his family lived in Lodz. When the war broke out they left and went somewhere. A few days later Yaacov Feivel was found hanged on a tree, close to Lodz, not far from village Yezew. His wife, Chaya, and their two children went to Czestochowa and they died there. Avraham Yechiel died in Lodz.

My parents lived in Klobuck until 1933. My father, Hersh Guterman, a Gerer Chassid, was involved in all of the Tzedakah (charity) institutions and in "Hevrat Bikur Cholim" (Society to visit the sick people). Later we moved to Lodz. We were seven children: Gitel, Arye, Baila, Chana, Kreindel, Mendel and Freidel.

The Germans deported my parents and several children to Czestochowa and from there to Treblinka, where they were killed. Their yahrzeit (anniversary of death) falls on Bet Chol Hamoe'd Sukkot (Second day of Chol Hamoe'd Sukkot).

The family survivors, who now live in Israel, are my aunt Chaya, with her husband Benzion Greenfeld, the writer of these lines, with his wife Feigel and a son.

[Page 355]

The Feige Family

by Zvia Mendelewicz–Feige, Canada

My old grandfather, Moshe Feige, lived in Klobuck. He had several sons and daughters, who held prominent positions in the Jewish life (of Klobuck). His eldest son, Shimon, was the landlord of the candle factory and was a representative in the Czestochowa city council. The second son, Avraham, lived in Klobuck, where he was the community representative and gabai (secretary) of the "Hevra Kadisha" (Jewish funeral society) for a substantial period of time. The third son, Shmuel Leib, my grandfather, was a grain merchant, and his wife, my grandmother Libe, sold milk. She wrote her accounts on the wall with a piece of chalk, and thereby recorded her debts. Both passed away at an advanced age with great honors. They were survived by several sons and one daughter. Of all of them, only my father died in his bed; the others perished in the Hitler's hell.

My father Daniel was an observant Jew, and on Shabbat and Chagim (Holidays) he wore a silk overcoat with a velvet hat. After WWI my father often repeated: "God should protect us from another war, because a war is a misfortune for Jews. The first victim is always the Jew." My father was a wood merchant. He was a partner in the sawmill of Itzik Chade.

Once, when he was visiting his sister in Wielun he became sick. He was immediately brought back to Klobuck, and a doctor from Czestochowa was called. His condition worsened. On the Friday evening before his passing away, the Rabbi came with several Chasidim to visit the sick man. On Shabbat before dawn, Shevat 17, he returned his soul to the Creator.

My mother, Feigel, passed away in Czestochowa.

My husband, Yossel Mendelewicz, was a confectioner. We had a confectionery store and made a good living. We had four children. All of them were good students. My husband helped many people. Whenever the peddlers couldn't sell their goods of butter, cheese, eggs, they brought their products to us. We always paid them immediately so that they would not suffer (financial) harm. We participated in all of the social institutions.

[Page 356]

Yossel Mendelewicz

When the dreadful war broke out, we went through the seven levels of hell. My husband fell ill in the Zagorz camp. My brother, Moshe, brought him to the Krzepice hospital. Later when the Krzepice camp was liquidated, my husband was sent together with all the Jews in the Direnport camp in Upper Silesia. He passed away there.

When the Klobucker Jews were deported to Blechammer, my brother looked after my two sons, who were with him in the same train carriage. When they got off the train, everybody walked in a single row. My eldest son, Levi, and my brother

[Page 357]

were sent to Aneiwer. My youngest son, Yechezekel, had to stay in Blechammer where he died.

My eldest son, Levi, was later sent to Kletendorf. I saw him there. I heard that he was killed just before the liberation. He was in a train that was bombarded by the Americans.

I live now in Canada with my two daughters, who survived.

Zvia Mendelewicz–Feige Canada

Levi Mendelewicz

**Yechezekel Mendelewicz
died in Auschwitz being 6 years old**

[Page 358]

Top Right: Feivel Feige with her grandchildren

Top Left" Feige Kreidel Ring, Hinde

Bottom: Chaim Feige

[Page 359]

Sarah Rachel daughter of Fishel Feige and Tovia Berkowicz

Daniel Reich, grandson of Daniel Feige

Szmulewicz family

by Yaacov Szmulewicz, Paris

Translated by Asher Szmulewicz nephew of the Yaacov Szmulewicz

My father Moshe Szmulewicz, born in Wielun, came from a family of Chasidic rabbis. My mother Ruchla née Zyscholc (Zissholtz) was born in Bor Zapilski. They lived in Klobuck for a long time. My father was a long standing spokesman (leader) of the Jewish community, and always worked for the interest of the community.

After the First World War, when Poland became an independent state, my father was elected to the city council (ratman), and to be a lay judge (lawnik) in the court. He spoke four languages fluently and was the comptroller (bookkeeper) for the Jewish community (kehilah).

We were a family of eight brothers and four sisters. My father passed away in 1936, when he was 74 old. My mother always helped poor people. She was active in the "Chevrat Beit Lechem" and in the "Chevrat Kadisha" for women. In 1942 when she was 75 years old, she was deported to Auschwitz by the Germans. She did not survive the deportation.

My sister Chaya-Sarah was killed in Maidanek along with her husband Getsil Fuchs and three of their children. Their eldest son, Gavriel, came to Israel in 1934.

My sister, Baila, married Genoch Rogowski. They had seven children. She perished along with her husband and six children in the concentration camps. Her eldest son, Avram, was also deported to German concentration camps, but he survived.

My brother, Avrum Asher, a former Beit Midrash student, married Chava Ring. He was a bookkeeper for a small commercial bank and for the Jewish community. When the Germans occupied Klobuck, they summoned the president of the community, Baruch Szperling, and my brother, Avrum Asher. They received severe cuts from bayonets; their hair was cut off; and they were forced to eat their own hair.

Later Avrum Asher and his son Shmulik were sent to the German deportation camps where they died. His wife and daughter were killed in Auschwitz.

My brother, Berl, was a communist, one of the founders of the Peretz library and of the society "Bildung" (Culture). He was married to Chana Szperling. They were killed together with their daughter, Tseshe.

The same fate befell my sister, Hinde, her husband, Mordechai Szperling, and their four children. They were all killed.

My brother, Leib, a former member of the Klobuck dramatic club, was married to Chana Sarah Granek from Krzepice. They had two children. In

1939 my brother was sent to Nuremberg by the Germans and later deported to Treblinka. During the revolt of Treblinka, he succeeded in escaping with other prisoners. He went into the underground. He fell during an attack in the Ukrainian forest. His wife and children succumbed in Auschwitz.

My sister, Macha, married Yechezkel Rosen. They had one daughter. Yechezkel Rosen was killed in the German concentration camps, and my sister and her daughter perished in Auschwitz.

My brother, Aaron, who before World War II was an active society member and a good speaker, was deported to Treblinka and perished there. My brothers, Shaya Itzik and Groynem, died from typhus after the First World War.

From the entire family only the two youngest brothers remained alive, myself and my brother, Yossel, who spent most of World War II with me in German concentration camps.

Szmulewicz family

[Page 361]

Rodel, the mother of the Unglick family

לזכר פון דעם פֿאָטער
פון דער משפחה
אונגליק — מאַנטשע ז״ל,
פון וועמען עס איז נישט
געבליבן קיין פֿאָטאָ־
גראַפֿיע

**In remembrance of the father
of the Unglick family: Mantshe, of
blessed memory
There is no remaining picture of
him**

[Page 362]

**Top: Daughter, Rivka Leah, and husband,
Simcha Yakubowicz, with their child**

**Bottom: The children of Simcha Yakubowicz and Rivka Leah:
Moshele, Nachmiele and Chanele**

[Page 363]

Mantshe Unglick (Manele)

He was from the observant Jews of the shtetl, with the fear of God. Throughout his life he was involved with Tzedakah (charity) and Chesed (benevolence). He had a butcher shop, and he was a butcher. The Pilczer Rabbi, who lived in Czestochowa, ate the meat that came only from Mantshe's butcher shop.

Every Shabbat afternoon you could see Mantshe in the Beit HaMidrash (House of study) with the "Midrash Tanchuma" (Torah commentary) open. He loved to speak with young people about Rabbis and Chasidut. His wife, Rodel, was known in Klobuck to be a virtuous woman, giving charity anonymously. Several poor families ate meat on Shabbat and Festivals, donated by Rodel, and she also added baked food. Their son, Gedaliahu, was a good student, and was a good–natured person. Their son–in–law, Simcha, was ordained as a rabbi. It was a house of God and people.

During the murderous German occupation the following were killed: Mantshe and his wife Rodel, their daughter, Rivka Leah, and her husband, Simcha, and the three children from this couple: Moshele 9 years old; Nachmiele 7 years old; and Chanele 6 years old. Gedalihu was shot together with Simcha, and was buried in Klobuck. Aaron and his wife were shot in Czestochowa, Feigel and Hertzke Szilit were killed in Treblinka.

Top: Their son, Avraham, and his wife, Golde.

Bottom: Their daughter, Chanele, her husband, Hartzke Szilit and child.

[Page 364]

From left: **Gedalihu Unglick, Sarah Unglick and their daughter, Blume**

Reb Shmuel David Shniur

by Eliyahu Rosenthal, Australia.

He was born in Czestochowa, and got married in Klobuck to Roize, the daughter of Shlomo Mordechai Green. Reb Shmuel ate "Kest" [1] at his father-in-law's table. During his "Kest" period he learned Torah and received a teaching diploma from Rabbi Yankele. He was a Gerer Chasid, who sat at the table (he was a diligent student) of the "Sefat Emet" [2]. His family was comprised of 5 daughters and 2 sons. He arranged good marriages (shiduchim) for his daughters, and his sons–in–law were: Aaron Hendel, the son of Yeshayu Chade, the son of the Truskolaser shochet (the ritual slaughterer); Yechiel Krimolowski and the grandson of the Komaner Rabbi, Meir Taub.

Reb Shmuel David Shniur was killed with his wife in Treblinka. His only son, Mendel, survived and lives now in Australia.

Translator's Footnote:

1. "Kest" is room and board that was offered to a new son–in–law to enable him to continue his studies without financial worries.

2. "Sefat Emet" Yehudah Aryeh Leib Alter (1847☐1905), also known by the title of his main work, the *Sfas Emes or Sefat Emet*, was the Gerer Rebbe from 1870 until his death. (source Wikipedia)

[Page 365]

Reb Yitzhak Djalowski

Reb Yitzhak Djalowski was an outstanding Klobucker landlord, and a Radomsker Chasid. He loved to read the book of ethics, and he had a son, who studied Torah. His son, Shimon, was the son–in–law of Reb Yeshuha Israel, and his second son, Moshe, was a good student and was shochet in Czestochowa. Reb Yitzhak was always the first secretary of the "Chevra Kadisha" (Jewish burial society).

Reb Yechiel Kraszkowski

He was a Radomsker Chasid, an honorable, good–hearted and affable man. He exhibited, by his attitude, courtesy to everyone. His wife, Feigel, had an outward personality, like her husband. Their two sons, Elyahu and Itshe, were killed. The following survived: one son and two daughters, Breidel and Gitel, both living in Australia.

Avraham Diamant

He was a hard worker Jew, and was the long time secretary of the Zagorz mill. Every Shabbat he traveled a long way to pray at the Radomsker "shtibel", together with his children. He was active in social institutions, in the community, and also in the charity fund. His wife, Rachele, was a hearty Jewish mother, and raised her children as proud and national Jews. From the entire family of the sons, David, Yaakov, and Motek and a daughter, only the daughter, Zissel, together with her husband, David Krakowski, survived. They live in Australia.

Avraham Maas

He was a peddler, always traveling, and going to markets. His principal objective was to give his children a good education. His wife, Ester, helped him achieve this goal and be national Jews. That was his goal in life, and the hope to witness "nachas" (satisfaction) from his children. They did not live to see satisfaction from their children. The German murderers killed the father and the mother.

Three sons of the Maas family survived: Berel, Kopel and Leib Baruch. All of them live in Australia.

[Page 366]

Krakowski family

Top left: Rachel Krakowski,Top Right: Yechiel Krakowski
Bottom left: Elie Krakowski. Bottom right: Yaakov Krakowski

[Page 367]

Mendel Granek

The son of Moshe Granek (Opatower). A hard working man, who made an honorable living for his family. He was a Radomsker Chasid, who performed many good deeds. He loved reading a good Yiddish book. His wife, Chaya Rivka, a daughter of Chaim Djalowski, helped her husband in all of his good deeds for the benefit of all.

From this humble family only one daughter, Rachele, remains, and she lives in Australia with her husband Israel.

Shimon Rosenthal by Eliyahu Rosenthal

The son of Moshe Yaakov was from one of the well–educated families in Klobuck. As a young man, several years before WWI, he started to actively spread the "Haskalah" (non–religious education and culture) in the shtetl. His colleagues were: Yitzhak Yaakov Buchweitz, Zalman Lapides, two Kerner brothers, Yitzhak Granek and Michael Rojewicz, who was born in Krzepice. Shimon opened the first Zionist library, which was located in a small room. In the library there was a large picture hung on the wall of "Yirmiahu, the prophet mourns the destruction of the Beit HaMikdash (temple)".

Because of his "Haskalah" activities Shimon was pursued by fanatics, but he calmly performed his diligent work, and established the foundation of the "Haskalah" in Klobuck. Later he became involved in Czestochowa in social and political activities.

[Page 368]

Shimon Rosenthal shared the fate of the persecuted Jews in Poland. He was killed in the Czestochowa ghetto with his wife and three children. Then my entire family was killed, my mother and sisters: Rivka, Feigel, Leah Sarah, Rachel Esther and their husbands and children.

His surviving brother,

Eliyahu Rosenthal, Australia.

My Parents (Unglick) by Masha Kurland (Unglick)

My father, Itche Unglick, and my mother, Chaya Sarah, always performed the two mitzvot (commandments) of "Gemilut–Chasadim" (charity) and "Hachnasat Orchim" (hospitality).

Itshe Unglick and Chaya Sarah

We lived on the "Shule"(synagogue) street, and we had the only soda water factory in Klobuck. Opposite our house was the "Hachnasat Orchim" place. Several poor passers–by knew that before they went to the "Hachnasat Orchim" to sleep, or before they left the "Hachnasat Orchim" in the morning, my mother would give them a meal to eat and a few groschen (pennies) for the road. My mother also looked after the cots, and made sure they were in order in the " Hachnasat Orchim". She fulfilled the mitzvah (commandment) to perfection.

[Page 369]

During difficult times my father always gave loans to people whenever they needed (help). When he suspected that the financial situation of somebody was not good he used to ask: "How do you manage with your living? Perhaps you need some money. Don't be ashamed to ask for a loan, when you have the money you will give it back to me".

After my father's passed away, people came to repay loans that we did not know about.

My father Yossel Szimkowicz by Baruch Szimkowicz

My father, Yossel Szimkowicz, was born in Krzepice. My mother, Libe, (was born) in Klobuck. From the time they married and throughout all of their many years, they managed a bakery in Klobuck, and made a living from it.

We were four children: My sisters, Tova and Malka, Michael and myself. Our house was for God and for people. My parents did a lot for poor people, and supported people either with money or with baked food. Our bakery was on a crossroad of Czestochowa and Krzepice. Passers–by, and peddlers who came to the fair in Klobuck, first came to our bakery, to warm up and drink a hot glass of coffee or tea that was always ready for the guests. They always could borrow a Talit (prayer shawl) and Tefilin (phylacteries) to pray and afterwards continue their journey.

On Shabbat at dawn, my father was close to the oil lamp, and read twice the weekly (Torah) portion and Rachi 's commentary. When emissaries from Jerusalem from the Yeshivat "Etz Chaim" came, the Rabbi immediately called on my father and Asher Goldberg to collect money for the sacred Torah institutions.

My parents passed away sometimes before the war, but my sister, Tova, died in Czestochowa (during the war). My brother, Michael, I was told, lived in Ozorkaw. During the Jewish extermination period he was sent by the Germans to the Lodz ghetto. When he escaped from the ghetto, he was caught by the Germans and hanged. He was always active in the "Poalei Zion"(Workers of Zion) party (right wing) in Ozorkaw. My sister, Malka, died in Belgium.

[Page 370]

Reb Shmuel Friedman by Yaakov and Yote Friedman

He was an Alexander Chasid, and a business man. Throughout the years, he managed the mill with his partner. As a member of the Judicial Court, he always took care of the poor Jews. He often argued with the Polish members of the Judicial Court because he did not want to yield and give up his fight to help the poor Jews. His wife, Esther Chaya, came from Rabbinical descendants, and she always looked after poor, sick people and sent food packages, for Shabbat, to needy households. She was also active in various women institutions.

We remember their children: Dvorah Feigel, Sarah, Chaim Moshe, and Hadassa. They all perished.

Pinchas Unglick by Baruch Szimkowicz

I knew the house of the Unglick family very well from my childhood, because I went to cheder (school) with their son Avraham, (who lives in Israel), and later we were together in "Chevra–Baruchim" (Society of teenagers). Meshulam Unglick, a cattle trader, honored his parents highly. On Shabbat and Festivals, he used to davenen (pray) in the small Beit–Hamidrash (House of Study). His wife, Fromet Sheindel, was modest, observant and good to people. She helped needy families in secret and silently supported everyone in their sorrow. Her sacred desire was to raise her children in the Jewish spirit. Their son, Pinchas, was known as a joyous, good–hearted man, with a nice smile on his face. He supported social institutions.

[Page 371]

A long time ago, during the years when we went to the Beit–Hamidrash–Bachurim (House of study for teenagers) on Rosh–Chodesh (First day of Jewish month), we gathered money to buy and repair books, he went unnoticed and he was very offended when he was asked: "Why do you not have money to buy books?" He indeed gave the largest amount of money. During a certain period Pinchas was a community representative in Klobuck.

He was killed by the German murderers.

My father Zalman Weichman by Batia Letzer–Weichman

He died on 12 Adar 1944 in the Griditz camp. My brother, Yitzhak, died in Buchenwald on 5 Lyar 1945. My brother, Nechemia, died in the "Hospital" (infirmary) in Mathausen. My sister, Rachel, was killed in Auschwitz in 1942.

**Nechemia (Memye)
Weichman**

Mantshe Unglick Family by Tova Unglick

My father, Mantshe Unglick, arrived in the Zamel camp. From a great fright he became sick and died in 1941. My mother, Fromet, continuously hid in a bunker with her grandchildren until the first "Aussiedlung" (deportation). Later the Germans shot them on the spot. Also my four brothers and my two sisters died during the war. The only thing left is a picture of my sister Hendel.

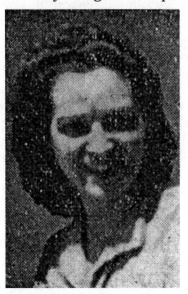

Hendel Unglick

[Page 372]

Karola Enzel by Avraham Enzel

She was born in Klobuck. During the liquidation of the ghetto she worked with sick people who had typhus in the Kamyk shtetl. Later she was transferred to the Zagorz work camp, and from there the Germans sent her to Czestochowa. She died as a heroine. By her death she wanted to save a bunker full of women and children. When the murderers discovered the bunker, she came out from the bunker with another young man, but the other women and children were still hidden. They pretended that they were alone there. The Germans shot them immediately.

**Karola Enzel with her husband
and a child from the Tzintzinatus family**

When your destiny is to die naturally by Avraham Enzel

My grandmother, Henia Enzel, at 70 years old, fled to Czestochowa with her two daughters just before the "Aussiedlung" (deportation). En route she stopped somewhere. First, ten days after the deportation, I received a notice that she was in the fields near Lobodne. In the middle of the night I left the Zagorz camp in order to find my grandmother in the fields. I found her, she was half dead. I brought her to the camp. There, Karola Green and Henia Wolkowicz took care of her. After a few days she recovered.

[Page 373]

In the camp, old people were not allowed, so I took her to Czestochowa with the help of Aryan papers. After six weeks I was informed that my grandmother was very sick. I immediately went to Czestochowa where I saw her. She smiled at me and with a nod of her head she expressed her thanks that she was passing away naturally. She died not long afterwards, and she was properly buried.

My brother, Feivel, together with 14 Jews from the shtetl, Miedzno, were taken away by the Germans on Rosh HaShana, 1939. He was executed in Buchenwald. We had to pay 5 Reichsmarks to receive his ashes, which were buried in Klobuck during 1941.

**Jews from Krzepice camp (close to Klobuck).
Between them several Klobucker Jews.**

[Page 374]

Photographs of Jewish Families from Klobuck

Photographs include those perished during the extermination period of the Jews. In certain family photographs there are individuals who survived and are still alive, (as of 1960).

Aaron Azjner, wife and children.

[Page 375]

Clockwise from the top: Zoltobrotzki Family – some of them survived, Dvorah Zoltobrotzki and Feigel Unglick, Zissel Groyman, Tseshe Abramowicz

[Page 376]

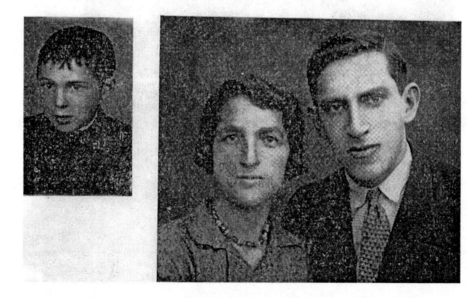

Clockwise from the top: Zisskind Mayerstock with his family, Groynem and Chaya Zoltobrotzki – Chaya lives in Israel, their son Yehuda (perished)

[Page 377]

From left to right: Rachel Gelbart with her children and grandchildren, Yitzik Gelbart and wife.

[Page 378]

Left to right: Mordechai Gelbart with his wife Libe, daughter of Wolf and Rachel Gelbart

[Page 379]

Clockwise from the top left: Sarah Rivka Zigelman, Mordechai Gelbart and his wife Eidel Leah, Shlomo Enzel, Avraham Szperling

[Page 380]

Clockwise from top right: Sarah Azjner, Berel Zigelman, Freide Zigelman, daughter of Berel and Freide, daughter of Sarah Azjner

[Page 381]

Top: Wolf Hersh Rosen
Bottom from left: Chaim Daniel Birenbaum and Rosa Pinkus

[Page 382]

Leizer Kleinberg and his wife, Rachel Nachtigal, Avraham Lieb Nachtigal, Asher Weichman, Wolf Szperling son of Itzik Leib, Pinchas Klopak

[Page 383]

Clockwise from top left: Ratze Berkowicz, Welvel Berkowicz, Breindel Bentshkowki, Daughter Frimet
Center: Standing from right: Grine, Groynem, Leah. Sitting: Avraham and Gutshe Unglick

[Page 384]

Clockwise from upper right: Elyahu Mass and family, Eizik Mass and family, Berel Mass, his wife and child.

[Page 385]

Clockwise from the top right: Freide Rypsztein, husband and child, son of Freide Rypsztein, Children of Chana Rypsztein, who perished together with their parents, Children of Freide Rypsztein

[Page 386]

ישראל זייבעל, מרדכי שפּערלינג און ראָזען,
ט בעת דער דייטשער צוואַנגס־אַרבעט אויף דער לאַנקע ג

Top: Israel Zeibel, Mordechai Szperling and Rosen, picture taken during the German forced labor in the meadow close to the Shul.
Bottom: The Shul Street during the war, the roof of the Shul can be seen.

[Page 387]

„חדר" יסודי התורה של אגודת ישראל

Top: Cheder Yesodei HaTorah of the Agudat Israel.
Bottom: The Firefighters' orchestra, which included a few Jews.

[Page 388]

שרה רחל בירנבוים   אַ גרופּע קלאַבוצקער מיידלעך

Clockwise from top left: Sarah Rachel Birenbaum, A group of women from Klobuck., Benzion Shwertzerski and Dvorah Jarzombek

[Page 389]

Clockwise from top right: Yaakov Davidowicz Yechiel Chaskelewicz and Chaim Bentshkowski's grandson, Golda Rosen

[Page 390]

די משפחה פון הערשל ראָטבאַרד

רייזל לאה דזשאַלאָװסקי

Clockwise from Upper Left: The family of Hershel Rotbard, Reisel Leah Djalowski

Berish and Yachet Rypsztein and their children.

[Page 391]

Tombstone of Rivka Kurland in the Klobuck cemetery, which was close to the tombstone of Reb Yossef Kurland and his daughters.

[Page 392]

Exhumation and Burial of 26 Murdered Jews

The following picture is from Gedalia Goldberg, who was shot in year 1943 in the Czestochowa ghetto, on Podjeczna street during a resistance uprising against the Germans. After the war, the Czestochowa Jewish committee undertook an exhumation (of the bodies) at the place where the mass murder took place. Twenty six corpses were exhumed. His photograph was found in a bottle near his body.

The murdered Jews were brought to rest in the Czestochowa cemetery. The two pictures on the next page are from the burial.

Gedalia Goldberg

[Page 393]

Top: The coffins with the dead ones.

Bottom: The burial.

[Pages 394-406]

Necrology

Translated by Ruth Wilnai

Note: Page numbers in the right column are the page numbers in the original Yizkor book, not this translation.

Surname	Given name	wife	Husband	Daughter	Son	Comments	Page number in Original Yizkor Book
Goldberg	Yitzhak Hanich					The Rabbi Yitzhak-Hanoch Goldberg, the local Rabbi, was the last Rabbi of the Klobuck Community. He went with his people on the death road and was murdered together with his family and with last holy people of Klobuck by the Germans	394
				Alef א			
Abramowicz						wife and children	394
Urbach	Hersz-Dawid					wife and children	394
Unglik	Meshulam	Frumat Sheindl					394
Unglik	Pinchas						394
Unglik	Alter						394
Unglik	Shlomo					wife and children	394
Unglik	Masha						394
Unglik	Chaya-Sara						394
Unglik	Baruch	Chaya					394
Unglik	Kopel						394
Unglik	Rikl					husband and children	394
Unglik	Leibish					wife and children	394
Unglik	Leibke					wife and children	394
Unglik	Kopel					wife and children	394

Unglik	Yissachar				wife and children	394
Unglik	Iczek				wife and children	394
Unglik	Idl					394
Unglik	Gdalyahu					394
Unglik	Miriam				Miriam and Sara are related	394
Unglik	Sara				Miriam and Sara are related	394
Unglik	Yeshayahu					395
Unglik	Yissachar					395
Ajzner	Baruch				and family	395
Ajzner	Shmuel				wife and children	395
Ajzner	Lipman				wife and children	395
Ajzner	Leib Baruch				wife and children	395
Ajzner	Miriam	Gershon Yankl			and family	395
Ajzner	Moshe				Moshe, Fraydl, Hendl, Chana-Laja, Reizl, Hershl are related	395
Ajzner	Fraydl				Moshe, Fraydl, Hendl, Chana-Laja, Reizl, Hershl are related	395
Ajzner	Hendl				Moshe, Fraydl, Hendl, Chana-Laja, Reizl, Hershl are related	395
Ajzner	Chana-Laja				Moshe, Fraydl, Hendl, Chana-Laja, Reizl, Hershl are related	395
Ajzner	Reizl				Moshe, Fraydl, Hendl, Chana-Laja, Reizl, Hershl are related	395
Ajzner	Hershl				Moshe, Fraydl, Hendl, Chana-Laja, Reizl, Hershl are related	395
Ajzner	Laja					395
Ajzner	Wolf				Wolf, Chaya-Sara, Dora are related	395
Ajzner	Chaya-Sara				Wolf, Chaya-Sara, Dora are related	395
Ajzner	Dora				Wolf, Chaya-Sara, Dora are related	395
Ajzner	Leib-Baruch				wife and relatives	395

Bet ב

Bochowicz	Yosef	Nacha				395
Bochowicz	Yitzhak-Yakov	Mania				395
Bochowicz	Berl	Rachel				395
Bochowicz	Shlomo-Yechiel					395
Bochowicz	Treina				and husband	395
Biber	Leibe					395
Birenbom	Yona				wife and children	395
Birenbom	Eliyahu	Chaya-Ester	Sara-Rachel	Wolf-Mendl		395
Birenbom	Itzek Leib				and wife	395
Birenbom	Mendl				wife and children	395
Birenbom	Mordechy				wife and children	395
Blau	Majer				wife and children	395
Blau	Yosef				wife and children	395
Blau	Radl				and children	395
Blau	Chaya		Sara-Rachel	Daniel-Leib		395
Blau	Israel	Radl	Bluma			395
Besser	Dawid				and family	395
Besser	Rachel				and family	395
Besser	Sheindl				Husband and children	396
Besser	Wolf Hersz				and family	396
Berliner	Yoske (yosef)				and family	396
Berkowicz	Velvel				and wife	396
Berkowicz	Ziser					396
Brat	Zalman				wife and children	396
Brat	Pinchas					396
Brat	Gitl					396

Gimel ג

Goldberg	Abraham Herszke					396
Godberg	Gdalyahu					396
Goldberg	Manas					396
Goldberg	Menachem					396
Gutman	Dotman				and family	396
Guterman	Mendl				and family	396
Guterman	Hirsz				Wife and children	396
Gwozdsz	Yizek				and family	396
Gliksman	Abraham					396
Gliksman	Shmuel					396
Gendelman	Leah				and family	396
Gelbert	Rachel				and children: Yitzhak-Mordechai, Eidl-Leah, Dvora-Chana, Aharon-Meir, Wolf-Leib, Liba	396
Gelbert	Moshe				and family	396
Gelbert	Zolka				and family	396
Gelbert	Yeshayahu-Leizer				and family	396
Gelbert	Mordechai				and wife	396
Gelbert	Yitzak					397
Gelbert	Yakl					397
Gelkep					and family	397
Ganyslaw	David-Meir				wife and children	397
Granek	Shlomo					397
Granek	Yitzak				and family	397
Granek	Leibel				and family	397
Granek	Zenwil				and family	397
Grouman	Abraham	Feigl			and children: Zisel, Chaim-Daniel, and daughter	397
Griwu	Ben-Zion				wife and children	397

Gryn	Berl				and family	397
Gryn	Leibusz				wife and children	397
Gryn	Hinda-Miriam					397

Dalet ד

Dawidowicz	Yakov				wife and children	397
Dawidowicz	Shlomo				Shochet	397
Dudek	Machl				wife and children	397
Dudek	Hanoch				wife and children	397
Dudek	Binem				wife and children	397
Dudek	Yosef				and family	397
Dzialowski	Chaim				and family	397
Dzialowski	Shimon				and family	397
Dyamant	Abraham	Rachel				397
Dyamant	Dawid					397
Dyamant	Yakov					397
Dyamant	Matek					397

Hey ה

Holczman	Lipman				and family	397
Holczman	Abraham-Itche				and family	398
Horowicz	Beinish				and family	398
Heyman	Moshe					398
Heyman	Efraim				Heyman Efraim, Berl and Ester are related	398
Heyman	Berl				Heyman Efraim, Berl and Ester are related	398
Heyman	Ester				Heyman Efraim, Berl and Ester are related	398

Vav ו

Wileczki	Moshe	Bryndle			and children	398
Willinger	Mordechai-Gershon					398
Willinger	Bryndle					398

Willinger	Baruch					398
Wien	Yechezkel				Wife and children	398
Wejs	Wolf				and family	398
Wejchman	Kopel	Betshe			and children	398
Wejchman	Aharon					398
Wejchman	Mordechai				Wejchman Mordechai and Leib are related	398
Wejchman	Leib				Wejchman Mordechai and Leib are related	398
Wejchman	Eliyahu	Sara			Children: Pinchas, Rikle, Asher, Yakov-Moshe, Chaya-Rivka	398
Wyman	Yakov-Itzhak	Hinda				398
Wejs	Shlomo	Chaya'le				398
Wejspelner	Grunem					398
Wejspelner	Ester-Rachel				and family	398
Wejspelner	Ester		Iyzik		and children: Mordechai, Groynim	398

Zayin ז

Zlatberski	Sheindl					398
Zlatberski	Chaya					398
Zlatberski	Zalman	Bryndle-Miriam			and six children: Moshe, Rachel, Alte, Beila, Wolf, Zelda	398
Zlatberski	Yehuda-Ber					398
Zlatberski	Beltshe				and Chiam Shlomo and four children: Itzhak, Perl-Rachel, Eliezer	398
Zlatberski	Groynem				and Yehuda	398
Zlatberski	Ben-Zion	Ester-Leah			and their children	399
Zlatberski	Veve				and family	399
Zlatberski	Sara-Leah				and children: Yacht, Dina, Zeev, Shulamit, Yehudith-Daba, Shmuel	399

Zlatberski	Herszl					and wife	399
Zlatberski	Eliyahu					and family	399
Zambek	Leib					and family	399
Zambek	?						399
Zambek	Rachel						399
Zambek	Yitzhak-Wolf					Zambek Yitzhak-Wolf, Shlomo, Zipora, Israel-Chaim, Mordechai, Yakov-Yitzhak, Ester, Dina and Zeev are related	399
Zambek	Shlomo					Zambek Yitzhak-Wolf, Shlomo, Zipora, Israel-Chaim, Mordechai, Yakov-Yitzhak, Ester, Dina and Zeev are related	399
Zambek	Zipora					Zambek Yitzhak-Wolf, Shlomo, Zipora, Israel-Chaim, Mordechai, Yakov-Yitzhak, Ester, Dina and Zeev are related	399
Zambek	Israel-Chaim					Zambek Yitzhak-Wolf, Shlomo, Zipora, Israel-Chaim, Mordechai, Yakov-Yitzhak, Ester, Dina and Zeev are related	399
Zambek	Mordechai					Zambek Yitzhak-Wolf, Shlomo, Zipora, Israel-Chaim, Mordechai, Yakov-Yitzhak, Ester, Dina and Zeev are related	399
Zambek	Yakov-Yitzhak					Zambek Yitzhak-Wolf, Shlomo, Zipora, Israel-Chaim, Mordechai, Yakov-Yitzhak, Ester, Dina and Zeev are related	399
Zambek	Ester					Zambek Yitzhak-Wolf, Shlomo, Zipora, Israel-Chaim, Mordechai, Yakov-Yitzhak, Ester, Dina and Zeev are related	399
Zambek	Dina					Zambek Yitzhak-Wolf, Shlomo, Zipora, Israel-Chaim, Mordechai, Yakov-Yitzhak,	399

						Ester, Dina and Zeev are related	
Zambek	Zeev						Zambek Yitzhak-Wolf, Shlomo, Zipora, Israel-Chaim, Mordechai, Yakov-Yitzhak, Ester, Dina and Zeev are related	399
Zander	Moshe						and family	399
Zaks	Ester							399
Zaks	Leib						and wife	399
Zaks	Yitzhak						and children	399
Zaks	Ita							399
Zaks	Zashna						Zaks Zashna, Lida and Madlene are related	399
Zaks	Lida						Zaks Zashna, Lida and Madlene are related	399
Zaks	Madlene						Zaks Zashna, Lida and Madlene are related	399
Zygelboym	Moshe	Masha					Children: Shlomo, Dawid, Sala, Rivka, Nacha'le	399
Zygelman	Kopel							399
Zygelman	Berl						and family	399
Zygelman	Shlomo						Zygelman Shlomo and Yosef-Aharon are related	399
Zygelman	Yosef-Aharon						Zygelman Shlomo and Yosef-Aharon are related	399
Zygelman	Abraham							399
Zygelman	Gabai							399
Zygelman	Yakov						and family	399
Zygelman	Zalman						Wife and children	399
Zygelman	Berisz						Wife and children	399
Zygelman	Itzik	Leah						399
Zygelman	Yehuda						Zygelman Yehuda, Yosef and Herszl are related	399
Zygelman	Yosef						Zygelman Yehuda, Yosef and Herszl are related	399

Zygelman	Herszl					Zygelman Yehuda, Yosef and Herszl are related	399
Zaybel	Meir						399
Zaybel	Beila					and children	399
Zaybel	Groynim						400
Zaybel	Itzik					and family	400
Zajdman	Chaim	Chana'le				Zydman Chaim and Chana'le are related to Zydman Yitzhak, Chaya-Rivka, Ester, Rachel, Yakov and Nathan	400
Zajdman	Yitzhak					Zydman Chaim and Chana'le are related to Zydman Yitzhak, Chaya-Rivka, Ester, Rachel, Yakov and Nathan	400
Zajdman	Chaya-Rivka					Zydman Chaim and Chana'le are related to Zydman Yitzhak, Chaya-Rivka, Ester, Rachel, Yakov and Nathan	400
Zajdman	Ester					Zydman Chaim and Chana'le are related to Zydman Yitzhak, Chaya-Rivka, Ester, Rachel, Yakov and Nathan	400
Zajdman	Rachel					Zydman Chaim and Chana'le are related to Zydman Yitzhak, Chaya-Rivka, Ester, Rachel, Yakov and Nathan	400
Zajdman	Yakov					Zydman Chaim and Chana'le are related to Zydman Yitzhak, Chaya-Rivka, Ester, Rachel, Yakov and Nathan	400
Zajdman	Nathan					Zydman Chaim and Chana'le are related to Zydman Yitzhak, Chaya-Rivka, Ester, Rachel, Yakov and Nathan	400
Zajdman	Pinchas					Zydman Pinchas, Rachel, Gitl, Perl, Rivka are related	400
Zajdman	Rachel					Zydman Pinchas, Rachel, Gitl, Perl, Rivka are related	400
Zajdman	Gitl					Zydman Pinchas, Rachel, Gitl, Perl, Rivka are related	400
Zajdman	Perl					Zydman Pinchas, Rachel, Gitl,	400

						Perl, Rivka are related	
Zajdman	Rivka					Zydman Pinchas, Rachel, Gitl, Perl, Rivka are related	400
Zajdman	Baruch					Zydman Baruch, Rivka, Arye, Ahron, Chaya are related	400
Zajdman	Rivka					Zydman Baruch, Rivka, Arye, Ahron, Chaya are related	400
Zajdman	Arye					Zydman Baruch, Rivka, Arye, Ahron, Chaya are related	400
Zajdman	Aharon					Zydman Baruch, Rivka, Arye, Ahron, Chaya are related	400
Zajdman	Chaya					Zydman Baruch, Rivka, Arye, Ahron, Chaya are related	400
Zajdman	Ester					Zydman Ester, Rachel, Chaya-Rivka, Mania, Abraham, Aharon and Pinchas are related	400
Zajdman	Rachel					Zydman Ester, Rachel, Chaya-Rivka, Mania, Abraham, Aharon and Pinchas are related	400
Zajdman	Chaya-Rivka					Zydman Ester, Rachel, Chaya-Rivka, Mania, Abraham, Aharon and Pinchas are related	400
Zajdman	Mania					Zydman Ester, Rachel, Chaya-Rivka, Mania, Abraham, Aharon and Pinchas are related	400
Zajdman	Abraham					Zydman Ester, Rachel, Chaya-Rivka, Mania, Abraham, Aharon and Pinchas are related	400
Zajdman	Aharon					Zydman Ester, Rachel, Chaya-Rivka, Mania, Abraham, Aharon and Pinchas are related	400
Zajdman	Pinchas					Zydman Ester, Rachel, Chaya-Rivka, Mania, Abraham, Aharon and Pinchas are related	400
Zajdman	Yitzhak					Zydman Yitzhak, Chaya-Rivka, Nathan, Ester, Rachel, Yakov are related	400
Zajdman	Chaya-Rivka					Zydman Yitzhak, Chaya-Rivka, Nathan, Ester, Rachel, Yakov are related	400

Zajdman	Nathan				Zydman Yitzhak, Chaya-Rivka, Nathan, Ester, Rachel, Yakov are related	400
Zajdman	Ester				Zydman Yitzhak, Chaya-Rivka, Nathan, Ester, Rachel, Yakov are related	400
Zajdman	Rachel				Zydman Yitzhak, Chaya-Rivka, Nathan, Ester, Rachel, Yakov are related	400
Zajdman	Yakov				Zydman Yitzhak, Chaya-Rivka, Nathan, Ester, Rachel, Yakov are related	400
Zalman	Abraham				Zalman Abraham, Yehuda and Ber are related	400
Zalman	Yehuda				Zalman Abraham, Yehuda and Ber are related	400
Zalman	Ber				Zalman Abraham, Yehuda and Ber are related	400
Zalman Arye	Bryndle				and their three children: Mantshe, Menachem and his wife and their two children	400
Zelkowicz	Moshe				and family	400
Zelkowicz	Zelig				and family	400
YUD						
Yazszamback	Leah				and daughter Dvora	400
Yakobowicz	Abraham				wife and children	400
Yakobowicz	Simcha					400
Yoskowicz	Herszl				wife and children	400
Kaf כ						
Chada	Herszl					400
Chada	Itzek				wife and children	400
Chada	Royse				and children	400
Chada	Yeshayhu				and family	400
Chaskelowicz	Yechezkel	Mindle-Yente				400
Chorzowski	Abraham-Leib	Gitl				400

Chorzowski	Imanuel	Matle-Roza			Imanuel's sister Frydle-Leah and her children: Itche-Ber, Moshe'le	400
Chlopak	Berl				and children	400
Chlopak	Yitzhak	Faygl			and children	401
Chlopak	Chana'le				Chlopak Chana'le, Tzasha and Bela are related	401
Chlopak	Tzasha				Chlopak Chana'le, Tzasha and Bela are related	401
Chlopak	Bela				Chlopak Chana'le, Tzasha and Bela are related	401

Lamed ל

Langer	Yosef-Meir					401
Lapides	Fayvel	Rachel-Leah				401
Lapides	Zisser					401
Lapides	Kryndl					401
Lowiczki	Zenwil				Wife and children	401
Lowiczki	Abraham					401
Lichter	Shimon				wife and children	401
Lichter	Yakov				wife and children	401
Lewkowicz	Baruch				wife and children	401
Lewkowicz	Isreal				wife and children	401
Lewkowicz					Leib Lewkowicz's wife and their children	401

Mem מ

Mantel	Yakov				and family	401
Mantel	Kopel				and family	401
Mass	Fayvel					401
Mass	Eliyahu					401
Mass	Berl				wife and children	401
Mass	Chaim-Mendle				and wife	401
Mass	Yakov				and family	401

Mass	Shmuel					wife and children	401
Mass	Iyzik						401
Mantel	Rachel					and her husband	401
Markowicz	Yosef					and his wife	401
Markowicz	Yerachmiel					and his family	401
Mintkewicz						wife and children	401
Meirsztock	Ziskind					wife and children	401
Mayersztock	Nechemya					wife and children	402
Mendlowicz	Chaim					wife and children	402
Martz	Yitzhak					wife and children: Yidle, Moshe, Leib	402

Nun נ

Nachtigal	Aharon-Pinchas	Rachel				and children: Abraham-Leib, Zvia	402
Neidziela	Chana-Rosa					Neidzila Chana-Rosa, Mirl, Zipora, Shlomo and Adela are related.	402
Neidziela	Mirl					Neidzila Chana-Rosa, Mirl, Zipora, Shlomo and Adela are related.	402
Neidziela	Zipora					Neidzila Chana-Rosa, Mirl, Zipora, Shlomo and Adela are related.	402
Neidziela	Shlomo					Neidzila Chana-Rosa, Mirl, Zipora, Shlomo and Adela are related.	402
Neidziela	Adela					and three children. Neidzila Chana-Rosa, Mirl, Zipora, Shlomo and Adela are related.	402
Neidziela	Abraham					wife and children	402
Neidziela	Pinchas	Sara				and children	402
Neidziela	Shlomo						402
Najman	Shlomo-Baruch					wife and children	402

Samech ס

Starzynski	Rivka-Leah					and family	402

Skarpa	Leah					402

Ayin ע

Adaniya					and children, Basha and children	402
Eliszewicz	Peretz				and family	402
Eliszewicz	Jonathan					402
Enzel	Cholke				wife and children	402
Enzel	Yakov				wife and children	402
Enzel	Yeshayahu				and children	402
Enzel	Shlomo					402
Enzel	Sara					402
Enzel	Rivka				and children	402
Epsztain	Yitzhak-Yakov				and wife	402
Epsztain	Moshe				wife and children	402

Peh פ

Patezki	Yudl				and daughter	403
Pinkus	Herszl					403
Pinkus	Yoma (Binyamin)					403
Fintkewicz	Shyndle				and husband	403
Fayga	Faygle-Adela		Chaim			403
Fayga	Yankl	Frida				403
Fayga	Bayle		Zalman		and children	403
Fayga	Chaya-Sara		Moshe-Yeshayahu			403
Fayga	Abraham-Aba	Eidle				403
Fayga	Hinda				Fayga Hinda, Yakov-Mordechai, Abraham-Dawid and Leah-Zelda are related	403
Fayga	Yakov-Mordechai				Fayga Hinda, Yakov-Mordechai, Abraham-Dawid and Leah-Zelda are related	403
Fayga	Abraham-	Leah-			Fayga Hinda, Yakov-	403

	Dawid	Zelda			Mordechai, Abraham-Dawid and Leah-Zelda are related	
Fayga	?	Ester				403
Fayga	Chaya				her son Daniel-Leib, her daughter Sara-Rachel	403
Fayga	Dvora					403
Pelta	Macha'le				and her daughter	403
Fridman	Eliyahu				wife and children	403
Fridman	Shlomo-Hirsz				wife and son	403
Fridman	Eliyahu					403
Fridman	Yona					403
Fraytag	Yosef				and family	403
Frank	Layzer				and family	403
Frank	Herszl				wife and children	403

Tsadek צ

Tzukerman	Yakov				and wife	403

Kof ק

Kanapnitzki	Abraham				and family	403
Korland	Yosef-Meir	Rivka'le				403
Korcbart	Jonathan				wife and children	403
Korcbart	Gershon				and son	404
Korcbart	Gronim				wife and children	404
Korcbart	Berl				and wife	404
Korcbart	Cholke				and family	404
Klejnberg	Layzer-Yehoshua				wife and children	404
Klejnberg	Fiszel				wife and children	404
Klejberg	Fiszel				wife and children	404
Kraszkowski	Eliyahu					404
Kroyze	Yankl				old man	404
Kaszpitzki	Alter				and family	404

Kaszpitzki	Eliezer					and family	404

Resh ר

Rozen	Yitzhak					and family	404
Rozen	Mordechai					wife and children	404
Rozen	Wolf-Hersz	Gelda				children: Chanina, Abraham-Leib, Shlomo-Yosef	404
Rozen	Eliyahu						404
Rozen	Yechezkel						404
Rozen	Fraydle				Moshe		404
Rozen	Yechiel					and wife	404
Rozen	Dawid					and wife and children: Shulamit, Sara and Rachel	404
Rozen	Ester						404
Rozenthal	Yakov-Fiszel					and wife	404
Rozenthal	Shlomo					and wife	404
Rozenthal	Abraham						404
Rozenthal	Yechiel	Bronia				and children	404
Rozenthal	Shimon						404
Rotbart	Mordechai-Dawid	Bryndle				and son	404
Rotbart	Leah					husband and children	404
Rotbart	Herszl	Gitl				and children	404
Ryfsztajn	Berisz					wife and children	405
Ryfsztajn	Shlomo	Frayda				and children	405
Ryfsztajn	Itzek	Rikle				children: Masha and Asher	405
Ryber	Abraham	Malka				and children: Moshe, Israel, Leah, Ester, Rozshke	405
Ryber	Shimon					wife and children	405
Ryber	Moshe					Moshe and Israel are related	405
Ryber	Israel					Moshe and Israel are related	405
Rajch	Daniel						405

Shin ש

Szwayerczerski	Zalman-Yosef				and family	405
Sztyler	Itche-Meir					405
Sztajer	Itzchak					405
Sztajer	Baruch				and family	405
Sztajer	Israel				and children	405
Szilit	Herszl				and family	405
Szilit	Mindle		Simcha		and children	405
Szperling	Meir					405
Szperling	Eliyahu	Yente			Children: Nacha, Anszel, Itzhak, Fraydle, Pesa	405
Szperling	Wolf				&wife, children Yosef, Kopel	405
Szperling	Izyk				wife and children	405
Szperling	Itzhal-Leib				and family	405
Szperling	Baruch	Sara				405
Szperling	Itzek				wife and children	405
Szperling	Herszl	Chana			and family	405
Szperling	Mordechi				and family	405
Szperling	Chana				and daughter	405
Szperling	Itzhak				and wife	405
Szperling	Eliyahu				and family	405
Szperling	Yosef				and family	405
Szperling	Yakov				and family	406
Szperling	Berl					406
Szperling	Batshe					406
Szperling	Eliyahu				and children	406
Szperling	Abraham					406
Szperling	Berl	Pesa			and children	406
Szperling	Chana				and children	406
Szymakowicz	Michael				wife and children	406
Szymakowicz	Tova				husband and children	406

The latest Klubuck's Community Heads

Surname	Given name	wife	Husband	Daughter	Son	comment	Page number in Original Yizkor Book
Szperling	Baruch						406
Dzialowski	Yakov-Yosef						406
Diamant	Abraham						406
Wejs	Wolf						406
Zlatwerski	Yosef-Leib						406
Chada	Yakov						406
Szperling	Mordechai						406

From the latest Klobuck's Community Heads

Surname	Given name	wife	Husband	Daughter	Son	comment	page in Yizkor Book
Zlatwerzki	Yosef-Leib					Lives in Israel	406

Klobuck's People Who Passed Away in Israel

Surname	Given name	wife	Husband	Daughter	Son	comment	Page number in Original Yizkor Book
Birnbaum	Shlomo						407
Goldberg	Asher	Gitl					407
Granek	Yakov						407
Dudek	Moshe						407
Wilinger	Imanuel	Beila				and their daughter - Rachel	407

Zajbel	Faiga					From the home of Besser	407
Zlatnik	Pesa					From the home of Chrozawoski	407
Hayman	Kaza						407

Klobuck's People Who Killed on Duty in Israel

Surname	Given name	wife	Husband	Daughter	Son	comment	Page number in Original Yizkor Book
Brat	Eliezer					Eliezer was killed on Duty with the Palmach in Kibutz Mishmar Ha'emek,	407
Zaks	Aharon					Aharon was killed on an IDF's duty	407

[Pages 407-416]

Klobucker Survivors in Israel, France and in Australia

Translated from Yiddish to English by Asher Szmulewicz

[Pages 408]

Like all the Jews from Eastern Europe, the Klobucker Jews, spread out all over the world. Even before the First World War, the Klobucker Jews traveled the world to find a livelihood and a better life. People went to America, England, Argentina and Eretz Israel.

Baruch Szimkowicz

Klobucker Jews in Eretz Israel

Just after the First World War when Poland became independent, the "Poznantshikes" and the "Haliertshikes"* threatened the Polish Jews with their anti-Semitic and hooligan actions, by cutting the beards of Jews and conducting pogroms. It was then that Klobucker Jews started to make Aliya to Eretz Israel. It was after the Balfour Declaration, (England's declaration that there should be a Jewish homeland in then Palestine), which spread the hope that Jews would receive Eretz Israel. Klobucker Jews also made their journey to Eretz Israel.

After the First World War, I lived in Warsaw and did not know exactly what was going on in Klobuck. In 1923 I left to go to Eretz Israel, as a member of the Warsaw "Young Mizrachi". I settled in Jerusalem.

In 1925 I went to Tel Aviv, and there I was informed

[Pages 409]

*Note of the Writer: "Poznantshikes", "Haliertshikes" : Polish military formations, the first called after the region of the city Poznan (Posen in German) and the second named after the General Haller. that Klobucker Jews were in Israel. My first encounter was with Feigele Skarpes and her husband, Godel, from Czestochowa.

In addition to Feigele, there were also the following Klobuckers in Israel: Shlomo Birenbaum, Kerner, Chaim Zeidman, Yaakov Dawidowicz, Esther Granek and Emmanuel Willinger. They all came with their families. Then life was very harsh in Israel, and it was very difficult from all sides. The only consolation was to say: "Troubles of the many are half of the consolation". Boats came with Polish Jews, people called it the "Rough Aliyah".

The Pioneers Aliya

When the British Mandate government stopped the Aliya to Eretz Israel, the Zionist Organization arranged for illegal Aliya, in which members of the Klobuck "Hitachdut" organization participated. Several Klobuckers (attempted to) make the journey, not in a single group, but in various groups. When they arrived close to the Eretz Israel coasts they were caught and send back to where they came from. The Olim traveled (by foot) through several countries, and later traveled with various false papers until they arrived safely in Eretz Israel.

Through this Aliya the following "Hitachdut" members entered the country (of Israel): Menachem Chadzeski, Yaakov Szperling, Avraham Goldberg, Yaakov Starjinski, Daniel Szperling, Chaim Kurland, Shmuel Goldberg, Rachel Chade, Batia Zeibel, Chava Walbram and Leah Birenbaum. When Hitler came to power in Germany, Avraham Unglick, who used to live in Berlin, left the Third Reich and came to Eretz Israel.

After the "Churban" (Shoah) came the survivors.

When the gates of the concentration camps opened, and we received information in Israel about the Klobucker Jews who survived, I received a letter from the camps through the Jewish Agency. The letter was written by a former friend from the time when I went to school in the "Beit-HaMidrash" (house of study), Yaakov Granek. He wrote in perfect Hebrew and described, in summary, the kind of sufferings he went through: his parents and wife were murdered. Granek asked to be allowed to come to Jerusalem to see the Gerer

Rebbe and become his secretary. When he arrived safely in Israel, he would become a Gerer Chasid.

[Pages 410]

**Klobucker committee in Israel, National Convention,
Chol HaMoed Pesach 5717 (1957)**

I filled out his request (application), and when he came to Eretz Israel, he went to Jerusalem for Shavuot to visit the Gerer Rebbe, and stayed by me during the "Yom Tov" (Holiday) with his son Berek.

Little by little the Klobucker Jews, survivors of the German extermination, started to come. Several went to various countries of Galut (Diaspora). We don't know how many Klobucker Jews live in the Diaspora. In Israel there are about 140 families (from Klobuck). Almost everybody had work. We work and earn, some more, some less. All of the Klobuckers took part in the Liberation War, and even earlier in the Haganah. Our children are good soldiers of Tsahal (Israel Defense Forces). We remember a son of a Klobucker who fell during the Liberation War: Eliezer Brat, the son of Shoshana Brat, the grandson of Emmanuel Willinger. He fell in the ranks of the Palmach (Elite unit) during the combat in Mishmar HaEmek.

[Pages 411]

Eliezer Brat who fell in the ranks of the Palmach during the combat in Mishmar HaEmek

We Did Not Forget the Kedoshim (Martyrs)

Every year on Tammuz 17, we duly organize the "Hazkarah" (Remembrance) for the Jews of Klobuck, who were murdered, and for the entire community of Klobuck. Also we carried out the task of perpetuating the Klobucker martyrs by writing a Yiskor (remembrance) book. This book will be a tombstone that will be transmitted from generation to generation, and will relate how Jews lived in Klobuck, and how they were persecuted by the Germans.

The Jews from Klobuck in Israel gather from time to time for familial happy events, such as for a Chanukah evening, and for a Chol HaMoed Pesach celebration and the like.

We also celebrated the 10th Year Jubilee of the State of Israel. The famous singer Sarah Yaari participated in this celebration.

We also received people from Klobuck who live in other countries, and who come to visit Israel from time to time. We also regret that some of the Jews from Klobuck do not find it necessary to participate in our celebrations, or even come to the "Hazkarah" for the martyrs.

[Pages 412]

Remembrance ceremonies for the Klobucker martyrs

Top: 5716 Remembrance Ceremony (1956) in Tel Aviv with the participation of Rabbi Spir

Bottom: Remembrance Ceremony in Tel Aviv for the 15th anniversary of the martyrdom of the Klobuck community (1957)

[Pages 413]

Banquets and Celebrations of Klobucker Jews in Israel

Top: The celebration of the 10th Independence Day
Bottom: A marriage celebration 1958

[Pages 414]

קלאָבוצקער קאָמיטעט אויף אַ חתונה־אָוונט 1959

Top: Klobuck committee during the Chanukah evening 1959

Bottom: Banquet in honor of a guest from Australia: Adele Unglick, Shmuel Goldberg welcomes the guest

[Pages 415]

Top: Conference to raise money for the Yiskor book

Bottom: President of the convention of Klobucker Jews in Tel Aviv. Chol HaMoed Pesach 5717 (1957). A. Wolf Jasny gave a conference about the Yizkor book

[Pages 416]

Chanukah evening of the Klobucker Jews in Israel

[Page 417]

Klobuckers in France

by Moshe Wajnman

Translated from Yiddish to English by Asher Szmulewicz

The emigration of Jews from Klobuck to France lasted for a few decades. Starting during the Czarist regime in Russia, Jews left Klobuck and went to France. In part (they left) to escape the military service, "Dinen Fonien" (Russian Service), which was characterized with blows and anti-Semitic insults, and partly for economic reasons, due to the inability to earn a living. In the aftermath of the 1905 revolution a third group left Klobuck and went to France. These were Jews with well-known political positions, and they joined the commoner emigration flow to France, and partly to Belgium. This emigration was mainly a political emigration. People exiled themselves because of the political repression.

A larger emigration flow of Klobucker Jews started before the outbreak of WWI, especially in 1912-1914, due to the boycott of Jewish trades by anti-Semitic elements, and the loss of their livelihoods by the Jews of Klobuck. The thought of emigration as a solution became more prevalent. The ones who left were those who had (financial) means or had relatives to go to. Those who had boat tickets went to America, but many others became stuck half-way in France. At that time it was not too difficult to get settled economically. Access to work or a trade in France for the newcomer was not restricted. During their first years in France, the Klobucker Jews were mainly working in trade and small businesses, primarily in the garment industry of women and menswear.

A new emigration flow from Klobuck occurred during the First World War. The famine in the Polish towns during 1914-1918 drove many young Jews out of Klobuck, and (forced many) to go to work in the coal mines of Germany, with the hope that later they would be able to settle abroad. The Jewish coal miners, in those years, were in Germany, and they also worked in various crafts (in Germany) until the rise of power of Hitler.

[Page 418]

In 1933 when Hitler came to power, the Klobucker Jews left Germany and settled in France.

In the beginning of the 1920's very few Klobucker Jews emigrated. The Polish economy had stabilized. The economic situation was not as bad. Jews traded and worked and made a living, but then the economic situation worsened, because Minister Grabski levied (excessive) taxes on Jews, and poverty increased in the shtetl every day.

The fortunate ones, who then had children abroad, especially in America, received a few dollars from time to time to get through the bad times. Then emigration again recommenced. Mostly those who emigrated were Jewish workers and middle class people, and also young people, who were active in the Communist movement, and were harassed and targeted by the police.

In view of the severe economic crisis, anti-Semitism took more threatening forms. The constant worry about the future didn't provide any peace of mind for people, especially for the young people. A large segment of the young people left the shtetl for larger cities, and went to Czestochowa, Lodz, Katowice, and those who had the means went to France. The Zionists found a way out by walking and traveling towards Eretz Israel.

Because of the political persecutions, the writer of these lines, together with a group, had to leave Poland, and for some time settled in Belgium, and then later in Paris.

[Page 419]

Klobuck Countrymen Organization in France

The emigration from Klobuck in France, in the beginning, was not organized in the form of a countryman association. The first emigrants did not have the idea of a countryman association, but almost all of them belonged to various "Societies" that dealt with social help, and provided (at 120 years) a grave. The thought to organize a countryman association grew out of the great (financial) hardship that was occurring in our home shtetl. The emergency need to send money home to deal with the hunger of the Klobuck children was becoming more urgent every day.

Our countryman, Benzion Green, who was a father of five children, devoted all of his energy to organize all of the countrymen. During the first meeting a help committee was elected, and a large amount of money was raised. The fundraising went on as planned.

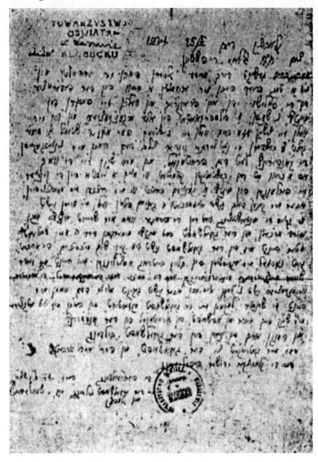

**Document concerning the action
conducted in France to help the
hungry Jewish children in Klobuck**

According to our plans, then in Klobuck we established a multi-party committee, in which the entire community was also represented. We linked ourselves with the "OSE"[1] (TOZ in Poland), who made an agreement with us that through our fundraising the "TOZ" in Poland will increase its projects.

Our help for Klobuck lasted until the outbreak of the war. But no stable countryman organization was established.

[Page 420]

Jews from Klobuck in France

When the war broke out in 1939, the Klobucker Jews who lived in France were drafted in the French Army, partly as volunteers[2] , to combat Hitler's fascism. In the army were: Moshe Wajnman; Leibel Azjner; Noach Rypsztein; Kopel Mas; Yankel Moshe Unglick; and others. Together with French soldiers, the Klobucker Jews became prisoners of war, and were held in captivity in German war prisoner camps until the end of the war. Only a few managed to escape from the prisoner of war camps, and participate in the Resistance movement: Moshe Wajnman, Noach Rypsztein and Yankel Moshe Unglick (Leibkes).

The terrifying bloodshed, carried out by the German murderers, against the Jewish people, did not spare our Klobucker Jews in Paris. In France those who were murdered included: Benzion Green and his wife, who was from Czestochowa and her maiden name was Yaskel, and their four children. Only one daughter survived. The daughters of our friend, Yossel Zachs (who passed away recently), were murdered; and the wife of Israel Azjner and their children. In the French Resistance Movement (Maquis), Klobucker Jews had important positions, in Paris: Yankel Moshe Unglick (Leibkes) (nowadays in Poland), and Moshe Wajnman in Toulouse (South of France).

[Page 421]

After the Liberation, the Klobucker Jews in Paris strove to reestablish their private and social life. The writer of these lines, who was active before the war in the Czestochowa countryman society activities, in which the Klobucker Jews joined, took part in the re-establishment of the society. The orderly flow of new countrymen, the survivors of the German death camps, imposed on us an important task to help them, both for those who were just passing through Paris, and for those who wanted to establish themselves there.

Today, although not organized, the Klobucker Jews form a pleasant family. The work of creating the Yiskor Book, to perpetuate the memory of our destroyed hometown, and the murdered individuals and families, brought together even more Klobucker Jews in France. The painful loss of our two countrymen, Aliye Szperling and Yossel Zachs, seriously affected all of us.

The Klobucker Jews in Paris, imbued with the feeling of brotherhood and assisting others, will continue performing these tasks.

[Page 422]

**Haskarah in Paris,
in remembrance of the murdered community of Klobuck**

[Page 423]

**Klobucker committee,
leading the Hazkarah, speech by Moshe Wajnman**

Translators footnotes

1. OSE (Oeuvre de Secours aux Enfants), in English "Organization to Save the Children".

2. The Jews who were French citizens were automatically drafted in the army; the foreigners had to volunteer.

[Pages 424-430]

Klobucker in Australia

by Eliyahu Rosenthal

Translated from Yiddish to English by Asher Szmulewicz

The first Klobucker who walked on Australian soil was Shlomo Granek z"l (of blessed memory), the son of Moshe Granek (from Opatow), a son-in- law of Shalom Lisek. Before then, for a long time he lived in Czestochowa. He arrived in Melbourne with his wife and two children in 1937. He pursued the traditional Klobuck life, and raised his children with this in mind. Shlomo brought his brother, Mordechai Granek, the son-in-law of Yechiel Kroszkowski z"l. Mordechai came with two of his children on the eve of WWII, and he left his wife Breindel, with their other three children in Poland. She survived the murderous disaster with one son. They came to Melbourne right after the war. Until today he is busy being a tailor.

Mordechai Granek also brought the survivors of his family: his brother-in-law and sister-in-law David and Esther Kroszkowski, and the children of his brother-in-law, Avraham Kroszkowski, Shlomo Mordechai, Gitel and Zissel, the daughter of Avraham Diamant and the wife of David Kroszkowski. They have three children today.

After the war others came to Melbourne, including: David Granek, with his son Mordechai; the daughter of Mendel and Chaya Rivka Granek, Rachele, with her husband, Israel Granek; and the daughter of Leibele Granek, Sarah with her husband Chaim Zeltzer. Thus, the survivors of the Granek family moved to Australia and continued their former Jewish traditional lives.

Adele Unglick was the first from her family to come to Australia after the war. She brought with her the surviving young girl, Bashe, daughter of her murdered brother Aaron.

Adele married Gedaliahu, the son of David Chajewski from Krzepice, and she brought her brothers: Leibush, with his wife and children; Meshulam, with his wife and child, and also the two surviving sons of her brother Aaron.

[Pages 425]

Klobucker countrymen in Australia

[Pages 426]

The Chajewski family took an honorable place in the Jewish social life in Melbourne and this applied also to some extent to the Unglick family.

*

Reb Yaakov Baruch, the son of Berel Baruch, who in his time in Klobuck was known as a Torah student, came to Australia before the war. His wife and two children stayed in Poland and shared the tragic fate of the majority of Polish Jews.

Today Yaakov lives alone in Sydney. He suffers from his personal tragedy and the Jewish tragedy.

*

Also Avraham Yehoshua, the son of Moshe Yaakov Rosenthal z"l, lives in Melbourne.

He came to Australia during the war, with deported Jews from Germany, where he used to live for many years. He lives a Jewish traditional life, like in the good old time before WWII in Poland.

During the last emigration flow of Polish Jews to Australia, he brought his brother, the writer of these lines, with his wife and two children. He also brought his sister's daughter, Libe, with her husband, Meir Davidowicz, and their two children.

*

First, the son of Wolf Hirsh Rosen, escaped to Russia during the Second World War, and later he lived in Germany from where he made Aliya to Israel. In 1955 he came to Australia and lives in Melbourne.

In Sydney lives Moshe, the son of Shimon Djalowski. He came right after the war, together with many other Jews.

In Melbourne lives the son of Aaron Szperling, Mordechai, and his brother is in America. They are the only ones who survived from the large Szperling family, grandchildren of Reb Meir Szperling. There are also two sons of Mordechai Gelbart, Yankel and Nathan, with their wives and children. They have a very good life.

[Pages 427]

*

In the later years after the war, a group of Klobuckers, who survived the German extermination, came to Australia. They live together in Melbourne: Aaron David Buchweicz with his wife and two children. He lives a Jewish well to do life, and takes part in Jewish social activities. He produces coats for women and makes a (good) living.

In Melbourne also live: the son of Avraham Maas, Berel with his wife Matel, and their child, Kopel, with his wife Chaya and three children.

Leib Baruch and Mendel Shniur, with his wife and three children, live in Sydney, and they live a Jewish traditional life. Also there are Sheindel Azjner (married to Goldfarin) with two children, and her brother, Berel Azjner.

They make a living from trade and live modestly.

[Pages 428]

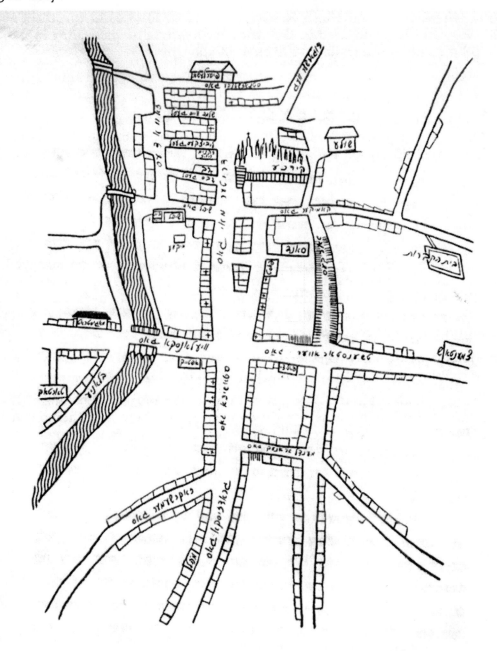

Map of Klobuck Drawn by Adele Unglick

[Pages 429]

[blank page]

[Pages 430]

[blank page]

[Page 431]

Final Remarks

Translated from Yiddish to English by Asher Szmulewicz

Coincidently, we finished writing the Yiskor Book of the murdered community of Klobuck during the days of the Adolf Eichman trial in Jerusalem. (Eichman was) the German mass murderer, who conducted, organized and implemented the extermination of hundreds and hundreds of Jewish communities. It is beyond human ability to present all of the testimonies before the Israeli court, or even of at least one representative from each community, to tell the Israeli judges, and the historical world judges, how the Germans in each town or shtetl specially devised bestial and cunning means to disguise their murderous and thieving intentions towards the Jewish population. Each Yiskor Book's contents of a murdered community is a special indictment by the Jewish people against the Germans. Those who actively or passively watched with indifference, benefited from the robbery, and took part in the extermination of the six millions Jews. The "Sefer Klobuck" that we present to the public is one of those indictments.

The "Sefer Klobuck", like all of the Yiskor Books, is a joint work of the "Organization of People Originating from Klobuck in Israel". It gathered the documents and the financial resources for the book from the Klobuckers who contributed to the purpose; it (located) the individuals who took a pen in their hand to describe the life and the death of their community; and (provided) the editor who condensed, filtered and reviewed (the text) to assure the use of proper Yiddish language, and prepared (the book) for print.

Each of the above mentioned participants in the "Sefer Klobuck" made additional efforts to ensure that the book was published in its completeness. The "Sefer Klobuck" included all the knowledge of the Klobuckers about the historical past of

[Page 432]

their former home in the Polish shtetl; and of the old time Jewish way of life, and their livelihoods and cultural activities until the disaster. A special place was made in the Yiskor Book for the Rabbinical traditions, social activists and the social political activities, in which there was wide spread participation, especially when viewed in relation to the relatively small number of Jews in Klobuck.

The tragic experiences of the Jews from Klobuck during the German Jewish extermination was brought to print from the memories of our countrymen, who experienced all of the seven levels of hell, and finally had the chance to be spared from the German annihilation.

Among the memories of 40 friends, often the same facts or stories are remembered. This was done on purpose, because everybody sees each event from his own point of view. The memories of many and their repetitions added to the completeness of the entire way of life of the old time, small, community of Klobuck. This was especially important about the memories of the time of the extermination, because it reinforced the truth of the barbarian events from that time, and according to the Talmudic rule: "two witnesses are needed to convict the indicted".

In spite of all the efforts made, the "Sefer Klobuck" is not complete to the fullest extent. Missing from the book is a description of the "Bund" activities in Klobuck. The request for an account to write and submit his memories was made from a Czestochower Bundist, who also was active in Klobuck. We did not receive any material from him. It is also our duty to remember in the section "Klobucker Survivors in Israel, France and in Australia" that the writings of the Parisian "Countrymen Union of Klobuckers and Czestochowers" are missing, and the role (in the union) of the well-known writer, editor, social activist and doctor in medicine, Leib Kurland, who had a close connection to the Klobuck Kurland family. From the above mentioned Countrymen Union we did not receive any documents or explanations.

[Page 433]

We write the last lines of the "Sefer Klobuck" with the belief that we erected a monument to the community, whose members conducted an honest and hardworking cultural and religious way of life in a small village in the Polish soil, which was tragically decimated. Their lives, sufferings, and deaths were respectfully described for Historic eternity.

May their memories be blessed

    A. Wolff Jasny

    Tel Aviv 19 Iyar 5721 (May 5th 1961)